Saracens and Franks in 12th – 15th Century European and Near Eastern Literature

Saracens and Franks in 12th – 15th Century European and Near Eastern Literature examines the tension between two competing discourses in the medieval Muslim Mediterranean and medieval Christian Europe: one rooted in the desire to understand the world and one's place in it, and another promoting an ethnocentric narrative. To this end, it examines the construction of an image of the Other for Muslims in the Eastern Mediterranean and for Christians in Western Europe in works of literature, particularly in the works produced in the centuries preceding the Crusades, and it explores the ways in which both Muslim and Christian writers depicted the Enemy in historical accounts of the Crusades.

The author focuses on medieval works of ethnography and geography, travel literature, Muslim and Christian accounts of the Crusades, and the romances of Western Europe to trace the evolution of the image of the Eastern Mediterranean Muslim in medieval Western Europe and the Western European Christian in the medieval Muslim world, first to understand the construct in the respective scholarly communities, and then to analyze the ways in which this conception informs subsequent works of nonfiction and fiction (in the Western European context) in which this Muslim or Christian Other plays a prominent role. In its analysis of the medieval Mediterranean Muslim and European Christian approaches to difference, this book interrogates the premises underlying the concept of the Other, challenging formulations of binary opposition such as the West versus Islam/Muslims.

Aman Y. Nadhiri is Assistant Professor of English and Arabic at Johnson C. Smith University, USA.

Saracens and Franks in 12th – 15th Century European and Near Eastern Literature
Perceptions of Self and the Other

Aman Y. Nadhiri

LONDON AND NEW YORK

First published 2017
by Routledge

2 Park Square, Milton Park, Abingdon, Oxfordshire OX14 4RN
52 Vanderbilt Avenue, New York, NY 10017

Routledge is an imprint of the Taylor & Francis Group, an informa business

First issued in paperback 2019

Copyright © 2017 Aman Y. Nadhiri

The right of Aman Y. Nadhiri to be identified as author of this work has been asserted by him in accordance with sections 77 and 78 of the Copyright, Designs and Patents Act 1988.

All rights reserved. No part of this book may be reprinted or reproduced or utilised in any form or by any electronic, mechanical, or other means, now known or hereafter invented, including photocopying and recording, or in any information storage or retrieval system, without permission in writing from the publishers.

Notice:
Product or corporate names may be trademarks or registered trademarks, and are used only for identification and explanation without intent to infringe.

British Library Cataloguing in Publication Data
A catalogue record for this book is available from the British Library

Library of Congress Cataloging-in-Publication Data
A catalog record for this book has been requested

ISBN: 978-1-4724-7235-9 (hbk)
ISBN: 978-0-367-88153-5 (pbk)

Typeset in Sabon
by Apex CoVantage, LLC

With sincere, humble thanks . . .

Contents

	Acknowledgments	viii
	Introduction	1
1	Saracens: Muslims as a concept in medieval Europe	11
2	*Al-iFranj*: Medieval Muslim perceptions of Western Europeans	38
3	The medieval travel narrative and the Other in Ibn Fadlān, *The Travels of Ibn Jubayr*, and *Mandeville's Travels*	63
4	The lesser evils: Familiar Saracens and Saracen Converts	80
5	Foreign Saracens	107
6	Foreign Saracens in accounts of the Crusades	126
7	Western Europeans in Muslim accounts of the Crusades	137
8	A familiar enemy: Salāh al-Dīn and Richard I in enemy sources	172
	Conclusion	191
	Bibliography	197
	Index	211

Acknowledgments

This work is the final step of a long, arduous journey, a journey I could not have completed without the help of numerous others, to whom I owe my undying gratitude. First, I would like to thank my beautiful wife, Racquel, who has provided inspiration, motivation, and when necessary, consolation. She has been the missing ingredient, lending me the balance necessary to complete the task. My parents, Asili and N.Y. Nadhiri, have been unflagging in their support and encouragement; I owe them thanks for this book, and so much more than words can express. It is a debt I will never be able to repay in full, but for the present I hope that my thanks will suffice. Likewise, my brother and sister, Muhammad and Iyesha, have made contributions to this and all of my other endeavors of a nature that defies quantification. My grandmother, Mrs. Ella J. Dinkins, has also been a source of inspiration throughout my life; her mind and spirit are unmatched. Mr. Walter Bennett, Mrs. Mary Neil Bennett and Mr. Harry Dinkins, while no longer with us, have nonetheless been present in spirit as sources of comfort and encouragement as well. I must also thank my Uncle Anthony and my cousins Nancy and Helen Bennett for the countless stimulating conversations we have shared over the years. Additionally, I would like to thank the Mackalo and Lugogo families, who have treated me as a member of their families over the years. However, any acknowledgment of family must include my newest relatives, the Lewis family (and Cheverdeen Williams and her daughter, Shari), in particular Nigel and Paula Lewis, who have been generous beyond description with their kindness, patience, and understanding, although those things pale in comparison to the gift they bestowed upon me just a few Januaries ago.

In addition to the support of loved ones, I have also benefited from the support of numerous others who guided me through the process of transforming *Saracens and Franks* from a dissertation to its current form. I am particularly grateful to Dr. Joseph Wittig and Dr. Carl Ernst at the University of North Carolina – Chapel Hill for their advice and support throughout the process. Likewise, Dr. Mbaye Lo of Duke University provided much-needed guidance and timely suggestions along each step of the way, and for that he has my thanks. I am also indebted to the countless individuals in the libraries at Davidson College, the University of North Carolina – Chapel Hill, and Johnson C. Smith University who assisted me in locating needed resources, often at their own inconvenience, and to Dr. Leslie Gutierrez for her input on my translations from Spanish.

Finally, I would like to thank Erika Gaffney and her staff at Ashgate for their guidance and patience throughout this process, and the anonymous reader, whose suggestions helped to uncover this work's true potential.

Introduction

This book seeks to examine the tension between two competing discourses in the medieval Muslim Mediterranean/Near East and medieval Christian Europe: the discourse related to the desire to understand the world and one's place in it, and the discourse that promotes an ethnocentric narrative that elevates one group at the expense of others. These competing discourses have each influenced the ways in which both Muslims of the Mediterranean and Near East and Christians of Western Europe viewed one another during the Middle Ages, inspiring attempts at objective examinations of foreign places, peoples, and cultures, but also leading to works that contributed to the "Othering" of a people through caricature and wholesale misrepresentation; in some instances, both phenomena can be observed in the pages of a single work. While it is tempting to categorize all attempts at objective analysis of foreign people and places as the work of scholars, and all attempts toward misrepresentation as works of fiction, this dynamic tension is evident in sober works of geography, ethnography, and history, just as it is present in some of the most popular works of fiction from the medieval period. This tension between the divergent goals of understanding the world as it is and forwarding an ethnocentric narrative is part of the larger, universal human experience; the peoples of the medieval Muslim and Christian worlds of the Mediterranean/Near East and Western Europe, respectively, are ideal subjects for this project in that their complicated, interconnected histories provide fertile ground for exploration. And so this book will examine these competing discourses and the ways in which the tension between them influenced Muslim and Christian writers as they looked to their neighbors to the North and West, or the South and East, throughout the course of the Middle Ages.

Chapter 1 explores the development of the idea of the Muslim, or rather Saracen,[1] Other in medieval Western Europe. In doing so, it poses the question, "What image of the Muslim (particularly the Muslim of the Mediterranean, Near East, and North Africa) did medieval European scholars provide, and what were the sources that informed this image?" From its origins in Classical/Late Antique works of geography/ethnography to the contributions of scholars in the High-Late Middle Ages, the chapter analyzes

2   *Introduction*

the ways in which Western Europeans perceived the Eastern Mediterranean/ Near East and its peoples prior to the advent of Islam, and whether and/or to what degree their perception of the region changed in the years and centuries after the expansion of Islam. To this end, the chapter discusses the contributions of some of the luminaries in the field of geography/ethnography from the Classical/Late Antique period to the Middle Ages, as well as the prevailing theories related to world geography and ethnography, and how they shaped Western scholars' understanding of their neighbors in the Eastern Mediterranean and Near East.

Chapter 2 continues the exploration of scholars' attempts to understand the Other scientifically, but from the perspective of the medieval Muslim approaching a Western European, Christian subject. The chapter follows a trajectory similar to that of the chapter that precedes it, identifying the geographic/ethnographic sources available to medieval Muslim scholars, from the Classical/Late Antique period to the High-Late Middle Ages, as well as the prevailing theories in the field, and their impact on the scholars' conception of the Western European. The chapter also examines the contributions of some of the masters in the field of geography/ethnography in the medieval Muslim world, and the ways in which their contributions informed Muslims' (particularly Muslims in the Mediterranean and Near East) understanding of Europe and Europeans. Like the chapter that precedes it, this chapter is as much an investigation of the scholars' perception of their society's place in the world as it is of their theories relating to the Other. From the tension between the desire to understand the world as it is, and the desire to reinforce an ethnocentric narrative that privileges one's society in the global hierarchy, emerge many of the most pernicious, intractable ideas about the Western Other, ideas that still resonate (albeit to varying degrees) in our time.

Chapter 3 explores a genre that can be described as resting at the intersection of scholarship and popular literature: the medieval travel narrative. As a work that is not "scientific" in either its tone or methodology, yet does present information not readily available to a lay audience (ostensibly as a result of the writer's travels), the travel narrative made distant parts of the world accessible to the public, and in a style more accessible to a wider audience. The role of the travel narrative was particularly important in the medieval world, in which travel was an arduous, dangerous, expensive, and time-consuming undertaking, a privilege generally reserved for merchants, sailors, soldiers, officials, and the wealthy. The travel narrative not only described foreign – often exotic – locales to an interested public, it focused on the areas of interest for an audience eager to learn about the outside world: notable natural and manmade landmarks; the size, stature, and atmosphere of foreign cities of note; and the physical appearance of the native people, as well as their customs, manners, religion, and "exotic" practices. In a sense, the medieval travel narrative was the medieval equivalent of popular scholarship, engaged in by individuals whose qualifications were their experiences.

This chapter approaches some of the most famous travel narratives of the medieval Mediterranean Muslim and Western European Christian worlds. In particular, it focuses on works that ostensibly describe the writer's experiences amongst the Muslim or Christian Other. The medieval travel narrative is invaluable, in that such works are the sites of production of knowledge vis-à-vis personal observation and insights (first hand or through informants; or in some cases, through research), and simultaneously sites of unabashed subjectivity, in which personal, cultural, racial, and religious prejudices are candidly expressed. The medieval travel narrative is vital to our discussion, as it is illustrative of the tension between understanding and "Othering" the Muslim or Christian; each traveler carries his culture – and its baggage – with him. As he observes other cultures, he is consciously and unconsciously measuring it against his own culture; he is constantly positioning and repositioning his culture within the wider context of the world. Each new experience requires an adjustment, and the audience is included in much of the process. These narratives are recorded instances in which the writers become public scholars; their works often transmit both theory (albeit in an indirect manner) and popular opinion within one text, in the process of contributing to the popular understanding of a particular Other (Muslim, Eastern or Christian, Western) in a meaningful way. It is for these contributions that some of the most famous medieval travel narratives are the focus of this chapter.

Chapters 4 and 5 focus on the portrayal of Muslims in the European literary tradition derived from the Old French *chansons de geste*; these epic texts were popular across medieval Europe, both in French and in translations/adaptations. By their nature, the *chansons de geste* lent themselves to exaggeration and hyperbole, and in the case of the "Muslim" characters, this often took the form of caricature and distortion. Within the *chansons de geste*, the caricaturing of Muslim (or Saracen) characters follows predictable patterns; this book argues that there are three distinct Saracen "types": the Foreign Saracen, who is wholly alien from a Western European audience in appearance and/or behavior; the Familiar Saracen, in whom an audience could find familiar traits (i.e., honor, loyalty, nobility); and the Saracen Convert, who converts to Christianity in the course of the tale and becomes(?) European.

Chapter 4 examines the Familiar Saracen and the Saracen Convert with respect to their distinguishing characteristics and the ways in which they function within the *chansons de geste*. Among the most widespread legends were those of *Fierabras* and *Otinel*, narratives in which converted Saracens play a significant role. We will investigate the ways in which the Saracen Convert and Familiar Saracen are identified within the texts, and their relationship to other Saracen and Christian characters through a close reading of the Middle English romances *The Romance of Duke Rowlande and Sir Ottuell of Spayne* (from the *Otinel* tradition), *The Sowdone of Babylone* (from *Fierabras*), and *The King of Tars*. This chapter also considers their

4 *Introduction*

broader implications for medieval Western European society vis-à-vis racial, cultural, and religious identity formation, and the ways in which they complicate simple binary formulations of Saracen and Christian, terms that are already laden with meaning.

Chapter 5 explores the Foreign Saracen, the most recognizable of all Saracen characters, a category that includes some of the most arresting figures in the romances. As the site upon which medieval stereotypes and fears of the Muslim Other are projected, the Foreign Saracen is the most important of the Saracen types; he is the point of reference for an audience vis-à-vis Islam, Muslims, and Muslim society. Moreover, the Foreign Saracen is crucial in delineating the boundaries of Saracen/Eastern and Christian/Western identity; he is as important in reaffirming the Western European Self as he is in marking the Saracen Other. The Foreign Saracen's role within the romances is crucial, as his defeat completes the narrative of Christian dominance within the text. Through a close reading of *The Sowdone of Babylone* and *La Chanson de Roland*, this chapter identifies the distinguishing features of the Foreign Saracen, as well as his relationship with other Saracen and Christian characters within the texts. The Foreign Saracens are often the most compelling figures in the texts; they became synonymous with Islam and Muslims in medieval Western Europe, contributing to a caricature of the Muslim that still resonates.

Before continuing on to a description of the sixth chapter, a word about the romances that are the source material for much of the discussion in Chapters 4 and 5: *La Chanson de Roland*, *The Romaunce of the Sowdone of Babylone and of Ferumbras His Sone Who Conquered Rome* (and the French original *Fierabras*), *Duke Rowlande and Sir Ottuell of Spayne*, and *The King of Tars*. *La Chanson de Roland* is the oldest extant,[2] most influential of the *chansons de geste*; it is not an exaggeration to say that *La Chanson de Roland* gave birth to the genre. *La Chanson de Roland* was the most well known of the Charlemagne legends; its narrative style, themes, and characters (principal and ancillary) informed many of the *chansons de geste* and derivative vernacular romances of the next four centuries. *La Chanson de Roland* is the definitive work of the genre; no discussion of medieval romances is complete without it.

After *La Chanson de Roland*, *Fierabras* was one of the most popular of the *chansons de geste*; the Middle English derivative, *The Romaunce of the Sowdone of Babylone and of Ferumbras His Sone Who Conquered Rome* was equally popular in England.[3] *The Romaunce of the Sowdone of Babylone and of Ferumbras His Sone Who Conquered Rome* incorporates into its rendition of *Fierabras* the post-written prequel, *La Destruction de Rome*,[4] thus producing a different work. The text presents two archetypical Saracen characters: the Convert Saracen Princess (Floripas) and the Saracen Monarch/Foreign Saracen (Laban, Balan in *Fierabras*); it is a brilliant example of the way in which the characters and themes of the *chansons de geste* are preserved and interpreted in the vernacular romances.

Duke Rowlande and Sir Ottuell of Spayne, a late-fourteenth/early-fifteenth-century Middle English derivative of the late-twelfth/early-thirteenth-century *Otinel*,⁵ is a product of the immense popularity of the Charlemagne romances; it appears to be a response to medieval audiences' demand for more stories about the exploits of Charlemagne and his knights.⁶ *Duke Rowlande and Sir Ottuell of Spayne* presents audiences with one of the most identifiable male Saracen Converts, Sir Ottuell. Moreover, it presents one of the few examples of a Saracen who is neither "Other" or Convert, Sir Clarell (Clariel in *Otinel*), who is respectable within the works as a Saracen. *Duke Rowlande and Sir Ottuell of Spayne* provides yet another demonstration of the ways in which the characters and concepts of the *chansons de geste* are appropriated in the vernacular romances.

The King of Tars is perhaps the most exceptional of the romances under discussion. The story, of a Christian princess who marries a Saracen king under duress, the subsequent birth of a misshapen infant, and the eventual conversion of the Saracen king as a result of the miraculous healing of the infant via baptism, is derived from a story in the *Flores Historiarum*.⁷ However, what distinguishes *The King of Tars* as a romance is the *nature* of the conversions which take place, in particular, the ways in which many of the underlying issues relating to Muslim–Christian identity, relations (intermarriage), and conversion are writ large within the text. These distinctive features make *The King of Tars* an ideal resource for a discussion of medieval Western European constructions of Muslim identity and Muslim–Christian relations. The same can be said in regard to all of the romances under discussion in Chapters 4 and 5; each work reveals fundamental aspects of the ways in which Muslims and Muslim societies were "Othered" in the popular discourse of medieval Western Europe.

Although Western European (or Frankish) Christian characters can be found in the literature of the medieval Muslim world, they do not appear with the same frequency as their Saracen counterparts. For some, this is indicative of a general lack of interest in Europe and Europeans on the part of medieval Muslims. There has been considerable speculation as to why this might have been the case; some interpret it as characteristic of a myopic civilization lacking the intellectual curiosity to approach other cultures, while others suggest that perhaps medieval Western Europe was not as important a presence on the world stage (compared to the civilizations of the Indian subcontinent and China, or the Muslim Mediterranean and Near East), and did not merit the type of attention given to the Muslim world in Western European literature. This book does not attempt to settle this argument; as Frankish Christian characters are not as strong a presence in Muslim literature as Saracens are in Western European literature during the Middle Ages, this book instead looks to medieval Muslim depictions of Western Christians in accounts of the crusades and the Crusades-era Levant, when many Muslims' attention was focused squarely on the intruders from the West.

6   Introduction

Chapter 6 explores the ways in which Muslims are portrayed in medieval Western accounts of the crusades. Using the template of Foreign, Familiar, and Converted Saracens from the discussion of the romances, this chapter examines the manner in which medieval crusade accounts appropriate these types—in particular, the Foreign and Familiar Saracens. Chapter 6 focuses on the utilization of the Foreign Saracen as a category into which Muslim opponents are placed as a means by which to dehumanize them and elevate the crusaders by evoking the pathos of the romances. Looking at accounts of the First Crusade in particular, the chapter examines the characterization of certain Muslim leaders as villains, and the techniques employed by the chroniclers to achieve the desired effects, as well as the factors that enabled them to frame these individuals, and the First Crusade as a whole, within the narrative framework of the romances. It also investigates the reasons behind the relative frequency with which the idea of the Foreign Saracen is evoked vis-à-vis Muslims in general, and Muslim leaders in particular, in accounts of the First Crusade, and the disappearance of the Foreign Saracen in accounts of subsequent crusades. Muslims remain the enemy in accounts of later crusades; however, after the First Crusade there is a noticeable divergence from the tone that marks the accounts of the events leading up to the initial Western conquest of Jerusalem in 1099. The First Crusade is unique among the crusades of the Middle Ages (whether to the Near East, Central/Eastern Europe, or against the Cathars in France), but it was the subsequent crusades to the Near East that generated a distinct genre of medieval Western European literature.

Chapter 7 turns its focus to medieval Muslim historians' portrayal of Western Europeans in accounts of the crusades, and in the case of the warrior and statesman Usāmah ibn Munqidh, the milieu of the twelfth-century Levant. At issue are the ways in which popular stereotypes of *al-iFranj* (Franks) are evoked in the works in question, and how the tension relating to the nature of the crusades informs (and influences) the use of these stereotypes. There were a number of stereotypes at the writers' disposal; however, the Crusades accentuated cultural and religious differences; Muslim writers were as keen to emphasize these differences as their Christian counterparts were, developing a caricature of "the Frank" that, like "the Saracen," still resonates in the dialectic between "East" and "West." The Frank of the Muslim accounts is not as monstrous or depraved as the Saracen of the romances, but Frankish customs and beliefs are clearly marked as inferior. The role of the Frank, like that of his Saracen counterpart, is to illustrate the inferiority of the group of which he is a caricature – racially, culturally, and religiously. This chapter identifies the ways in which medieval Muslim writers use the Frank as a means by which to Other Western Europeans, and the ways in which this narrative of "Frankish Otherness" is reinforced within the works in question.

Chapter 8 approaches the subject of the enemy as familiar in accounts of the crusades, but from two distinct vantage points. Unlike Chapters 6 and

7, in which the perspective is exclusively that of Western European and Muslim chroniclers, respectively, this chapter explores the issue from the perspective of writers from both sides of the conflict as they record the activities of famous leaders from the ranks of the enemy. The chapter focuses on two of the most well known and universally respected individuals from the crusades: Richard I and Salāh al-Dīn (Saladin in Western sources). Both individuals are principally known as heroes of the crusades (in this case, the Third Crusade); moreover, both emerged as admirable, heroic figures in the literature of the medieval Muslim Mediterranean/Near East (Richard I) and Christian Western Europe (Salāh al-Dīn). Both figures also crafted their image as warriors for the faith assiduously, images that obscured their political and territorial ambitions, which were generally realized at the expense of coreligionists. In the accounts, we observe the ways in which Muslim and Christian chroniclers approach individuals who because of their abilities and success cannot be easily dismissed as the Other, but who cannot become heroes within the narratives. The chapter also addresses the unique quality the matching of two accomplished individuals imparted to the Third Crusade, and the ways in which the accounts reveal the writers', and the two leaders', awareness of the historical circumstances in which they found themselves.

In its discussion of the Other as a signifier, this work is indebted to the work of Edward Said, particularly *Orientalism*, and his analysis of the construction of the Muslim in Western discourse. In *Orientalism*,[8] Said argues that the Western construction of the "Middle East" is a concept that is wholly disconnected from both the historical and contemporary Middle East; it is an amalgamation of ideas, stereotypes, and theories originating in the West that have evolved into a discourse that is both self-referential and self-perpetuating. According to this critique, the literature of the past concerning the Middle East, both fiction and nonfiction, is informed by and, both implicitly and explicitly, reaffirms this pre-existing Western construct of the Orient, which is not reliant upon factual support as proof of its validity. Rather, it is the work of the individual writer that must conform to a Western concept of the region, a concept not only divorced from the Middle East as it actually is, but that is for its audience more relevant than either the area itself or any attempt to provide a realistic representation of it. In explaining his perception of Orientalism as a discipline, Said writes:

> the essential aspects of modern Orientalist theory and praxis (from which present-day Orientalism derives) can be understood, not as a sudden access of objective knowledge about the Orient, but as a set of structures inherited from the past, secularized, redisposed, and reformed by such disciplines as philology, which in turn were naturalized, modernized, and laicized substitutes for (or versions of) Christian supernaturalism. In the form of new texts, the East was accommodated to these structures.[9]

Due to the self-affirming, self-referential nature of the Orientalist construct of the East, and in particular the Eastern Mediterranean, the language of an Orientalist text does not present images of the East as it exists in fact, nor is this an expectation for the audience of such a text.[10]

However, Said's analysis reflects the discourse between the "West" and the Muslim Near East over the last three centuries, a discourse heavily influenced by the ascendant, then-dominant position of the Western, Christian powers. During this period, the subordinate position of the Muslim Near East, and the Muslim world in general, meant that they, like all peoples subjugated as a result of European expansion, felt the implications of their Otherness. But in his investigation of the roots of Western (mis)conceptions of Islam and Muslims, which Said accurately locates in the Middle Ages (as have others, notably Daniel Norman in *Islam and the West*), he projects the present state of affairs back to earlier eras, irrespective of the power dynamic in place at the time. Christopher Tyerman is correct in his assertion that despite the proclamations of nineteenth-century historians and modern extremists in the Near East, the Crusades were not a precursor to the Colonial Era.[11] The Crusades were largely successful because of the extent to which ineptitude and internecine warfare dominated politics in the Muslim Levant; the unification of Muslim resources and political will against the crusaders[12] spelled the end of the Western European presence in the Muslim Levant. It is correct to assert that the Muslim was the Other for medieval Western Europeans; it is incorrect to imply that the Muslim was "Othered" by medieval Western Europeans.

In a manner of speaking, this book does not approach the Other as a corollary of subjugation, but as a reflexive response in the formation of group identity, as an articulation of Self in encounters with difference. This book attempts to understand the competing impulses (to understand a part of the world and its peoples and to dismiss it as alien, inferior) at work in the medieval West and Mediterranean/Near East. In this context, the Other is not primarily a signifier of power (although power is undeniably, inextricably linked with the idea of the Other, particularly as it renders subjugated groups as "Other," a phenomenon witnessed in medieval Western Europe and the Muslim Mediterranean and Near East); rather, it is a signifier of difference and perceived difference. It is within this framework that the idea of the Other is evoked in the pages of this book.

The Other as a concept has become indelibly linked to discourses of dominance and oppression, of asymmetrical relationships of power. In particular, it has a strong association with the "East–West" or "Islam–West" dialectic.[13] In this context, the influence of the colonial legacy is undeniable; past and present events are inevitably interpreted through the prism of the last three centuries. However, the Other as a concept is not bound to the power to dominate. Asymmetries of power enable one group to impose its worldview upon another group, to "Other" it, but the concept itself is enabled by the power of an individual or group to formulate a perspective of the world in which their characteristics, customs, and beliefs are normative. Gayatri

Spivak once famously wondered if the subaltern could speak. However, one might also be justified in querying whether the oppressor can hear. Our concept of who is the Other is often colored by our perception of who occupies the dominant position; as the late Chinua Achebe reminds us in *Things Fall Apart*, the colonizer is also the Other to the colonized; they only differ inasmuch as the colonizer is able to project his perspective through the application of military, political, and economic force.

The question of the Other, of "who is Othering whom," is often fraught with the baggage of historical systemic oppression, and discussions have a tendency to devolve into exercises in censuring or exonerating individuals or groups. Understanding the historical consequences of the utilization of this concept as justification for conquest and exploitation is vitally important; however, it is also important to understand the concept itself, to recognize it as a frame of reference common to all, a corollary to the concept of the Self. This book endeavors to do just that, to examine the ways in which the Other was employed by two cultural and religious regional entities as a means by which to comprehend a neighbor in the world beyond their borders, and the tension between the desire to render a foreign entity the Other and the need to understand it. To this end, this book's focus is on the medieval worlds of the Muslim Mediterranean and Near East and Christian Western Europe, and how they perceived and portrayed one another through several genres of literature, ranging from the scientific to the wildly imaginative. We will examine the origins of the Other in the medieval East–West dialectic; and then we will examine the origins of its Other.

Notes

1 "Saracen" was the term most commonly used to refer to Muslims in Western European works of the time.
2 The consensus for the date of production for *La Chanson de Roland* is the final years of the eleventh century (1098–1100). "Introduction," *The Song of Roland*, Trans. Glyn Burgess (London: Penguin, 1990) 8.
3 For Dorothee Metlitzki, it was the most popular of the romances dealing with the theme of Christian-Muslim conflict/relations in medieval England. Dorothee Metlitzki, *The Matter of Araby in Medieval England* (New Haven: Yale UP, 1977) 169. The "Ferumbras group," Middle English derivatives of *Fierabras*, includes *Sir Ferumbras*, *Firumbras*, and *The Romaunce of the Sowdone of Babylone and of Ferumbras His Sone Who Conquered Rome*. *Sir Ferumbras* and *Firumbras* were both composed in the last quarter of the fourteenth century; *The Romaunce of the Sowdone of Babylone and of Ferumbras His Sone Who Conquered Rome* is a product of the fifteenth century. Janet M. Cowan, "The English Charlemagne Romances," *Roland and Charlemagne in Europe: Essays on the Reception and Transformation of a Legend*, Ed. Karen Pratt (London: King's College, 1996) 159–62.
4 Emil Hausknecht (Ed.), *The Romaunce of the Sowdone of Babylone and of Ferumbras His Sone Who Conquered Rome* (London: N. Trübner, 1881) xxiii.
5 Anna Hunt Billings, *A Guide to the Middle English Metrical Romances: Dealing with English and Germanic Legends, and with the Cycles of Charlemagne and*

Arthur (New York: Henry Holt and Company, 1901) 69, 73. The early fourteenth century *Otuel* is another Middle English descendent of *Otinel*; however, *Duke Rowlande and Sir Ottuell of Spayne* more closely approximates the French original. Ibid, 70, 71–2.
6 Ibid, 69–70.
7 The earliest iteration of *The King of Tars* theme is found in the *Reimchronik*, produced before 1290. The story found in *Flores Historiarum* is attributed to Matthew Paris. Laura Hibbard Loomis, *Mediæval Romance in England: A Study of the Sources and Analogues of the Non-Cyclic Metrical Romances* (New York: Burt Franklin, 1969) 45–6.
8 While there have been numerous vocal critics of the work and the ideas of *Orientalism*, it has unquestionably altered the nature of the discourse regarding both the representation of the foreign and the dialectic between the East and West.
9 Edward Said, *Orientalism* (New York: Vintage Books, 1978) 122.
10 "[W]e need not look for correspondence between the language used to depict the Orient and the Orient itself, not so much because the language is inaccurate but because it is not even *trying* to be accurate." *Orientalism*, 71. Emphasis added.
11 Christopher Tyerman, *Fighting for Christendom: Holy War and the Crusades* (Oxford: Oxford UP, 2004) 199–208.
12 Individual leaders like 'Imād al-Dīn Zengi, Nūr al-Dīn and Salāh al-Dīn were successful in uniting Muslims under their banners against the crusaders, but the crusaders were of secondary consideration to their dynastic ambitions. In the end, it was the trauma of the Mongol invasions and depredations (which included the killing of the last 'Abbasid caliph) that inspired the Mamlūk Turks, who defeated the Mongols at 'Ain Jalūt, to rid the Near East of any "foreign" presence.
13 The binary formulation of Islam and "the West" is addressed in detail in Chapter 4.

1 Saracens
Muslims as a concept in medieval Europe

The term most commonly used in reference to Muslims in medieval Western European literature is "Saracen." The *Middle English Dictionary* defines the term "Sarasin" (the anglicized version of Saracen) as follows:

> A Turk; also an Arab; also, a M[u]sl[i]m; – often with ref. to the Crusades; ~hed, the head of a Saracen; (b) a heathen, pagan; an infidel; (c) as a type of non-Christian; ~or jeu, jeu and (or, other) ~, paien and ~, **painimes and sarasines, sarasines and (ne) jeues**, etc.; (d) the language of the Saracens; (e) one of the pagan invaders of England, esp. a Dane or Saxon; – also coll.; (f) a member of a non-Hebrew tribe, esp. a desert nomad; – also coll.; (g) pagandom; – ?=**Sarasin** n.(2); (h) **sarasines flesh**, mummy, a substance taken from embalmed corpses; **brouet sarasines**, a stew of some kind [cp. **Sarasin** adj.(b) & **Sarasinesse** n.(b)]; (i) in surnames; (j) **sarasines hed**, the name of an inn.[1]

The very definition suggests the multiplicity of meanings called forth by "Saracen," and the liminal space Muslims occupied in medieval European literature as non-Christians. As a designation that came to encompass not only Turks and Arabs in medieval literature, but also pagan Danes and Saxons, and non-Christians in general, the term appears to convey a sense of the distant and vaguely defined, an image of masses of undifferentiated faces rather than individuals, masses identifiable primarily by their Otherness.

However, by the very nature of its polyvalence, "Saracen" becomes a term of infinite utility for medieval writers, providing a blank slate, a vague outline of a figure, which can be filled in to suit the needs of the work in question. It can be used to evoke a sense of the distant yet familiar (Danes and/or other pagan Europeans of the past or present) or the wholly alien (Muslims of the Eastern Mediterranean and Africa). Moreover, the term can be subject to multiple acts of conflation, as the Mediterranean Muslim can be conflated with the Persian or African Other, and yet fit comfortably within the parameters of Saracen-ness. Yet despite the inherent polyvalence of the term, writers are able to differentiate between the multiple connotations to convey a specific image, and to evoke specific emotional reactions

12 *Saracens: Muslims as a concept*

from their audiences that are dependent on the type of Saracen to whom the writer is referring, which is identifiable within the context of the behavior of the Saracens in question. For example, in *King Horn*, the writer elicits a heightened response from his audience by ascribing perceived Mediterranean/African Muslim "behavior" to the Danish/Saxon "Saracens" of the text through the testimony of an old knight, who informs the audience that not only have the Saracens conquered and pillaged the land, but that *they have forced the Christians to abandon their faith*.[2] In this instance, the idea of forced conversion recalls a charge commonly leveled against Muslims, serving as a marker for the audience, which would likely have associated such behavior with Mediterranean Muslims as opposed to pagan Danes. In this instance, "Saracen" as an identifier is of great utility to the writer precisely because of its ambiguity, which offers infinite possibilities.

However, specificity and historical accuracy were not immediate concerns in medieval popular fiction. Whether or not an audience was able to distinguish a pagan Dane from a North African Muslim, the true distinction of importance was the fact that both were non-Christians, and therefore enemies. Details of ethnicity could be and were often conflated to achieve the greatest dramatic effect. Specificity could at times be constricting, and the medieval romances which dealt with Christian – non-Christian interaction and conflict often called for a suspension of disbelief that did not lend itself to the pursuit of historical or factual accuracy or specificity. Inasmuch as this was the case, a term such as "Saracen" that provided a greater range of possibilities was inherently more valuable, and an obvious choice for the writers of medieval works of popular fiction.

But discussions of the use of "Saracen" as a term in medieval works of popular fiction and nonfiction can obscure the role it played in describing the world as it was understood by the writers and readers of the time. Despite the imaginative nature of many of the accounts in medieval popular fiction (and, at times, the historical works), they are based in part on a certain understanding of the world, particularly the world beyond Western Europe, which was considered accurate in a "scientific" sense by reader and writer alike.[3] This worldview was based in part on the works of Early Medieval and Crusades-era thinkers, who were themselves often clerics, and in part on works and a worldview stretching back to the writers and thinkers of Antiquity.

The geographical information that constituted much of the understanding of the outside world in Western Europe during the early Middle Ages (eighth through eleventh centuries) and into the Crusades was based on the works of Roman writers such as Pliny, Pomponius Mela, and Julius Solinus in the first centuries C.E. and late antique scholars like Macrobius, Martianus Capella, Orosius, and Isidore of Seville, who wrote in the late fourth (Macrobius), fifth (Martianus Capella and Orosius), and sixth (Isidore of Seville) centuries C.E.[4] Many of the works of the classical geographers such as Ptolemy, along with those of the great thinkers such as Aristotle and Plato, had been lost (although in Ptolemy's case, a few of his works survived). Moreover, Greek was largely unknown to Western scholars during the Early Middle Ages (and for much of the era of the Crusades as well), making both Byzantine texts and classical works on geography inaccessible to them. As a result, the works that were available (i.e., the works of Pliny and Solinus, along with those of other lesser-known geographers from the final centuries of the Roman Empire) became the foundation of first Late Antique, and later medieval scholars' understanding of world geography.

Many of the works produced by geographers such as Solinus in the last centuries of the Roman Empire were not of the quality of the works of earlier geographers such as Ptolemy. Writers in the latter years of the Empire were constrained by the circumstances in which the declining and contracting state found itself. The diminution of the Roman sphere of influence brought with it a reduction of Roman access to and information about areas of the world with which Roman citizens had previously been familiar; without direct access, the boundaries of the known world contracted for Roman geographers. This phenomenon manifested itself in the works of later Roman geographers in a twofold manner: (a) in the decrease in the amount and quality of information about the outside world (in comparison with their predecessors); and (b) in a fascination with the "marvels" and "Monstrous Races" that were imagined to exist in the most distant regions.[5]

In addition to the available classical texts, the works of Late Antique scholars and theologians were also very influential. Among the Late Antique works, the works of Paulus Orosius and Isidore of Seville were perhaps the most instrumental in shaping a medieval geographical worldview. Orosius and Isidore of Seville, who were both Spaniards, dealt with questions of world geography and ethnography in their works, Orosius in his *Historiarum adversus paganos libri septem* and Isidore of Seville in his *Etymologiae sive originum libri XX*. Writing in the fifth century,[6] Orosius' *Historiarum adversus paganos libri septem* is a response to the charge that Christianity was to blame for the disintegration of the Roman Empire; it catalogs the various instances of human suffering from the Creation to his time,[7] with a focus on what he identified as the great empires from the four corners of the earth – Macedonia (North), Carthage (South), Babylon (East), and Rome (West)[8] – in an attempt to demonstrate that the suffering which accompanied the fall of Rome was not as extreme as popular opinion held it to be when compared to the suffering of others during previous calamities. The value of *Historiarum adversus paganos libri septem* to future geographers was that it provided an image of the world which was of great utility to subsequent Christian writers in a variety of disciplines, while also establishing a precedent for providing geographical information in historical works.[9]

In describing the world, Orosius follows the example of his predecessors, imagining three continents, Africa, Asia, and Europe, surrounded by the ocean.[10] However, in his description of the world and its people, the two groups principally associated with Islam in the Middle Ages – the Arabs (or

Saracens) and Turks – receive scant attention. This lack of attention is likely due to the peripheral status of both groups in Christian salvation history, and both groups' lack of prominence as military and political actors in the Mediterranean world of his time. Of the area that would in later years comprise the "Islamic heartland," Orosius writes:

> Between the Tigris and Euphrates rivers is Mesopotamia, beginning in the north between the Taurian and Caucasian ranges. To the south we meet in order, first Babylonia, then Chaldea, and lastly Arabia Eudaemon, a narrow strip of land facing east and lying between the Persian and Arabian gulfs. Twenty-eight peoples live in these lands.[11]

The only reference to Arabs/Saracens comes in his description of Syria, the area that either includes or shares a border with many of the most famous places in the medieval Muslim world. Of Syria, he writes:

> Syria is the name generally given to the land that extends from the Euphrates River on the east to Mare Nostrum on the west, from the city of Dagusa on the boundary between Cappadocia and Armenia near the place where the Euphrates rises on the north, as far south as Egypt and the end of the Arabian Gulf. This gulf extends southward in a long and narrow furrow which abounds with rocks and islands; from the Red Sea, that is, from the Ocean, it stretches in a westerly direction. The largest provinces of Syria are Commagene, Phoenicia, and Palestine, *not including the lands of the Saraceni and the Nabathaei, whose tribes number twelve*.[12]

Outside of passing references to them as passive witnesses to historical events,[13] this is the only time in which Arabs/Saracens are mentioned as a people in the *Historiarum adversus paganos libri septem*.

Writing in the sixth century, Isidore of Seville borrowed from Orosius' *Historiarum adversus paganos libri septem*, as well as the works of Solinus, in composing the parts of *Etymologiae sive originum libri XX*[14] that dealt primarily with geographical information; he also drew from Solinus for some of his ethnographic information.[15] However, in its ethnographic information *Etymologiae* stands apart from Orosius' work, providing genealogies for the races of the world that extend back to Ham, Japheth, and Shem.[16]

Among the many groups that Isidore of Seville includes in his genealogies are the Arabs, who appear on a number of separate occasions in Book IX (which focuses on languages, nations, regimes, the military, citizens, and familial relationships).[17] Isidore locates the Arabs among the descendants of Ham, who, according to the theologian, account for the largest number of nations in the known world:[18]

> 10. There were four sons of Ham, from whom sprang the following nations. Cush, from whom the Ethiopians were begotten. Mesraim (i.e.

Egypt), from whom the Egyptians are said to have risen. 11. Put, from whom came the Libyans – whence the river of Mauretania is called Put still today, and the whole region around it is called Puthensis. 12. Finally Canaan, from whom descended the Africans and the Phoenicians and the ten tribes of Canaanites. 13. Again, the sons of Cush, grandsons of Ham – the grandchildren of Ham were six. The sons of Cush: Saba (i.e. Seba), Havilah, Sabtah, Raamah, Seba and Cuza. 14. Saba, from whom the Sabeans were begotten and named . . . These are also the Arabians . . . 17. But Raamah, Seba, and Cuza gradually lost their ancient names, and the names that they now have, instead of the ancestral ones, are not known. 18. The sons of Raamah were Saba (i.e. Seba) and Dedan. This Saba is written in Hebrew with the letter shin, whereas the Saba above is written with a samekh, and from him the Sabeans were named – but now Saba is translated "Arabia."[19]

In another passage, he explains the significance of the name assigned to the Arabs: "[49.] The Sabeans were named after the word . . . that is, 'supplicate' and 'worship,' because we worship the divinity with Sabean incense. They are also called Arabs, because they live in the mountains of Arabia called Libanus and Antilibanus, where incense is gathered."[20] The reader is provided with both the genealogical background of the Arabs as well as an explanation of the origins of the name by which they are known.

The explanation provided by Isidore is surprisingly detailed, given the status of the group to whom he is referring at this time (existing at the intersection, yet simultaneously on the periphery, of the Byzantine, Ethiopian, and Persian empires, and almost a century away from the expansion and conquest that would transform the character of the Mediterranean littoral). However, it is even more interesting in light of a later reference to a group by a name that has been traditionally "translated" as "Arab":

> 57. The Saracens are so called either because they claim to be descendants of Sarah or, as the pagans say, because they are of Syrian origin, as if the word were Syriginae. They live in a very large deserted region. They are also Ishmaelites, as the Book of Genesis teaches us, because they sprang from Ishmael. They are also named Kedar, from the son of Ishmael, and Agarines, from the name Agar (i.e. Hagar). As we have said, they are called Saracens from an alteration of their name, because they are proud to be descendants of Sarah.[21]

This passage complicates the explanation of the name and genealogy presented in prior sections of Book IX. However, it appears to be in accord with the general image of the Arabs prior to the advent of Islam held by Western historians of the Middle Ages, as an enigmatic people existing on the fringes of the global consciousness. To a certain extent, it appears that Isidore of Seville's more detailed explanations were largely disregarded by future scholars in favor of explanations that accorded with the above excerpt, which could be interpreted in an unfavorable manner relative to the group in question.

In the context of its time, the *Etymologiae* approaches ethnographical and genealogical questions relating to the peoples of the Arabian Peninsula in an objective manner, especially when compared with the works of subsequent Western writers on the subject. If anything, the *Etymologiae* appears to lack the type of vitriol of many of the subsequent works in regard to issues of race and ethnicity, and even in dealing with potential regional biases. Instead, the work provides a systematic explication of the various nations and races (both real and imagined) of the known world (among other things), which later scholars would then adapt and interpret to suit the circumstances of their current situation.

However, Isidore of Seville also transmitted a number of erroneous ideas from the Classical and Late Antique ages, ideas that would play a large role in Western Europe's perception of the outside world. Among them, and perhaps one of the most important for its implications for the development and intensification of regional and racial biases, was his endorsement of the theory of the influence of climate upon the physical features and racial characteristics of individuals:

> 105. People's faces and coloring, the size of their bodies, and their various temperaments correspond to various climates. Hence we find that the Romans are serious, the Greeks easy-going, the Africans changeable, and the Gauls fierce in nature and sharp in wit, because the character of the climate makes them so.[22]

This theory of climatic influence would be revisited on countless occasions, and was not absent from the discourse of political/military tensions between the Latin West and the nations of the Eastern Mediterranean and North Africa.[23]

In addition, the *Etymologiae* contains references to various types of monstrous races, among them the Troglodytes ("so called because they run with such speed that they chase down wild animals on foot") and the Anthropophagians (who "feed on human flesh and are therefore named 'maneaters'"),[24] locating many of them in Ethiopia and India. Perhaps of equal interest for its influence on subsequent literature is the explanation provided in the *Etymologiae* regarding the relationship between Ethiopians and Indians:

> 127. Ethiopians are so called after a son of Ham named Cush, from whom they have their origin. In Hebrew, Cush means "Ethiopian." 128. This nation, which formerly emigrated from the region near the river Indus, settled next to Egypt between the Nile and the Ocean, in the South very close to the sun. There are three tribes of Ethiopians: Hesperians,

Garamantes, and Indians. Hesperians are of the West, Garamantes of Tripolis, and the Indians of the East.[25]

The explanation Isidore offers appears to derive in part from the Greek definition of an Ethiopian as a "burnt-face person,"[26] in accordance with the theory that blackness as a defining racial characteristic was attributable to overexposure to the sun. This explanation of the genealogy of the Ethiopians would contribute to the conflation of Ethiopian and Indian in the West throughout the Middle Ages, a conflation that would occasionally include the Muslims of the Eastern Mediterranean/North Africa.

Western scholars did not inherit a prejudice against Arabs from the scholars of the Classical and Late Antique periods, but they did inherit a regional bias against the peoples of the East and South, which they then applied to their observations of the Muslims of the Levant, North Africa, Asia Minor, and Central Asia. As peoples of either the East/South, Muslims of these areas were subject to the popular regional stereotypes of being intelligent and crafty, yet timid, cruel, and vengeful, and lacking in an overall hardiness of spirit, all of which was attributable to the effects of excessive exposure to the sun.[27] Pope Urban II recalls the regional stereotype of cowardice as a characteristic of the peoples of the South in his call to arms at Clermont when, according to William of Malmesbury, he declared that Muslims are:

> feeble men, who, not having courage to engage in close encounter, love a flying mode of warfare. For the Turk never ventures upon close fight; but, when driven from his station, bends his bow at a distance, and trusts the winds with his meditated wound; and as he has poisoned arrows, venom, and not valour, inflicts the death on the man he strikes. Whatever he effects, then, I attribute to fortune, not to courage, because he wars by flight, and by poison. It is apparent, too, that every race born in that region, being scorched with the intense heat of the sun, abounds more in reflexion, than in blood; and, therefore, they avoid coming to close quarters, because they are aware how little blood they possess.[28]

In this example the South and East are conflated, and Turks are described in terms traditionally used when referring to the peoples of the distant South.

Along with the bias against groups from the South and East, Muslims of the Levant, North Africa, Asia Minor, and Central Asia were also described in derogatory terms by Western writers on the grounds of their generally dark complexions, and the negative connotations such complexions carried in the eyes of Westerners stretching back to pagan antiquity. The association of the color black with bad fortune, and evil in general, pre-dated the advent of Christianity,[29] but in the hands of many Christian scholars it came to be associated with the outward manifestation of sin, appearing as an ethnic/racial feature either as a result of God's curse on Cain, or Noah's curse on Ham (who was identified as the progenitor of Africans and other groups identified as being racially "adjacent" to Africans). As a number of the nations comprising the Muslim world either bordered Sub-Saharan Africa, were a part of it, or bordered lands that were believed to contain monstrous races, Muslims were often conflated with members of these respective groups in medieval works of both fiction and nonfiction, and in their representation in works of art.

Beyond the general information regarding the places and peoples of the world which were shared amongst medieval writers, there were several individuals who made substantial contributions to the popular understanding of world geography and ethnography of the time. Building on the surviving works from the Classical Period, the works of Late Antique authors like Orosius and Isidore of Seville, and to a lesser extent upon Early Medieval authors, these writers helped preserve and transmit information from the past, and in some cases, predicted future developments in the areas of geography and ethnography. In particular, their works reflected the increased amount of attention directed toward the peoples of the Eastern Mediterranean, due in large part to the emergence of the region as a political, military, and economic power. These scholars helped to situate Western Europe and its peoples within the larger world, and to define the relationship between the peoples of the Eastern Mediterranean and Western Europe, which influenced relations between the two regions during the Middle Ages and beyond. Moreover, many of the most famous contributors to medieval geographical and ethnographical knowledge were amongst the greatest minds of the medieval period; in most cases their reputations stemmed from their contributions in other fields.

One such writer was William of Conches. William of Conches (c.1085–c.1154)[30] was one of the great European scholars and writers of the twelfth century. Although his works tended to be representative of the surviving tradition as opposed to original contributions to the fields of geography and ethnography, his role in preserving and transmitting information from Antiquity was invaluable to the study of these areas. He studied at the renowned school of Bernard of Chartres and later taught there for a time, and he was able to count such luminaries as John of Salisbury among his students.[31] Later, when political maneuvering on the part of others led to his early retirement, the Norman theologian returned to his homeland to work under the patronage of Geoffrey Plantagenet, most likely as a tutor for his two sons.[32]

Of his many works, his greatest contribution to medieval geography was the *Dragmaticon Philosophiae* ("Dialogue on Natural Philosophy"), which he likely composed between 1147 and 1149, during his years as tutor for the young Plantagenets.[33] The work is structured as a dialogue between the Duke of Normandy and an unnamed "philosopher." It identifies as its objectives: (a) revising the *Philosophia*, so as to retain the accurate portions, delete the inaccurate or obsolete portions, and add certain new material; (b) renouncing his errors in areas of doctrine in *Philosophia* (i.e., to make a profession of his adherence to the orthodox views espoused by the Church, so as to satisfy those whose ire he had aroused as a result of certain ideas he had put forward in *Philosophia*); and (c) providing both his patron and pupils with answers to certain philosophical questions, as well as an understanding of specific scientific principles.[34] *Dragmaticon Philosophiae* is not encyclopedic in its scope; however, it does address a number of issues related to the natural sciences, including many of the most fundamental questions pertaining to the field of medieval geography.

Within the *Dragmaticon Philosophiae* there is a brief discussion of world geography. In this discussion, he first advances several arguments in support of the theory of a round, spherical earth, and then proceeds to a dialogue concerning the nature of the earth and its regions. Here he proposes that the earth's true nature is characterized by coldness and dryness; the middle of the earth is the one exception, and this is a result of the fact that it is directly underneath the sun and is thus extremely hot.[35] The result of the two aforementioned conditions is that the earth is comprised of five climatic zones: to the extreme north and south are two frozen zones, which, along with the "torrid" zone in the middle of the earth are uninhabitable (as a result of their extreme cold and heat); on either side of the torrid zone, and between it and the frozen northern and southern regions, are two temperate zones which are suitable for habitation.[36] However, although the temperate zone between the torrid zone and the frozen zone in the south (which was commonly referred to as the *Antipodes*)[37] is capable of sustaining human life, William of Conches does not hold the opinion that it is inhabited.[38]

The temperate zone, which is home to the nations and peoples of the known world, is divided into three continents: Africa, Asia, and Europe. Asia is the largest of the three continents, occupying the Eastern half of the temperate zone from the frozen zone in the North to the Torrid Zone in the South, with the Don River in the North and the Nile in the South as its western borders. Africa occupies the Southwestern portion of the temperate zone; to the South it extends to the Torrid Zone (Libya and Ethiopia are identified as being the closest to the Torrid Zone), and the Mediterranean Sea and the Nile serve as its boundaries to the North and East, respectively. Europe is located in the Northwestern quadrant of the temperate zone; to the North its boundary is the frozen zone, and the Mediterranean Sea and the Don River mark its limits to the South and East, respectively.[39]

Beyond this description of the northern temperate zone, William of Conches does not go into detail regarding the nations and peoples of Africa, Asia, or Europe. The *Dragmaticon Philosophiae* is largely silent on the subject of world geography.[40] However, in the sections in which there is some discussion of this subject, William of Conches provides a concise description of the earth – in particular the areas of the then-known world. In the next century, scholars would do much to expand upon this foundation.

One of the scholars who would continue the work of William of Conches was the thirteenth-century scholar and theologian Albertus Magnus,[41] who was one of the most important theologians of the High Middle Ages.[42] During his lifetime he served as a lector at the University of Paris and taught in Cologne, he contributed to and oversaw the expansion of the Dominican order in Germany, established the first *studium generale* in Germany at Cologne,[43] and also served as a mentor to Thomas Aquinas.[44] However, his greatest and most enduring accomplishment as a scholar was his paraphrases of the known works of Aristotle (including those which had recently entered the Latin West via Spain), in which he included commentaries that integrated both his own opinions and those of the previous Muslim commentators such as Ibn Sīna (Avicenna) and Ibn Rushd (Averroes).[45]

In the field of geography, Albertus' most important work was his *Liber de natura locorum* ("Book of the Nature of Places"),[46] in which he examines both the theories of the classical philosophers and philosophers from the recent past (including those from the Muslim world), presenting them in tandem with his own ideas and, where he deems it necessary, correcting them in light of new evidence and/or his own contradictory opinions. In particular, *De Natura Locorum* addresses the subject of the division of the earth into different climes, the habitable and uninhabitable regions of the earth, the extent and nature of the habitable quarters, and the question of whether the Antipodes are inhabited. As Albertus was able to draw upon the most recent translation of the works of Aristotle (along with the accompanying commentaries), *De Natura Locorum* stands as one of the best offerings of medieval European geographical knowledge.

In *De Natura Locorum*, Albertus acknowledges the traditional division of the earth in its entirety into five regions, two of which are habitable, and the remaining three uninhabitable (like William of Conches).[47] However, in his discussion of world geography, he further divides the habitable world into seven climes.[48] In so doing, he acknowledges the position of the fourth clime (the region in which Iraq and Iran are located)[49] as being in the exact center of the habitable world.[50] But despite this fact, Albertus contends that the sixth and seventh climes, in which most of Europe, and all of Western Europe, can be found, occupy the central position in the earth relative to all of the regions, habitable and uninhabitable:

> There is, however, a certain doubt about these things that have been said, whether, indeed, the fourth clime is temperate among habitable places. The place of exceeding cold is not the seventh clime, but rather an uninhabitable place beyond the northern region. Similarly, the place exceeding in heat is not beneath the equator and a little to this side in the latitude of the first clime, but rather beneath the tropic, which latitude is semicircular. Therefore, it seems that the midpoint between the coldest place which is 90° in latitude, or a little less, and the hottest which is 24°, has a latitude of more than 40°. These are the sixth and seventh climes.[51]

This is an important assertion, as the centrally located clime was viewed as being the best of climes, conferring the greatest number of intrinsic benefits to its inhabitants, and the most conducive to the development of high civilization. Albertus Magnus seems to have these ideas in mind, and does not hesitate to compare the inhabitants of the fourth, sixth, and seventh climes as part of his argument that the latter two climes are in fact the most temperate:

> Of this place there seems to be evidence that men of those climes are very handsome of body, are of noble and fair stature, and they are beautiful in color, while the men of the fourth clime are small and dark. The place where men grow strongest seems to be most suited for habitation. For where men are more generally handsome and brave and noble of stature, there man thrives more readily. This is, as it appears, in the sixth and seventh climes.[52]

In his argument for the centrality of the sixth and seventh climes, Albertus Magnus also addresses the climate of the regions in question. In his estimation, the most centrally located, and thus temperate, region will feature a balance between the extremes of heat and cold, with cold winters and hot summers. If this is the case, then for him the fourth clime cannot be the most temperate clime:

> The greatest heat of the fourth clime seems to come in the summer, and a lessening of rains. For if it were temperate simply, as the philosophers say, there would be equally excessive cold there in the winter, as there is excessive heat in the summer. But we experience the opposite, because the heat of summer is above normal in that place, and there is no excessive cold there. According to these reasons the ideal winter temperature seems to be the temperature of the sixth clime, where there is neither an excess of heat in summer nor of cold in winter.[53]

In making this argument for the designation of the sixth and seventh climes as the centrally located, and thus most temperate climes, Albertus Magnus is in fact asserting a worldview that establishes Western Europe as the standard, the locus of what should be perceived as normative relative to the rest of the world. In so doing, he is following in the footsteps of the classical and Muslim geographers of the distant and recent past, who in their times argued for the centrality of their region (the fourth clime) based in part on an ethnocentrism which favored their places of origin. In this case, his stance identifies the location of the most temperate region as being further to the North and West than was previously imagined.

While Albertus Magnus fully considers the theory of the climes, *De Natura Locorum* does not offer much information about the various racial groups of the world, particularly in regard to the peoples of the East. This is especially true of the various Muslim ethnic/racial groups of the East, and in particular Arab Muslims; as a whole, they receive scant attention. The first reference to a group traditionally associated with Islam and Muslims occurs in a discussion of the Torrid Zone, in which he repeats a comment by Lucan regarding one of the groups inhabiting this zone:

> Lucan has written concerning the Arabs who live in the Torrid Zone, saying that the shadows on the right which they have in their own land when they turn toward the east in their own meridian (south) coming into the northern quarter, seem to go left; and therefore, he says speaking about them: "You Arabians have come into a world unknown to you."[54]

The next reference comes in his discussion of the eastern quarter of the habitable world and the famous cities to be found therein. After identifying the cities, he informs his audience that the listed names of the cities were the names that were in usage during the times of the Greek, and later Roman, conquests. "Later, however, when they were seized by the Saracens very many of them were destroyed and others of different names were built, and their names were changed."[55] Thus, while this reference does little to shed any light on the Saracens as a group, it is an acknowledgment of the impact that the Arab/Muslim presence has had on the eastern quarter.

The final reference to Saracens as a group in *De Natura Locorum* comes in a list of the "fifty-three" ancient tribes of the East. In the course of this list Albertus identifies the Saracens, but curiously later identifies the Arabs as another separate tribe. Though no information is provided apart from the list, there is an interesting addendum to the list: after identifying the tribes in question (which include the Anthropophagi), he writes "many names of all these tribes have changed either from war, or from the depopulation of the lands, or they changed them, perhaps, because of new sects and religions."[56] On some level, this statement might be a reflection of his awareness of the widespread changes which had taken place subsequent to the advent of Islam and the rise of the Muslim states.

While *De Natura Locorum* does not provide a great deal of information about medieval European scholars' perceptions of Muslims, it is valuable for the insight it provides concerning their worldview as it related to the science of geography, as well as the ways in which they were able to appropriate the existing classical and Muslim information at their disposal and employ it, and at times refute it, in order to promote their own ethnocentric conception of the world. It is also informative in its identification of its sources, as it reveals the names and types of classical works that had survived, along with Muslim works that geographers of his time would have had at their disposal. Finally, it clearly identifies the limits of medieval geographical knowledge, implicitly, when the information it provides is vague or inaccurate, and explicitly, when it admits to a dearth of information on a subject or group. *De Natura Locorum* provides an excellent perspective into the medieval European understanding of world geography and ethnography, and the often nebulous area occupied by Muslims therein. The information provided in *De Natura Locorum* had a profound impact in medieval Western Europe, and in Albertus Magnus' lifetime an English contemporary would develop it further in his own master work.

Roger Bacon (c.1214–1292)[57] was a lifelong scholar and a member of the Franciscan Order from 1257 until his death;[58] he was also an indefatigable advocate for reform in the educational system, at times at great personal cost to himself.[59] He was the author of a number of important works, including *De multiplicatione specierum*, *De speculis comburentibus*, the *Compendium Studii Philosophiae*, and *Compendium Studii Theologiae*; but his most well-known work was the *Opus Majus*.[60] As impressive as it is as a work, the *Opus Majus* was but a proposal for a reformation of the manner of teaching natural philosophy,[61] including a greater emphasis on the seven areas of inquiry.[62] One of these areas of scientific inquiry, astronomy, included within its confines the subject of geography.[63]

Although the *Opus Majus* presents a lengthy discussion of geography, what Bacon says is largely derivative, is not informed by personal observation, and has received less attention than other parts of the work. However, while his reliance on outside sources may not make the geographical portions of the *Opus Majus* as appealing to the modern scholar, its use of numerous texts – Classical, Late Antique, and Muslim – makes it invaluable as a collection of medieval geographical and ethnographical knowledge. In the course of his discussion of world geography, Bacon cites Æthicus Ister's *Cosmographia*, Aristotle's *De Caelo* and *Meteorologica*, and Jerome's *De situ et nominibus locorum Hebraicorum*, along with the works of Sallust, Seneca, Pliny, Ptolemy, Orosius, Isidore of Seville, al-Farghānī, Ibn Sīnā (Avicenna), the Bible, and Apocrypha.[64]

In his treatment of issues relating to geography, the *Opus Majus* is reminiscent of Albertus Magnus's *De Natura Locorum*. However, Bacon's work provides more ethnographic information, and does not adhere so closely to the ideas of geographical determinism, as does *De Natura Locorum*.[65] In certain ways, particularly in its instructions relating to the designing of a systematic map, the geographical portion of the *Opus Majus* anticipates the developments of the fifteenth century, when the quality of European cartography would improve substantially as a result of the translation of Ptolemy's *Geography*.[66] As such, Bacon's *Opus Majus* proved to be an invaluable work in the subjects of medieval geography and ethnography, while also pointing to future developments in these fields.

In his discussion of world geography, Bacon divides the earth into first the habitable and uninhabitable; he then identifies the three habitable continents (Africa, Asia, and Europe), and then posits the existence of seven climatic zones in the three continents.⁶⁷ For Bacon, location is one of the main determinants of a people's defining characteristics:

> And we see that all things vary according to different localities of the world not only in nature, but also men in their customs; since the Ethiopians have one set of customs, the Spaniards another, the Romans still another, and the Greeks yet another.⁶⁸

To this end, a portion of the *Opus Majus* is devoted to a detailed description of the habitable regions of the world, the natural features (mountains, rivers, etc.) for which they are known, and the groups for whom they are home. Moreover, in the case of the places that are mentioned in the Bible, he never fails to remind his audience of their scriptural significance. In discussing the natural features of an area, Bacon frequently addresses peculiarities which have elicited the attention of previous authors, such as questions relating to the source of certain famous rivers (e.g., the Tigris and Euphrates), and in the case of the Nile, the reason for its annual inundation of the Egyptian countryside.⁶⁹ For each of the three habitable continents, he cites the available sources – Scriptural/Exegetical, Classical, and Muslim – in the course of his discussion of them, and rarely excuses himself on the grounds of a lack of information.

In his discussion of the land of the Saracens, Bacon begins with a very specific account of the area in question:

> All this part of Aethiopia around Meroë, Syene, and Heliopolis toward the east is included under Arabia; and not only this section, but whatever there is around the tongue, that is, the extremity of the Red Sea and beyond its shore eastward from the point of its tongue to its Persian Gulf. It extends from the Red Sea as far as Pelusium in Egypt to the west, and spreads to the north through the whole of the desert in which the children of Israel wandered as far as the land of the Philistines above our sea bounded by Egypt, and extending eastward until the region of the Amalechites is reached, which lies to the east of the land of Philistia, and as far as the land of Edom, of Idumea, lying to the east of Amalech and reaching as far as the land of Moab. Then it turns more to the north through the land of Sehon, king of Esebon, and of Og, king of Bashan, as far as Mount Galaad and Lebanon, and turns still more to the north as far as Cilicia and Syria Commagene, and as far as the Euphrates.⁷⁰

In another passage, Bacon identifies Baghdad ("Baldac" in the *Opus Major*) as the place in which the "caliph lord of the sect of Saracens" has established the capital of the empire.⁷¹

His discussion of the lineage of the inhabitants of "Arabia" is characterized by an attention to detail and reference to Classical and patristic sources.

In one example, he uses Scripture and the writings of Jerome and Pliny to construct a portrait of the region:

> In this region, then, and likewise in Pharan, dwelt the children of Kentura and Agar, descendants of Abraham, of whom mention is made in Genesis, chapter XXV. And first from the Euphrates begins the Nabathaean country, so named from the first son of Ishmael, who was called Nabaioth, as Jerome states on Genesis, chapter XXV, and Pliny agrees with the statement in his first book, except that he calls one part of the Nabathaeans Nomads, who wander about the Euphrates near the Chaldeans. After these toward the desert of Pharan is the region of Cedar, which is named from the second of Ishmael's sons, who was called Cedar. Although other regions belonging to children of Ishmael are named as far as Sur, for he dwelt from Evila as far as Sur, as the Scripture states, yet all these regions are called Cedar, as Jerome maintains in his fifth book commenting on that Burden upon Arabia in Isaiah, chapter XXI. He says, "Here he is speaking for Kedar, which is the country of the Ishmaelites, who are called Agareni and Saracens by a wrong name." In the seventh book, commenting on Isaiah, chapter IX, he says in regard to these regions of Cedar and Nabathaena that Cedar is the country of the Saracens, who in Scripture are called Ishmaelites, and Nabaioth is one of the sons of Ishmael, from whose names the desert is called, which lacks crops, but is filled with cattle.[72]

In this instance, Bacon situates the inhabitants within a context that is familiar to and relevant for his audience, that of the greater Biblical narrative. As the descendants of Ishmael and Abraham, the Saracens take on a greater significance than they might as the current inhabitants of a significant portion of the Middle East.

For Bacon, the singular characteristic of the Saracens is their status as non-Christians. While there are relatively few references to the Saracens in terms of ethnographical information, there are numerous references to Saracens as a religious group, and still other references to Islam as a distinct religion. One of the first references to the Saracens within the context of religion in the *Opus Majus* occurs in Bacon's explanation of the need for the Church to have knowledge of various foreign languages. At one point he lists the most well known of the "schismatic" groups, and then elucidates on the way in such divisions are exacerbated and perpetuated by issues of language: "Then the Greeks and Rutheni and many more schismatics likewise grow hardened in error because the truth is not preached to them in their tongue; and the Saracens likewise and the Pagans and Tartars, and the other unbelievers throughout the whole world."[73] In another instance, Bacon identifies what he considers to be the six major sects from the beginning of time to the present: "Jews, Chaldeans, Egyptians, Agarenians or

Saracens, who descended from Agar and Ishmael, the Church of Christ, and the sect of Anti-Christ."[74]

In perhaps the most interesting moment of his discussions of religion in the *Opus Majus*, Bacon examines the influence exerted by the heavenly bodies over the various religions of the world:

> They [the mathematicians and authorities] say, then, that Jupiter and Venus are benevolent and fortunate planets, Saturn and Mars malevolent and unfortunate ones. Mercury, they say, is in a middle position, because he is good with the good, and evil with the evil, since he is of a changeable nature. Of the benevolent and fortunate planets they say that Jupiter is the better and that greater good fortune is owed to him, and the less to Venus . . . Venus has significance regarding the fortunes of this life, as far as pertains to games, pleasures, joy and the like, and Jupiter has respect to the blessings of the other life, which are greater.[75]

Having established the characteristics of the planets, Bacon then describes the pattern in which the planets are arranged in the heavens, identifying the planet that is of the greatest importance in matters of religion:

> Moreover, they divide the whole heavens into twelve parts, called houses, which are separated by the meridian circle and the horizon, and by four other circles intersecting one another at their points of meeting . . . The first house they assign to Saturn, the second to Jupiter, and so on according to the order of the planets, so that the eighth again is assigned to Saturn, and the ninth to Jupiter. All have agreed in considering the ninth house as that belonging to religion and faith . . . They say, then, that the planets are in conjunction and embrace one another in turn, and this happens when they are in the same sign and especially when they are in the same degree and in the sixteenth minute of that degree or below it. Therefore the philosophers maintain that Jupiter, from his conjunction with other planets, has signification regarding the division of religions and faith. Since there are six planets with which he can be united and in conjunction, they therefore assert that there must be six principal sects in the world.[76]

From this point, he now examines the religions that are signified through the conjunction between Jupiter and the various planets. Included in his analysis is the religion of the Saracens:

> If he is in conjunction with Venus, his reference is said to be the law of the Saracens, which is wholly voluptuous and lascivious. Although Mahomet reduced this law to writing, yet through long ages it was regarded by its votaries as the rule of life. Whence the book *De vitae sua*

mutatione, attributed to Ovid the poet, speaking of the lascivious sect, which the book stated was the law of the people in the poet's time, says

> "In which anything pleasing is considered lawful,
> Although a written law regarding it is not yet found."

This law more than six hundred years later Mahomet reduced to writing in a book called Alcoran.[77]

Thus, Bacon asserts a common charge leveled against Islam by medieval Christian theologians, that it was a religion that emphasized the pleasures of this life, doing so in the context of a discussion of the influence and movements of the planets.

According to Bacon, the religion of the Saracens will enjoy a fixed period of time before its eventual demise; he claims that evidence for this assertion exists in the works of previous scholars:

> Concerning the destruction of the law of Mahomet they speak clearly and with certainty. For according to what Albumazar says in the eighth chapter of the second book, the law of Mahomet cannot last more than 693 years . . . It is now the six hundred and sixty-fifth year of the Arabs from the time of Mahomet, and therefore it will quickly be destroyed by the grace of God, which must be a great consolation to Christians . . . Already the greater part of the Saracens have been destroyed by the Tartars, as well as the capital of their kingdom, which was Baldac [Baghdad], and their caliph, who was like a pope over them. These things happened twelve years ago.[78]

Perhaps with the imminent demise of the Saracen religion in mind, Bacon is prompted to render a final verdict on the religion. In so doing, he does not display the same level of hostility so often found in the writings of many of his contemporaries on the same subject:

> Although all things do not suffice to show fully the secrets of that sect, yet they give convincing evidence on the question of whether this is a sect, and also in regard to its quality in general, so that in our admiration of the wisdom granted to them we can easily excuse their ignorance in falling short of full certification of Christian rite, since they had not been instructed in it. We should praise them because they agree with us and confirm our profession.[79]

In his analysis of the religion of the Saracens, Bacon goes into greater detail than he does in either his discussion of the lands they inhabit or of their genealogy. As a group, they are but one of many found within the known world, and they do not have the historical pedigree of some of the others. However, as a religious community, they account for one of the six major historical religious movements, and are relevant both in the present context, and in the immediate and distant future. In the end, for Roger Bacon the Saracens as an ethnic/racial group are most relevant because of, and are thus defined by, their religion.

Bacon's focus on religion as the Saracens' defining characteristic reflects a common tendency among medieval Europeans, and theologians in particular, found in both fiction and nonfiction. The cultural, ethnic, and racial complexities inherent in the construct of "Arab" identity, the penetration of aspects of Arab culture into Muslim states (particularly in the initial stages of Islamization), and the heterogeneous nature of the Muslim world make, and have made, ethnographic studies difficult even for scholars familiar with the Eastern Mediterranean, to say nothing of medieval European scholars who were largely unfamiliar with it. Their attempt to categorize Muslims, and Arab Muslims in particular, often resulted in the conflation of race and religion, traces of which survive in the modern discourse. The fact that there were not easily discernible boundaries between the different ethnic and racial groups that comprised the medieval Muslim world, particularly in the Eastern Mediterranean and North Africa, often complicated the issue in a way that made the Muslim world ethnographically incomprehensible. As such, the common denominator for Western scholars and writers became Islam.

If the religion of the peoples of the Eastern Mediterranean and North Africa was what linked them in the eyes of Western writers, it was also what made them alien, even monstrous, as well. The adoption of Islam alienated these peoples from the Latin West, and particularly painful for some Western scholars was the fact that places that had once constituted the Christian heartland, places that were in some cases of central importance to the birth and rise of Christianity, were now populated by adherents of another faith. In the span of a few centuries the birthplaces of Augustine of Hippo, Athanasius, and John of Damascus had become foreign to the Latin West, and in place of these familiar figures now stood a people who were culturally and religiously foreign.

The loss of the Holy Land to Islam was especially problematic for Western scholars, who struggled to reconcile the advance of Islam with the traditional narrative of triumphant Christianity. In his *Summa totius haeresis Saracenorum*, the famous abbot Peter of Cluny (Peter the Venerable) attempts to explain the spread of Islam as a product of the intersection of favorable historical circumstances and opportunism:

> Forthwith, while the Roman Empire was declining, nay nearly ceasing, with the permission of Him through who kings rule [Prov. 8:16; Eccles. 24:9] there arose to power the dominion of the Arabs or Saracens, who were infested with this plague. And occupying by force of arms little by little the greater parts of Asia, with all Africa and a part of Spain, just as it transferred its rule upon its subjects, so also did it transfer its error.[80]

The archbishop William of Tyre describes the spread of Islam in his *History of Deeds Done Beyond the Sea* in a similar manner, although he attributes a greater role to the use of violence, striking a familiar chord with other Western accounts of this subject:

> This first-born son of Satan falsely declared that he was a prophet sent from God and thereby led astray the lands of the East, especially Arabia. The poisonous seed which he sowed so permeated the provinces that his successors employed sword and violence, instead of preaching and exhortation, to compel the people, however reluctant, to embrace the erroneous tenets of the prophet.[81]

Such accounts served to explain away, or rather to minimize, the apparent success of another religion in displacing Christianity from its ancestral homeland, focusing attention on the malevolence of the Saracens, who, through violence and deceit, were able to lead so many into "error."

For these scholars, the effects of the Islamization of the Eastern Mediterranean and its inhabitants, as well as its effects on other areas and peoples, were clear. It had transformed these formerly Christian peoples, remade them into something unrecognizable. When referred to as a nation or race by medieval commentators, Saracens were often depicted as monstrous, savage, and/or demonic. In the fourth book of his treatise *Against the Pagans*, Alain de Lille characterizes the religion and its adherents in the following terms:

> Muhamm[a]d's monstrous life, more monstrous sect and most monstrous end is manifestly found in his deeds. He, inspired by the evil spirit, founded an abominable sect, one suitable for fleshly indulgences, not disagreeable to the pleasures of the flesh; and therefore these carnal men, allured by his sect, and humiliated by the errors of various precepts, have died and continue to die miserably; the people call them with the usual appellation Saracens or pagans.[82]

In a similar vein, Fulcher of Chartres recounts Pope Urban II's warning (during his famous call to Crusade) of the resulting shame that would accompany Christian soldiers "if a race so despicable, degenerate, and enslaved by demons should thus overcome a people endowed with faith in Almighty God and resplendent in the name of Christ."[83]

The challenge posed by the Muslims was unique because of the threat posed by the religion they carried with them, a threat whose capacity to effect change within the Christian world had been demonstrated by the conquest and ultimate conversion of the lands of the Near East. The eventual response to Islam and Muslims would be marked by both intentional and unintentional misinterpretation and distortion of facts on the part of Western scholars, who often confused and conflated race, culture, and religion. In the process of describing Saracens, Western scholars rarely made the effort to differentiate between Saracens and Islam in such a way as to clearly identify what constituted Saracen-ness. In reading their writings, one is left with a perplexing question: is one *born* a Saracen (i.e., as the offspring of Saracen parents) or does one *become* Saracen (i.e., through the affectation of Saracen customs and/or conversion to the "Saracen religion")? Because of the complex nature of the Muslim societies upon which the concept of Saracen-ness was loosely based, the answer to this question was never clearly articulated; rather, religion, the one constant regardless of race, language, or location, was adopted as *the* defining characteristic for all who were included under the "Saracen" umbrella. And as the religion of the Saracens was viewed as aberrant and monstrous, it followed logically that its adherents would too become monstrous in the eyes of Western scholars.

In the end, it was religion that emerged as the defining characteristic of the Saracens, filling the gaps left by ethnographic and historical accounts, while also providing a framework within which such aspects of Saracen identity (or Saracen-ness) could be approached and discussed. But perhaps even more importantly, religion provided an amorphous context in which specificity was not required, which was of great utility for writers approaching a group about which accurate, specific information was in short supply. The cover of religion allowed writers to approach the myriad groups of the Eastern Mediterranean and North Africa not as individual groups but as a monolithic religious entity; Saracens were Saracens because they followed the Saracen religion. As such, the parameters of Saracen-ness were flexible; when necessary, even pagan Europeans could join the ranks of the Saracens (a phenomenon that occurs in some works of popular fiction).

Moreover, the Saracen racial/religious construct, nebulous as it was, never clearly distinguished between the concepts of race and religion, conflating the racial Other and religious Other in a manner that allowed writers to evoke either and/or both ideas at their discretion. And for Western scholars, the monstrous nature of the Saracen religion transformed the Saracen adherent, for whom religion was the singular defining characteristic, into something similarly monstrous. This approach toward the peoples of the Muslim world, and the Eastern Mediterranean and North Africa in particular, was as ubiquitous as it was simple, and resurfaced in some form in medieval texts on this topic regardless of author or genre.

Notes

1 Robert E. Lewis (Ed.), "Sarasin(e)," *Middle English Dictionary: Volume 10 (S-Sl)* (Ann Arbor: The U of Michigan P, 1986) 86.
2 George H. McKnight (Ed.), *King Horn, Floriz and Blauncheflur, the Assumption of Our Lady* (London: Kegan Paul, Trench, Trübner & Co., 1866) ll. 1413–16. Emphasis added. Diane Speed provides a thorough analysis of the portrayal of the Saracen characters of *King Horn*, arguing persuasively that "Saracen" was not a generic term for medieval non-Christians, but rather was primarily

affiliated with Muslims of the Middle East and North Africa. Diane Speed, "The Saracens of *King Horn*," *Speculum* 65 (1990) 564–95.
3 The information would have been scientific, or rather authoritative, in that it was in accordance with that of previous (Classical and Late Antique) authorities on the subject. A scholar's ability to access information from such sources was thus more indicative of his status as an expert, and of the "scientific" or "authoritative" nature of his work, than his ability to shed new insight on the subject matter.
4 Natalia Lozovsky, *"The Earth is Our Book": Geographical Knowledge in the Latin West ca. 400–1000* (Ann Arbor: U of Michigan P, 2000) 7.
5 George H.T. Kimble, *Geography in the Middle Ages* (London: Methuen & Co., Ltd., 1938) 13.
6 Orosius appears to have been born in the 380s, although the exact date is unknown. Paulus Orosius, *Seven Books of History against the Pagans: The Apology of Paulus Orosius*, Trans. Irving Woodworth Raymond (New York: Columbia UP, 1936) 3.
7 A.H. Merrills, *History and Geography in Late Antiquity* (Cambridge: Cambridge UP, 2005) 39.
8 Ibid, 51.
9 Ibid, 98–9.
10 "Our elders made a threefold division of the world, which is surrounded on its periphery by the Ocean. Its three parts they named Asia, Europe, and Africa. Some authorities, however, have considered them to be two, that is, Asia, and Africa and Europe, grouping the last two as one continent." Orosius, *Seven Books of History against the Pagans*, 34.
11 Ibid, 36.
12 Ibid. Emphasis added.
13 On two occasions (pp. 275, 347), Arabs are numbered among the groups conquered by Pompey and Severus Septimus, respectively.
14 *Etymologiae sive originum libri XX* will henceforward be referred to by the abbreviated title *Etymologiae*.
15 Kimble, *Geography in the Middle Ages*, 28.
16 Isidore of Seville also includes the "monstrous races" in his ethnographic survey of the world; these races are the subjects of a lengthy exposition. Both the passages concerning the monstrous races and the genealogical information pertaining to the other races of the world were very influential on later medieval scholars' treatment of the same groups.
17 Isidore of Seville, *The Etymologies of Isidore of Seville*, Ed. and Trans. Stephen A. Barney (Cambridge: Cambridge UP, 2006) 191.
18 By his estimation, thirty-one of the seventy-two known nations of the world are the descendants of Ham, twenty-seven of Shem, and fifteen of Japheth. Ibid, 192.
19 "Filii Cham quattor, ex quibus orate sunt gentes haec: Chus, a quo Aethiopes progeniti, Mesaim, a quo Aegyptii perhibentur exorti. Phut, a quo Libyi.Vnde et Mauretaniae fluvius usque in praesens Phut dicitur, omnisque circa eum region Phuthensis. Chanaam, a quo Afri et Phoenices et Chananeorum decem gentes. Item ex nepotibus Cham filii Chus, nepotes Cham sex. Filii Chus: Saba et Havila, Sabatha, Rhegma, Seba, Cuza. Saba, a quo progeniti et appellati Sabei . . . Hi sunt Arabes . . . Rhegma vero et Seba et Cuza paulatim antique vocabula perdiderunt, et quae nunca a veteribus habeant ignorantur. Filii Rhegma, Saba et Dadan. Hic Saba per Sin litteram scribitur in Hebraeo; ille autem superior Saba per Samech, a quo appellatos Sabaeos: interpretatur autem nunc Saba Arabia." Isidori Hispalensis Episcopi, *Etymologiarum Sive Originum Libri XX*, Ed. W.M. Lindsay (Oxford: Oxford UP, 1911) Bk. IX, Sec. II. 10–19. See also Isidore of Seville, *Etymologies*, 193.

32 *Saracens: Muslims as a concept*

20 "Saba, ei dicti . . . quod est supplicare et venerari, quia divinitatem per ipsorum tura veneramus. ipsi sunt et Arabes, quia in montibus Arabiae sunt, qui vocantur Libanus et Antilibanus, ubi turi colliguntur." Isidori Hispalensis Episcopi, *Etymologiarum*, Bk. IX, Sec. II. 49–50. See also Isidore of Seville, *Etymologies*, 194.

21 "Saraceni dicti, vel quia ex Sarra genitos se praedicent, vel sicut gentiles aiunt, quod ex orgine Syrorum sint, quasi Syriginae. Hi peramplam habitant solitudinem. Ipsi sunt et Ismaelitae, ut liber Geneseos docet, quod sint ex Ismaele. Ipsi Cedar a filio Ismaelis. Ipsi Agareni ab Agar; qui ut diximus, perverso nominee Saraceni vocantur, quia ex Sarra se genitos gloriantur." Isidori Hispalensis Episcopi, *Etymologiarum*, Bk. IX, Sec. II. 57–8. See also Isidore of Seville, *Etymologies*, 195.

22 "Secundum diversitatem enim caeli et facies hominum et colores et corporum quantitates et animorum diversitates existent. Inde Romanes graves, Graecos leves, Afros versipelles, Gallos natura feroces atque acriores ingenio pervidemus, quod natura climatum facit." Isidori Hispalensis Episcopi, *Etymologiarum*, Bk. IX, Sec. II. 105–6. See also Isidore of Seville, *Etymologies*, 198.

23 Just such an example can be found in Pope Urban II's famous call to Crusade in Clermont (1095); which is cited in Chapter 6.

24 Isidore of Seville, *Etymologies*, 199. A further discussion of the monstrous races (in particular the Cynocephali) of the *Etymologiae* and of the possible implications of their being located in Africa and India relative to Western perceptions occurs in a later section of this chapter. However, the main thrust of the discussion revolves around the Cynocephali and their connection to Western depictions of Muslims.

25 "Aethiopes dicti a filio Cham, qui vocatus est Chus, ex quo originem trahunt. Chus enim Hebraica lingua Aethiopes interpretatur. Hi quondam ab Indo flumine consurgentes, iuxta Aegyptum inter Nilum et Oceanum, in meridie sub ipsa solis vicinitate insiderunt, quorum tres sunt populi: Hesperi, Garamantes et Indi. Hesperi sunt occidentis, Garamantes Tripolis, Indi orientis." Isidori Hispalensis Episcopi, *Etymologiarum*, Bk. IX, Sec. II. 127–9. See also Isidore of Seville, *Etymologies*, 199.

26 The Greek word for "burnt-faced person" is "Aethiops," from which Ethiopian is derived. Frank M. Snowden, Jr., "Greeks and Ethiopians," *Greeks and Barbarians: Essays on the Interactions between Greeks and Non-Greeks in Antiquity and the Consequences for Eurocentrism*, Eds John E. Coleman and Clark A. Walz (Bethesda: CDL, 1997) 103.

27 Debra Higgs Strickland, *Saracens, Demons, & Jews: Making Monsters in Medieval Art* (Princeton: Princeton UP, 2003) 36.

28 William of Malmesbury, *William of Malmesbury's Chronicle of the Kings of England (From the Earliest Period to the Reign of King Stephen)*, Trans. J.A. Giles (London: Henry G. Bohn, 1847) 360–1.

> Numquam enim Turchus pede concerto martem audit, sed pulsus loco longe tendit nervos et permitil vulnera ventis, et quoniam habet tela mortifero suco ebria, in homine quem percutit non virtus sed virus mortem facit. Quicquid igitur, fortunae, non fortitudini attribuerim, quod pugnat fuga et veneno. Constat profecto quod omnis nation quae in Eoa plaga nascitur, nimio solis ardore siccata, amplius quidem sapit, sed minus habet sanguinis; ideoque uicinam pugnam fugiunt, quia parum sanguinis se habere norunt.

Willelmi Malmesbiriensis Monachi, *Gesta regum anglorum, Volumen II* (Londini: Sumptibus Societatis, 1840) 529.

29 Strickland, *Saracens, Demons, & Jews*, 83–4.

30 H.C.G. Matthew and Brian Harrison (Eds.), "Conches, William de," *Oxford Dictionary of National Biography: From the Earliest Times to the Year 2000, Volume 12 (Clegg-Const)* (Oxford: Oxford UP, 2004) 916.

31 William of Conches, *A Dialogue on Natural Philosophy (Dragmaticon Philosophiae)*, Trans. Italo Ronca and Matthew Curr (Notre Dame: U of Notre Dame P, 1997) xv.
32 Ibid, xv–xvi.
33 Ibid, xvii.
34 Ibid, xxiii.
35 Ibid, 120–8.
36 Ibid, 124.
37 The Antipodes were so named because they were believed to occupy a position that was the exact opposite of the northern temperate zone, in which the habitable areas of the known world were located.
38 William of Conches, *A Dialogue on Natural Philosophy (Dragmaticon Philosophiae)*, 125–6.
39 Ibid, 127–8.
40 However, the *Dragmaticon Philosophiae* does contend that Jerusalem is located at the center of the earth. Ibid, 110.
41 Albertus Magnus (Albert "the Great") was also known as Albert of Cologne, Albert the German, Albert von Bollstadt, and Albert the Teuton. Sr. Jean Paul Tilman, *An Appraisal of the Geographical Works of Albertus Magnus and His Contributions to Geographical Thought* (Ann Arbor: U of Michigan P, 1971) 14.
42 There has been a great deal of speculation as to the exact date of Albertus' birth, with some proposing a date as early as 1193, and others favoring a date as late as 1206/7. However, it is maintained by most scholars that the most likely date of birth for Albertus Magnus is circa 1200, and the general opinion is that his life spanned the years circa 1200–1280. James A. Weisheipl, O.P., "The Life and Works of St. Albert the Great," *Albertus Magnus and the Sciences: Commemorative Essays, 1980*, Ed. James A. Weisheipl, O.P. (Toronto: Pontifical Institute of Medieval Studies, 1980) 15–16.
43 Ibid, 28.
44 Ibid, 25–8.
45 Ibid, 14.
46 *Liber de natura locorum* will henceforward be referred to by the abbreviated title *De Natura Locorum*.
47 Tilman, *An Appraisal of the Geographical Works*, 50.
48 Ibid, 76.
49 See the discussion on the status of the fourth clime in the works of Muslim geographers (esp. Ibn Khaldūn) in Chapter 2.
50 Tilman, *An Appraisal of the Geographical Works*, 76.
51 "Est aute dubitation de his qua(?) dicta sunt. vtrum videlicet locus quarti climatis veresit s teperatior inter loca habitabilia, quoniam exceeds in frigidissimo non est clima septimu, sed potius locus inhabitabilis sub polo aglonari. Similiter aute exceeds in calidissimo non est locus sub egnoctial, & citra par in latitudine primi climatis, sed potius sub tropico qua(?) latitude est secudi climatis, mediu ergo per equidistatiam acceptam inter frigidissimu, quod est latitudinis nonaginta graduu vel paru minus, & inter calidissimu quod est. 24. graduu, vider esse op est latitudinus amplius [?] 40.graduu & hoc est sextu & and septimu clima." Albertus Magnus, *Liber de natura Locorum* (München: Bayerische StaatsBibiothek, 1515) 46. See also Tilman, *An Appraisal of the Geographical Works*, 77.
52 "[C]uius indiciu videt quod hoies il loru climatu pulcherrimi sunt in corpore, procure stature, & uenusti coloris, cu hominess quarti climatis sint parui, & susci coloris, vbi eni coplexio hois maxime coualescit illud videre magis cogruere hoi ad habitandu, coualescit aut maxime ubi generalius pulchriores & fortiores & procerioris stature sunt hoies, & hoc est in septimo & in sexto climate

sicut apparet" Albertus Magnus, *De natura Locorum*, 46. See also Tilman, *An Appraisal of the Geographical Works*, 77.
53 "[A]d hoc videt esse quarti climatis calor maximus in æstate, & diminution pluui arum. Si enim esset temperatu simpliciter, vt inquiut philosphi, tatus deberet in eo esse excessus frigoris in hyeme, qua tus est excessus caloris in eo in æstate, & opposite huiusmodi experimur ad sensum, quia excedit in ipso calor estates, & no excedit in ipso frigus hyemis, & secundum has ratios temperatum in medio videt esse clima sextu, in quo nec sentitur excessus caloris in æstate, neq frigoris in hyeme" Albertus Magnus, *De natura Locorum*, 47. See also Tilman, *An Appraisal of the Geographical Works*, 77–8.
54 "[E]tia Lucanus de Arabibus, qui in torrida habitant, scribat dicens, quod vmbras quas habebat dextras, in terra sua, quado se conuertebat ad orietem, in meridie suo, venientes in quarta aquilonare, videbant ire sinistras, &ideo dicit loques ad eos. Ignotu vobis Arabes venistis in orbe." Albertus Magnus, *De natura Locorum*, 36. See also Tilman, *An Appraisal of the Geographical Works*, 63.
55 "[P]ostea aute quado a Sarracenis occupate sunt, plurimæ ear fracte sunt, & aliæ ædificatæ alior nominu, & quobusdam(?) etia earu noia sunt mutata." Albertus Magnus, *De natura Locorum*, 74. See also Tilman, *An Appraisal of the Geographical Works*, 117.
56 "Haru autem gentium noia multa mutate sunt, aut ex bellis aut depopulationibus terrar, aut forte propter nouas sectas, & religiones nomina mutauerut." Albertus Magnus, *De natura Locorum*, 74–5. See also Tilman, *An Appraisal of the Geographical Works*, 117–18.
57 H.C.G. Matthew and Brian Harrison (Eds.), "Bacon, Roger," *Oxford Dictionary of National Biography: From the Earliest Times to the Year 2000, Volume 3 (Avranches-Barnewall)* (Oxford: Oxford UP, 2004) 176.
58 David C. Lindberg, *Roger Bacon's Philosophy of Nature* (Oxford: Clarendon, 1983) xx–xxi.
59 During the 1260s Bacon was transferred from Oxford to Paris, apparently against his will, so that his activities could be more closely monitored by his superiors. It was during this time, and as a result of his correspondence with Guy de Foulques (who later became Pope Clement IV), that he composed the *Opus Majus*. Brian Clegg, *The First Scientist: A Life of Roger Bacon* (New York: Carroll & Graf, 2003) 95–9.
60 John Henry Bridges, *The Life & Work of Roger Bacon: An Introduction to the Opus Majus* (London: Williams & Norgate, 1914) 12.
61 Clegg, *The First Scientist*, 99.
62 The seven sciences included perspective (optics), astronomy (which also included geography and astrology), a field he identified as the "science of weights," alchemy, medicine, and experimental science. Ibid, 99–100.
63 Ibid, 100.
64 David Woodward and Herbert M. Howe, "Roger Bacon on Geography and Cartography," *Roger Bacon and the Sciences: Commemorative Essays*, Ed. Jeremiah Hackett (New York: Brill, 1997) 200–1.
65 Ibid, 211.
66 Ibid, 217.
67 Roger Bacon, *The Opus Major of Roger Bacon, Vol. 1*, Trans. Robert Belle Burke (New York: Russell & Russell, 1962) 203.
68 "Et nos videmus, quod omnia variantur secundum loca mundi diversa non solum in naturalibus, sed homines in moribus; quoniam alios mores habent Æthiopes, alios Hispani, alios Romani, & alios [Graeci]." Roger Bacon, *Fratris Rogeri Bacon, ordinis minorum, opus majus ad Clementem quartum, pontificem romanum. Ex MS. Codice Dubliniensi, cum aliis quibusdam collato, nunc primum editit* (Londini: Typis Gulielmi Bowyer, 1733) 46. See also Bacon, *Opus Major*, 159.

69 Bacon, *Opus Major*, 339–43.
70 "Tota igitur haec pars Æthiopiæ citra Meroen & Syenem & Heliopolim versus orientem sub Arabia continetur, & non solum hoc, sed quicquid est circa linquam, i.e. extremitatem maris Rubri & super littus ejus versus orientem a cuspide linguæ usque ad finum ejus Persicum: & extendit se a mare Rubro usque ad Pelusium Ægypti ad occidentem, & dilatat se ad septentrionem per totum desertum, in quo vagati sunt filii Israelis usque ad terram Philistinorum super mare nostrum conterminam Ægypto, & extensam ad orientem donec occurat Amalechitarum region, quæ est ad orientem terræ Philistiem, & usque ad terram Edom, seu Idumæam, quæ ad orientem Amalech & usque ad terram Moab. Deinde flectit se magis versus septentrionem per terram Seon Regis Esebon, & Og Regis Basan usque ad montem Galaad & Libanum, & adhuc magis flectit se ad Septentrionem orientalem usque ad Ciliciam & Syriam Comagenam, & usque ad Euphratem." Bacon, *Fratris Rogeri*, 204–5. See also Bacon, *Opus Major*, 343–4.
71 "Et est Baldac civitas regia, in qua Caliph Dominus Saracenitæ sectæ sedem sua dignitatis constituit." Bacon, *Fratris Rogeri*, 209. See also Bacon, *Opus Major*, 351.
72 "In hac igitur regione pergrandi similiter & in Pharan habitaverunt filii Kethuræ & Agar, quos generavit Abraham, de quibus sit mention XXV capitulo Genesis. Et primo ab Euphrate incipit regio Nabathena a filio primo Ismaelis, qui vocatur Nabaioth, sicut dicit Hieronymus, super Gen. xxv capitulo, & nunc dicto concordat Plinius I libro, nisi quod unam partem Nabathenorum vocat Nomades, qui vagantur circa Euphraten prope Chaldæos; post hos, versus desertum Pharan, est Cedar region, quæ ab altero filiorum Ismael nominator, qui Cedar vocatus est. Et quamvis aliæ regiones filiorum Ismael nominentur usque Sur, nam habitavit ab Evila usque Sur, sicut dicit scriptura, tamen omnes vocantur Cedar, sicut vult Hieronymus 5 libro super illud Isaiæ XXI. onus in Arabia, dicens, hic loquitur pro Cedar, quæ est region Ismaelitarum, qui dicuntur Agareni & Saraceni nominee perverso & 7 libro super capitulum Isaiæ LX. dicit de his regionibus Cedar & Nabathena, quod Cedar est region Saracenorum, qui in scriptura vocantur Ismaelitæ, & Nabioth est unus filiorum Ismael, quorum nominibus solitude appellatur; quæ frugum inops, pecorum plena est." Bacon, *Fratris Rogeri*, 207–8. See also Bacon, *Opus Major*, 348–9.
73 "Deinde Graeci et Rutheni et multi alii schismatici similiter in errore perdurant quia non praedicatur eis veritas in eorum lingua, et Saraceni similiter et Pagani, ac Tartari, et caeteri infidels pertotum mundum." Bacon, *Fratris Rogeri*, 111. See also Roger Bacon, *The "Opus Majus" of Roger Bacon*, Ed. John Henry Bridges (London: Williams & Norgate, 1900) 121.
74 "& sunt secta Hebræorum, & Chaldæorum, & Ægyptiorum, & Agarenarum seu Saracenorum, qui fuerunt de Agar & Ismaele, secta Christi, ac secta Antichristi." Bacon, *Fratris Rogeri*, 160. See also Bacon, *Opus Major*, 276.
75 "Dicunt igitur Jovem & Venerem esse planetas benivolos & fortunatos, Saturnum & Martem malivolos & infortunatos; Mercurium dicunt medio modo se habere, quia cum bonis est bonus, cum malis malus, quia convertibilis naturæ est. De benivolis vero fortunatis dicunt Jovem meliorem esse, & majorem fortunam ei deberi, minoremque Veneri . . . dicunt Venerem significare super fortunas hujus vitæ, quantum ad ludos & gaudia atque lætitiam & hujusmodi, & Jupiter respectum habet ad bona alterius vitæ, quæ majora sunt." Bacon, *Fratris Rogeri*, 160. See also Bacon, *Opus Major*, 276–7.
76 "Prætera distinguunt totum cælum in XII partes, quæ vocantur domus, quæ distinguuntur per meridianum circulum & horizontem, & alios quatuor circulos intersecantes se in eorum sectionibus . . . Primam igitur domum dant Saturno, secundam Jovi, & ulterius secundum ordinem planetarum, ita quod VIII iterum

datur Saturno, & nona Jovi. Consideraveruntque omnes concorditer quod domus nona est domus religionis & fidei . . . Dicunt igitur planetas conjungi & complecti sibi invicem, & hoc est quando fuerunt in eodem signo & præcipue quando in eodem gradu & in XVI minuto illius gradus & infra. Volunt ergo philosophi Jovem ex sua conjunctione cum aliis planetis significare super sectam religionum & fidei. Et quia sunt VI planetæ, quibus complecti & conjungi potest, ideo affuerunt VI fore debere in mundo sectas principales." Bacon, *Fratris Rogeri*, 160–1. See also Bacon, *Opus Major*, 277–8.

77 "Si Veneri, significare dicitur super legem Saracenorum, quæ est tota voluptuosa & venereal, quam licit in scriptis Mahometus redegit, ipsa tamen per longa tempora in usu vitæ habebatur a suis cultoribus; unde in libro qui ascribitur Ovidio de vitæ suæ mutatione, cum loqueretur de secta venereal, quam hominibus fui temporis legem dixit esse, dixit in metro suo,

'In qua, si libeat, quodcunque licere putatur,
Scripta licet super hoc nondum lex inveniatur;'

Quam postea per sexcentos annos & amplius scripsit Mahometus in libro, qui dicitur Alcoran." Bacon, *Fratris Rogeri*, 161–2. See also Bacon, *Opus Major*, 278–9.

78 "Et de destructione legis Mahometi pulchre & certitudinaliter loquuntur. Nam secundum quod Albumasar dicit VIII capitulo secundi libri, non potest lex Mahometi durare ultra sexcentos Nonaginta tres annos . . . Et nunc est annos Arabum sexagesimus sexagesimus quintus a tempore Mahometi, & ideo cito destruetur per gratiam Dei, quod debet esse magnum solatium Christianis . . . Et jam major pars Saracenorum destructa est per Tartaros, & caput regni qoud fuit Baldac, & Caliph qui fuit sicut papa eorum. Jam hæc facta sunt XII annis clapsis." Bacon, *Fratris Rogeri*, 167. See also Bacon, *Opus Major*, 287. Bacon's citation of the destruction of Baghdad and the murder of the caliph is a reference to the Mongol destruction of the city, which took place in 1258.

79 "Sed quicquid dicunt in hac parte, hoc ad regulam fidei reducendum est, ut a catholica veritate non discordet. Et licet omnia & ad plenum non sufficient ostendere secreta istius sectæ, tamen an sit hæc sectæ, & quails sit in universali pulchre attestantur, ut fatis admirantes sapientiam eis datam facile excusemus eorum ignorantiam, quia defecerunt a plena certificatione ritus Christiani, cum in eo non fuerant instructi. Et laudare debemus, quod nobiscum concordant & confirmant nostrum professionem." Bacon, *Fratris Rogeri*, 168–9. See also Bacon, *Opus Major*, 289.

80 "Nam statim Romano languescente immo pene deficiente imperio, permittente eo "per quem reges regnant," [Prov. 8:15] Arabum uel Sarracenorum hac peste infectorum surrexit principatus, atque ui armata maximas Asiae partes cum tota Africa ac parte Hispaniae paulatim occupans, in subiectos sicut imperium sic et errorum transfudit." Peter the Venerable. *Summa Totius Haeriesis Saracenorum*. A 2vd in James's Kritzeck's *Peter the Venerable and Islam*, 208. See also James Kritzeck, *Peter the Venerable and Islam*, (Princeton: Princeton UP, 1964) 140.

81 "Mahumet primogeniti Sathane, qui se prophetam a domino missum mentiendo Orientalium regiones et maxima Arabium seduxerat, ita invaluerat doctrina pestilens et disseminatus langor in universas occuperavat provincias, ut eius successors non iam exhortationibus vel predicatione, sed gladiis et violentia in suum errorem populus descendere compellerent invitos." R.B.C. Huygens (Ed.), *Guillaume de Tyr: Chronique* (Turnholti: Typographi Brepols Editores Pontificii, 1986) 11. 105. See also William of Tyre, *A History of Deeds Done Beyond the Sea, Vol. 1*, Trans. Emily Atwater Babcock and A.C. Krey (New York: Columbia UP, 1943) 60.

82 "Cuius Machometi monstruosa vita, monstruosior secta, monstruosissimus finis in gestis manifeste reperitur; qui, maligno spiritu inspiratus, sectam abhominabilem inuenit, carnalibus voluptatibus consonam, a carnalium voluptatibus non dissonam; et ideo multi carnales, eius secta illecti, et per errorum varia precipitia deiecti, miserabiliter perierunt et pereunt; quos communi vocabulo vulgus Saracenos vel paganos nuncupat." Alan of Lille, *Liber quartus contra paganos, Opinio paganorum qui dicunt Christum conceptum fuisse de flatu Dei* in Michael Uebel, "Unthinking the Monster: Twelfth-Century Responses to Saracen Alterity," *Monster Theory: Reading Culture*, Ed. Jeffrey Jerome Cohen (Minneapolis: U of Minnesota P, 1996) 274.
83 Cf. Fulcher of Chartres, *Historia 3* (Trans. Ryan, 66) in Hillenbrand, *Saracens, Demons, & Jews*, 169.

2 Al-iFranj
Medieval Muslim perceptions of Western Europeans

Muslims of the Medieval Eastern Mediterranean world shared a perspective on the outside world and their place within it that differed in important aspects from that of their counterparts in Western Europe. As inhabitants of a world that extended from the outer edge of China in the East to Spain south of the Pyrenees in the West, medieval Muslims in general, and Eastern Mediterranean Muslims in particular, were the inheritors of much of the ancient Greek and Roman empires, as well as that of the Sassanian Empire in modern-day Iran and Iraq. The Muslim world at the eve of the First Crusade consisted of the 'Abbāsid Empire (by then a loose confederation of kingdoms ruled by Turkish sovereigns extending from the Levant to Central Asia, but nominally subject to the Caliph in Baghdad); the Fatimid Empire of Egypt; the Party Kings (al-Mulūk al-Tawā'if) of Spain, who inherited the spoils of the recently fallen Umayyad dynasty; and a number of independent and quasi-independent kingdoms of varying size and strength in North Africa. As inhabitants of a powerful, dynamic, albeit fragmented world, medieval Muslims reaped the benefits of their combined military, political, and economic strength, all of which infused them with a great degree of confidence, a confidence that was informed by centuries of growth in each of the aforementioned areas. All of this was especially true of Eastern Mediterranean Muslims, who inhabited the "Islamic heartland," living in proximity to many of the most powerful institutions and individuals in the Medieval Muslim world.

During the first century of expansion (c.640–740 C.E.) for what was then largely an Arab/Islamic polity, very little changed in the geographical outlook of the Arab Muslims, who looked primarily to the Qur'ān, the Traditions of the Prophet (hadīth), and pre-Islamic Arabic poetry as sources of knowledge.[1] The conquest of much of the Eastern Mediterranean and parts of the Indian subcontinent provided them with access to the accumulated knowledge of the Persian, Hellenic, Mesopotamian, and Indian civilizations, among others,[2] but it was not until the reign of the 'Abbāsid Caliph al-Mansūr (753–775 C.E.), under whom a two-centuries-long process of translation of foreign texts was initiated, that the acquisition of this ancient knowledge was begun in earnest.[3] Greek, Indian, and Persian geographical concepts all exercised a tremendous influence on Muslim geographical thought, with the Greek and Persian ideas having the greatest effect on the development of medieval Muslim geography.[4] From the Persian sources, Muslim geographers adopted a concept that would feature prominently in their conception of the world: the idea of the earth being divided into seven *kishwars*, or equal geometric circles, with the fourth *kishwar* (which was the most favorably situated, and included the Iranian and Iraqi heartland) in the center, surrounded by the other six.[5] From the Hellenic works, Muslim geographers acquired the concepts[6] and astronomical findings which informed much of the science which lay at the foundation of medieval Muslim geography, and which was most observable in their human, mathematical, and physical geography.[7]

The works of celebrated scholars such as Aristotle and Plato, and lesser-known figures like Marinos of Tyre (70–130 C.E.), were very influential within the emerging field of geography in the Muslim world during the eighth through the tenth centuries; however, the influence of Claudius Ptolemy was unmatched, and among his works *Geographikê Hyphêgêsis*, the *Almagest*, *Tetrabiblon*, and *Apparitions of Fixed Stars* were all utilized by Muslim geographers, with *Geographikê Hyphêgêsis* receiving the greatest amount of attention.[8] The works of Ptolemy remained largely unchanged in the hands of Muslim writers, and exerted an unparalleled influence on Muslim thought in the field of geography for centuries.[9] From Ptolemy, Muslims received the classical concept of the climatic zones, or "climes," of the earth, and their influence on both the physiological and psychological make-up of the peoples who inhabited them, although their division of the earth into seven latitudinal zones[10] was actually in accordance with the aforementioned Persian *kishwar* system.

Among the many early Muslim geographers, a few individuals are distinguished by their extraordinary achievements. Muhammad ibn Mūsā al-Khwārizmī (d. after 847 C.E.), known to future generations as al-Khwārizmī, translated Ptolemy's *Geography*, incorporating the additional information that had been gathered by Muslim scholars up to his time.[11] Ya'qūb ibn Ishāq al-Kindī (801–873 C.E.) further developed the Greek idea of the climes and the sun's influence on the various regions via its proximity, causing areas that were either too near or distant to be infertile and sparsely populated as a result of the excessive heat or cold, and providing the "intermediate" zones with an optimal environment for the cultivation of food and civilization.[12] Abū 'l-Qāsim 'Ubayd Allāh ibn 'Abd Allāh ibn Khurradādhbih (820–912 C.E.), known commonly as ibn Khurradādhbih, produced the first Muslim geographical reference work on the various fiefdoms and principalities in the 'Abbāsid empire, *Kitāb al-Masālik wa 'l-mamālik* (*The Book of Itineraries and Kingdoms*), which would serve as a model for future geographers attempting to describe the Muslim and non-Muslim world;[13] the title itself would be used for numerous subsequent works in the same vein by other authors. While this list is far from exhaustive, and omits some of the brightest minds of the era, these scholars made seminal contributions to the field of geography in the early medieval Muslim world, and their works paved the way for later writers who would focus on the distant places and peoples of the world, places such as medieval Western Europe.

In addition to the works of theoretical geography and the *Masālik wa 'l-mamālik* literature, another genre emerged: *'ajā'ib* literature, which focused primarily on faraway places and peoples. "*'Ajā'ib*" is generally translated as "marvels," and in the case of the study of distant lands, *'ajā'ib* literature during the tenth and eleventh century was characterized by its oscillation between realistic travel accounts and flights of fancy.[14] One of the earliest works of *'ajā'ib* literature was the *'Ajā'ib al-Hind (Marvels of India)* (ca. 953),[15] attributed to a captain Burzug ibn Shahriyār, which is comprised of the tales of sailors who had traveled to East Africa, India, and some of the islands of Southeast Asia; it is a blend of accurate accounts and stories of the marvelous.[16] The *'ajā'ib* literature produced during the formative years of medieval Muslim geography (and through some of its greatest development during the tenth and eleventh centuries) reflects the state of geographical thinking to some degree, as there is a balance between fact and the fantastic in the various works within the genre. However, in the centuries that followed there was a marked shift toward the fantastic, and by the fourteenth century this shift was so profound that the work of Burzug ibn Shahriyār had been reformulated into a new cycle of stories that featured a new character: Sindbād the sailor.[17]

Throughout the development of geographical thought in the medieval Muslim world between the eighth and tenth centuries through both the adaptation of foreign works and the observations of Muslim navigators, the focus was on (a) the areas and peoples comprising the Muslim world; (b) the lands adjacent to Muslim lands (primarily in the area of the Eastern provinces, but also certain parts of East Africa); and (c) the East, and India in particular. Even in the *'ajā'ib* literature, much of the focus was on the East. A result of this particular focus was a general lack of attention toward Europe, and Western Europe in particular.[18] While there were periodic accounts of Muslim travel to certain parts of Europe, such as that of Ibn Fadlān to the Upper Volga in the early tenth century and that of Ibn Ya'qūb's journey from Spain to Germany in the mid-tenth century,[19] such accounts were rare, and the peoples and places of Europe were not given the same type of attention by Muslim geographers as the peoples and places of the East.

Because medieval Muslim geographers largely ignored Europe, the information on these areas and their inhabitants was often vague or erroneous. In some instances, different groups were conflated, with one name being applied to multiple ethnic groups.[20] In the case of Western Europeans, or the *iFranj* ("Franks"), as they were known in the Muslim sources,[21] very little was known of or written about them for much of the early years of the Islamic empires. Al-Khwārizmī provided some geographical information regarding Western Europe via his Arabic adaptation of Ptolemy's *Geographikê Hyphêgêsis*,[22] and Ibn Khurradādhbih informed Muslim readers that the

Al-iFranj: *Medieval Muslim perceptions* 41

lands of the *iFranj* were "polytheist," and adjoined Spain.[23] Writing in the early tenth century, Ibn Rusta provided an account of the city of Rome and mentioned the British Isles; all of his information was based on the account of Hārūn ibn Yahyā, a former prisoner of war.[24] However, this was the extent of available information about Western Europe and its peoples through the earliest years of the tenth century. With the exception of the Byzantine Empire, little attention was given to the lands and peoples of Europe in the works of the Muslim geographers throughout the early Middle Ages. Of course, there were a few notable exceptions.

One of the greatest contributors to the field of medieval Muslim geography, particularly as it pertained to non-Muslim nations and peoples, was the tenth-century scholar Abū 'l-Hasan 'Alī ibn al-Husayn ibn 'Abd-Allāh al-Mas'ūdī (circa 896–956). Known to later generations as al-Mas'ūdī, he was one of the most important, yet one of the most enigmatic literary figures of the classical Islamic period.[25] A polymath who lived during turbulent times for an 'Abbāsid caliphate that, though embattled, remained relevant in a way it would not be by the time of the Crusades, al-Mas'ūdī wrote on a variety of subjects: religion,[26] including but not limited to objective and polemical treatments of Zoroastrianism, Christianity, Judaism, and Manichaeism; philosophy and science; historical traditions in general; and general knowledge within the context of history.[27] As a member of a minority sect within Islam,[28] he brought a perspective to religious questions and controversies not found within the mainstream of Muslim opinion.[29] Unfortunately, of his estimated thirty-six works, including books and epistles, only two survive, *Murūj al-Dhahab wa 'l Ma'ādin al-Jawhar* (*Meadows of Gold and Mines of Gems*) and *Kitāb al-Tanbīh wa 'l-Ishrāf* (*Book of Indication and General View*); information concerning the nature and content of the other works can be gathered only through references contained within the two surviving works.[30]

In composing the *Murūj al-Dhahab wa 'l Ma'ādin al-Jawhar* and *Kitāb al-Tanbīh wa 'l-Ishrāf*, al-Mas'ūdī drew upon a wide variety of sources, Islamic and pre-Islamic, for his discussion of the earth's geography, and the influences of the various sources and particular authors is evident in both works.[31] Among his various sources, the most important contributors to al-Mas'ūdī's understanding of world geography in the theoretical sense were the Greek and Muslim astronomers and geographers of the distant and recent past,[32] while his understanding of the physical geography of the world was largely influenced by Greek and Muslim philosophers.[33] Other sources also informed al-Mas'ūdī's writing on geography, but none of them exerted as great an influence as those of his Greek and Muslim predecessors.

Among the Greek sources, the works of Ptolemy and Aristotle had the greatest impact on al-Mas'ūdī's understanding of the earth's geography, both in terms of theoretical geography and physical geography. Al-Mas'ūdī appears to have been well acquainted with Ptolemy's *Almagest* and *Geographikê Hyphêgêsis*, and to have been at least familiar with his

Quadripartitum and *Appearance of the Stationary Stars*.[34] From these works, he derived his theories regarding the circumference, diameter, and shape of the earth; the division of the earth into three continents (Africa, Asia, and Europe); the climatic zones; the seas, and of particular importance, the limits of the habitable areas of the world. On this question, al-Mas'ūdī cites Ptolemy's calculations regarding the northern and southern limits, although he also includes the theories of al-Kindī in his discussion of the extent of habitable land south of the equator.[35]

Aristotle was known to al-Mas'ūdī in terms of his insights on the physical geography of the world in *Meteorology*, *De Caelo*, *Metaphysics*, and his letter to his most famous pupil (who was in India at the time, adding to his legend). From Aristotle, al-Mas'ūdī derived his ideas on the existence of ether, the relative size of the earth and the connected nature of the ocean, the notion that land and sea were in a constant state of change, and his theories on the mutual reaction of heat and cold.[36] In addition, al- Mas'ūdī learned of the theory that the polar and equatorial regions were incapable of sustaining life due to their extreme cold and heat, respectively, which was likely the basis for his division of land into the categories of inhabited and barren. Al-Mas'ūdī also references the works of Marinos of Tyre, Geminos, and Hermes,[37] but they did not exert an influence on his understanding of world geography proportionate to that of Aristotle and Ptolemy.

In addition to the Greek elements, the *Murūj* and *Tanbīh* also reveal al-Mas'ūdī's acquaintance with the works of earlier Muslim astronomers, geographers, and philosophers. In the area of astronomy, al-Mas'ūdī was familiar with the works of al-Farghani, al-Battani, al-Khwārizmī, and al-Balkhī,[38] as well as the works of the Caliph al-Ma'mūn's astronomers. From these works he derived many of his ideas regarding the latitudes and longitudes of the earth, the curvature of its surface, and its circumference, diameter, and shape. These works are especially relevant to any discussion of al-Mas'ūdī's description of the places and peoples of the world, in that he also derived both his approach of dividing the earth into four distinct quarters (North, South, East, and West), and its inhabitants into different groups according to color and "character" (which was attributed to the influence of the climate of the respective regions) from these earlier Muslim astronomers.[39]

From the Muslim geographers, al-Mas'ūdī acquired a great deal of material relating to descriptive and regional geography. While he consulted a number of works, Ibn Khurradādbih's *al-Masālik wa 'l-mamālik*, and to a lesser extent, al-Jāhiz's *Kitāb al-Amsār wa 'Ajā'ib al-Buldān*, appear to have been most influential, although he criticizes Ibn Khurradādbih's work for its lack of sufficient detailed information regarding the areas it describes, and al-Jāhiz's work because he had not traveled to the places he describes.[40] Al-Mas'ūdī was also well-acquainted with al-Kindī's *Rasm al-Ma'mūr min al-'Ard* and *Risāla fī 'l-Bihār wa'l-Madd wa 'l-Jazr*, as well as Ahmad ibn al-Tayyib al-Sarakhsī's *al-Masālik wa 'l-mamālik* and *Risāla fī 'l-Bihār wa* 'l-Miyāh wa 'l-Jibāl;⁴¹ from these sources he obtained information regarding the sizes of the various bodies of water and other types of oceanographic information.⁴²

Beyond the influence of Greek and Muslim scholars, al-Mas'ūdī's works also bear the stamp of other systems of thought. Following the example of his Muslim predecessors, al-Mas'ūdī bases his description of the various climes on the Persian *kishwar* system.⁴³ Al-Mas'ūdī's works also incorporate histories and legends into his descriptions of places and peoples;⁴⁴ clearly fantastic details can be found interspersed among the historical accounts. In recounting the history of a particular group, al-Mas'ūdī valued the accounts provided by the group's own historians, and availed himself of such sources whenever possible. As a result, he was able to gain greater insight into particular aspects of certain groups (e.g., the Persians), such as genealogical accounts. The use of a wide variety of sources is one of al-Mas'ūdī's particular strengths, and contributes to the overall quality of both the *Murūj* and *Tanbīh*. In the case of the *Murūj*, this willingness to consult foreign sources is relevant to his discussion of Western Europe and its peoples, as it enables him to provide his audience with a glimpse into the political system of the *iFranj*.

In addition to the aforementioned sources of information, al-Mas'ūdī had recourse to another easily accessible repository of information about many of the distant areas of the then-known world: his own experiences as a traveler. Like many of his predecessors, al-Mas'ūdī made use of informants, generally Muslim sailors, merchants, and others who were familiar with the lands in question,⁴⁵ to fill in the gaps in areas in which his knowledge was insufficient. However, al-Mas'ūdī was a traveler in his own right, and a substantial portion of his life was spent in foreign lands. One of al-Mas'ūdī's principal complaints regarding the works of other Muslim geographers was that they were often not informed by the types of personal observation that could only result from travel, and he took great pride in the fact that he was able to incorporate his own observations into his discussion of foreign territories and peoples.⁴⁶ Al-Mas'ūdī traversed the medieval Muslim world and beyond; his travels occurred during the greater part of his life, beginning in 915 with his journey to Persia and India, and ending with his death in Fustāt (present-day Cairo) in 956.⁴⁷ He traveled across his native Iraq; the majority of Persia; Azerbaijan; Armenia; India, including the Indus valley and its Western coast; parts of the East African coast; Arabia; Egypt; and Syria; he could boast of having sailed on the Indian Ocean, and the Caspian, Mediterranean, and Red Seas,⁴⁸ along with a multitude of rivers and smaller bodies of water. The information gathered by al-Mas'ūdī through his travels figures prominently in both the *Murūj* and *Tanbīh*, serving as an example of the way in which personal experience and practical observation could be used in conjunction with, and when necessary as a corrective for, information taken from outside sources when writing about distant places and peoples. These experiences were not directly applicable to his discussion of the places and peoples of Western Europe; however, they did inform his approach toward this subject in some aspects, particularly as it related to his desire to incorporate direct and indirect accounts about the area from native informants.

Al-Mas'ūdī was one of the first Muslim writers to provide a detailed account of the Western European political system, and in the *Murūj* he goes so far as to provide a list of the names of the kings of the *iFranj* from the reign of Clovis to Louis IV.[49] In providing the list, al-Mas'ūdī also demonstrates his willingness to consult non-Muslim sources; he explains that the source of the aforementioned list is a book composed in 939 by a bishop for the future sovereign of Spain, the Umayyad Caliph al-Hakam.[50] In consulting non-Muslim sources and incorporating material from these sources in his works, in actually making use of material produced by the group under investigation, al-Mas'ūdī (like al-Idrīsī after him) displays a desire to understand the different peoples of the world as they understand themselves, something that separates him from the majority of his peers. Although the information gleaned from the bishop's book does not significantly alter al-Mas'ūdī's impression of the *iFranj*, it does provide him with a more nuanced understanding of Western European politics, making his work all the more valuable to his contemporary Muslim audience for the information it contains about the Franks in particular, and to modern scholars for the insights it provides into the medieval Muslim perspective on the peoples of the outside world.

For al-Mas'ūdī, the *iFranj* share a common lineage with the Slavs, Lombards, Galicians, and Bulgarians, all of whom are identified as the descendants of Japheth.[51] Interestingly, the Turks, Khazars, and the "peoples of Gog and Magog" are also included amongst the descendants of Japheth. However, within this larger "family," the *iFranj* are identified as being among the most courageous in battle; only the Galicians are more formidable in combat. Moreover, according to al-Mas'ūdī, the *iFranj* are the most numerous, the possessors of the largest expanse of territories, and practice the best form of government of all the nations of Japheth. They are also distinguished by their loyalty to their sovereigns, above and beyond what is to be found amongst the other nations of Japheth (p. 36). Al-Mas'ūdī also informs his readers that the term "*iFranj*" is applied not only to the group as a whole, but is also the name given to their empire. This information serves as an introduction to the *iFranj*; further details and analysis come in the subsequent pages of the *Murūj*.

One of the most interesting sections of the *Murūj*, and a shining example of al-Mas'ūdī's attention to detail in approaching the subject, is the list of Frankish kings he provides in the final portion of his discussion of the Franks. Beginning with the reign of Clovis and continuing to his day, the list contains the names of each of the sovereigns, the length of his rule, and other pertinent information and noteworthy facts. Al-Mas'ūdī informs the reader that the first king, Clovis, was a pagan, but was eventually converted to Christianity through the efforts of Clotild, his Christian wife (p. 37). Al-Masʿūdī also mentions the fact that Charlemagne ruled during the time of the Umayyad caliph al-Hakam (p. 37). Charlemagne's son, Ludrick, is identified as the Frankish king who besieged Tortosa, while Ludrick's son, Carl, is reported to have made peace with the Umayyads (p. 37). In turn Carl's son, also named Ludrick, is reported to have come to peaceful terms, not with the Muslims to the South, but rather with pagans living in his own country, purchasing a truce for seven years with six hundred "ratls" of gold and six hundred "ratls"[52] of silver (p. 37). In al-Masʿūdī's own time, he reports that according to the most recent accounts from abroad, yet another Ludrick, son of Carl, has been king of the Franks for the last ten years (p. 38). This last piece of information is singular for its accuracy and for the insight it provides into the indefatigable researcher who composed this work.

The very inclusion of the list serves as proof of al-Masʿūdī's dedication to his craft. At the beginning of the section in which the list is presented, al-Masʿūdī informs the reader that he came upon a list containing the names of the Frankish kings in a Frankish book in Fustat (present-day Cairo) in the year 336 A.H. (947 C.E.).[53] All indications point toward the fact that al-Masʿūdī had completed work on the *Murūj* when he came upon this foreign source, and then revised his work to include the new information.[54] If true, this is a demonstration of both al-Masʿūdī's willingness to consult and use foreign sources, and the lengths to which he would go in order to ensure that his works presented the most current information on the subjects they covered.

In his later work, *Kitāb al-Tanbīh wa 'l-Ishrāf*, al-Masʿūdī takes up the subject of the climatic divisions of the world and their effects on people's nature and temperament. In discussing the climes, he divides the earth into two parts, and then proceeds to describe the inhabitants of both regions. Al-Masʿūdī's description of the peoples of the North (of whom the Franks are one group) enumerates many of the stereotypical attributes associated with Europeans in medieval Muslim literature:

> As for the northern quarter, which is farther away from the sun, in the extreme north, and which is the abode of the *Saqāliba*, the *Afranja* [Franks] and the neighboring races, and where the influence of the sun is rather alleviated and the region is cold, moisture and snow, the people are characterized by good physique, rude behaviour, slow wit, harsh tongue, white complexion, thick flesh, blue eyes, thin skin, curly and red hair. All these characteristics are found due to the predominance of moisture in their lands, and their cold nature does not encourage firmness of religious belief. Those living farther north are characterized by dullness of mind, harsh behaviour and barbarism. These characteristics increase proportionately as we proceed further north.[55]

In this passage, al-Masʿūdī reinforces what was already quickly becoming a widely held belief about the "character" of the *iFranj*, identifying barbarity and lack of intelligence as principal characteristics of this group and its culture. The *Tanbīh* was in many ways a revised edition of the *Murūj* and largely reflects the thinking of the prior work, as well as contemporary thought regarding the Northern regions. The *Tanbīh* condenses much of the information of the *Murūj* and other previous works, presenting it in a concise manner; this passage presents al-Masʿūdī's ideas regarding the nature of the *iFranj* in their essential form.

With his breadth of knowledge regarding the distant places and peoples of the world, in part due to his extensive consultation of Muslim and non-Muslim sources and his wide-ranging experiences abroad, al-Masʿūdī's works were invaluable for the information they contained about the Muslim and non-Muslim worlds. Al-Masʿūdī's attention to detail as a geographer was in part a reflection of his interest in history, and his belief that a people's history could not be understood outside of the context of the environment – cultural and physical – of the group in question;[56] this idea found further expression in the works of some of the best minds of the medieval Muslim world in subsequent centuries.[57] Al-Masʿūdī's interest in both pre-Islamic and non-Islamic societies, along with his interest in the various denominations within Islam and other religions, was also of great value to those who would follow in his footsteps, as he amassed a wealth of information in the pursuit of these interests. In addition, his philosophy of privileging knowledge based on personal observation and practical experience was not only a source of motivation for his travels abroad, but also resulted in a few discoveries that challenged widely held beliefs.[58] Al-Masʿūdī's inquiries into the culture, history and religion of the peoples with whom he came into contact during his travels yielded vast quantities of information in a variety of fields, particularly geography and history, and a research model for future scholars in the medieval Muslim world to emulate.

Another contributor to the corpus of literature on Western Europe and its inhabitants was the eleventh-century Andalusian writer Abū ʿUbayd ʿAbd Allāh b. ʿAbd al-ʿAzīz b. Muhammad b. Ayyūb al-Bakrī (c.1014–1094), who wrote from the perspective of a Muslim living in Europe, near the frontier of the Muslim and Christian worlds. In *Kitāb al-masālik wa-l-mamālik*, al-Bakrī attempts to describe the known world; what survives of his work covers North Africa and the *bilād al-Sudān* (Sub-Saharan Africa), Egypt, Iraq, Spain, and Syria.[59] Writing as a geographer in the Westernmost part of the Muslim world, al-Bakrī writes from the vantage point of a resident of a frontier territory,[60] with a greater awareness of non-Muslim Western Europeans than his peers writing in the East, while also praising the qualities of al-Andalus that distinguish it within the Muslim world and beyond.[61]

As part of his description of the Iberian Peninsula and its peoples, al-Bakrī writes of the Galicians and the Bretons. Al-Bakrī identifies the Galicians as the "enemies of the Franks," and "the most fearsome of all the people of al-Andalus" (p. 21). After identifying the greatest kings from among the Galicians,[62] he recounts King Ramiro's participation in the political intrigue between the then-Caliph 'Abd al-Raḥmān III and Umayya b. Isḥāq b. Muhammad b. 'Abd al-Raḥmān, and the ensuing military and political repercussions (pp. 21–2). He also includes the description of the Galicians provided by Ibrāhīm b. Ya'qūb al-Isrā'īlī al-Turṭūshī, who traveled throughout Western, Central, Northern and Eastern Europe in the tenth century (p. 22). Of the Galicians, al-Turṭūshī writes "Its people are treacherous and vile by nature; they do not clean or wash themselves more than once or twice a year, with cold water" (p. 23). However, despite these inherent shortcomings, the Galicians are indomitable warriors: "They have great courage, they do not accept [taking] flight in encounters in war, and consider death suitable in its place" (p. 23). Al-Bakrī's description of the Bretons is succinct; he fails to find any positive qualities in them: "They have a language that repulses the ears, repulsive appearance, and bad customs. Part of them are thieves, who attack the Franks and rob them" (p. 23). For al-Bakrī even courage, a characteristic commonly attributed to Franks and other Western European groups, is not applicable to the Bretons.

In the portrayal of the Galicians and the Bretons in *Kitāb al-Masālik wa-l-Mamālik*, al-Bakrī reinforces the idea of non-Muslim European filth and barbarity, including a propensity toward being dishonest. The courage of the Galicians is implicitly linked to their barbarism; like other "barbarians" (e.g., the Turks and Franks), their lack of refinement contributes to their ferocity as warriors. Through his descriptions, al-Bakrī situates the Galicians and Bretons well within the traditional framework of medieval Muslim discourse relating to Western Europeans.

Written at or around the height of the golden age of classical Islamic civilization, the works of al-Mas'ūdī, al-Bakrī, and al-Turṭūshī are largely devoid of the types of *ajā'ib* (marvels) found in even respectable works produced in the medieval Muslim world. The three were well situated to discuss the groups described in their respective works, al-Mas'ūdī as a result of his travels and research, and al-Bakrī through his proximity to non-Muslim Europeans and his research (including the account of Ibrāhīm b. Ya'qūb al-Isrā'īlī al-Turṭūshī). Their works provided insight into the people and places of Europe, drawing from their personal experiences, the experiences of other Muslim travelers (particularly merchants and sailors) and from the writings of past authorities, Muslim and non-Muslim. But for all the information their works provide about the various peoples of medieval Europe, it is the ways in which each work reinforces the stereotypes of the day that endured in the works of others and in the popular consciousness, stereotypes of European filth, barbarity, dishonesty, and predisposition toward violence (which manifested itself in a positive manner in battle as courage), which remained a constant theme in medieval Muslim works of all genres. Al-Mas'ūdī and al-Bakrī did not originate but rather inherited aspects of their worldview from classical scholars and their Muslim predecessors (including al-Turṭūshī); in their capable hands, these ideas were developed, buttressed, and transmitted to their successors, who would enshrine these ideas in the medieval Muslim discourse about the regions and peoples to the North and North-West.

Building on the work of previous Muslim geographers, including al-Mas'ūdī, the twelfth-century scholar al-Idrīsī contributed to a greater understanding of Western Europe among Muslims during the era of the Crusades. Abū 'Abdullah Muhammad ibn Muhammad ibn 'Abdullah ibn Idrīsī al-Sharīf (1099–1165 C.E.), or al-Idrīsī as he came to be known, is held by some to have been the greatest cartographer and geographer of the medieval period.[63] A politically important figure as a member of the powerful 'Alawī Idrīsīds of Morocco,[64] he is nonetheless best known for his masterpiece of geography and cartography, the *Kitāb Nuzhat al-Mushtāq fī' Khtirāq al-'Āfāq*[65] (*The Book of Pleasant Journeys and Far Off Lands*), which came to be known as the *Book of Roger* to later generations, so named for the patron who commissioned its production. The *Nuzhat al-mushtāq*, which was completed in 1154,[66] includes a preface and a map of the world (along with seventy smaller sectional maps), with descriptions of each region in terms of its physical, political, and cultural features.[67] While al-Idrīsī is more at home in describing Europe, Western and Central Asia, and North Africa than China and other parts of Southeast Asia,[68] the value of *Nuzhat al-mushtāq* was unquestionable in the eyes of later Muslim writers. During the Middle Ages, it was used by such luminaries as the historian and sociologist Ibn Khaldūn,[69] who referred to al-Idrīsī by his honorific title "al-Sharīf" (the Noble).[70] *Nuzhat al-mushtāq* would remain a relevant text for its geographical information for Muslim writers into the nineteenth century.[71] However, despite its obvious value as a product of both Christian European and Muslim Mediterranean geographical insight, and its availability as a result of its having been composed in Norman Sicily, *Nuzhat al-Mushtāq* would go largely unnoticed by Europeans throughout the Middle Ages and the Renaissance.[72]

In composing the *Nuzhat al-mushtāq*, al-Idrīsī drew from a number of different sources for his information. Al-Idrīsī does not appear to have used the works of some of the most important early Muslim geographers, including al-Mas'ūdī; he also failed to take advantage of many of the recorded accounts of earlier Muslim merchants and sailors, which worked to his detriment in his descriptions of the lands in the East.[73] He borrowed heavily from Ibn Khurradādhbih, particularly for his information regarding the earth's sphericity, the equator, the earth's circumference, and the inhabited regions of the earth.[74]

In most cases, al-Idrīsī looked to the accounts of merchants and sailors that were at his disposal in Sicily for information about Europe and the Mediterranean; he relied on both his own experiences and the accounts of Muslim merchants and sailors for his information about Africa and certain parts of Asia; and he made exclusive use of the works of Ptolemy for information about the remainder of Asia.[75] For his maps of the world, al-Idrīsī looked primarily to maps derived from Ptolemy's works.[76] In addition to works in the Ptolemaic tradition, al-Idrīsī also made use of the work of Ibn Hawqal in constructing some of his maps; this is significant because Ibn Hawqal came out of the Balkhī School of cartography, which differed considerably from the Ptolemaic school in some aspects of cartography.[77] However, al-Idrīsī relied most heavily on maps following the Ptolemaic tradition, along with the information he obtained from the aforementioned types of sources, for the lion's share of the information relating to the known world and its inhabitants, including the peoples and places of Western Europe, found in the *Nuzhat al-mushtāq*.

Al-Idrīsī's focus in describing Western Europe is to provide an accurate representation of the region's physical geography, accompanied by a description of the cities and other densely populated areas of note one might encounter while traveling through the area, and in this respect he is masterful in his work. In describing Western Europe, al-Idrīsī enumerates the myriad settled areas (including cities and large villages), describes the topography of each of the regions in question, provides an account of both the natural and manmade wonders, and includes the distance between the settled areas of note. For example, in his account of Tortossa, al-Idrīsī writes, "the city of Tortossa is a beautiful city on the Ebro River, between it and the Mediterranean Sea."[78] From there, al-Idrīsī goes on to mention that it possesses an impenetrable fortress, and that it boasts of pine trees of unmatched quality which it ships to lands near and far, concluding with the fact that it is forty-five miles from the city of Tarragona (p. 734).

Al-Idrīsī offers similar detail in his descriptions of the Frankish territories, enumerating the many nations, provinces, cities, and settlements that comprise the "lands of the Franks," such as Toulouse ("a beautiful, noble city that has villages and farms") (p. 739), Bourges, Clermont, and Dijon (pp. 739, 742). The same type of attention to detail can be found in his description of the individual Frankish territories; he is meticulous in enumerating the various characteristics of each of the settled areas (cities, villages, provinces) of note, and never fails to provide the reader with an indication of the distance from one province to its nearest neighbor. The city of Nevers is described as an important, noble city, possessing populated townships and ample harvests; Mâcon is described as a beautiful, well-populated city and region that possesses an abundance of wealth, and is amply provisioned with farms, vineyards, and bountiful harvests (p. 742). Collectively, the lands of the Franks and the lands that are under their dominion are described as being more fertile, more beneficial in terms of producing revenue, in better condition, and more productive in terms of annual yields than the German territories (p. 874), which are also the subject of al-Idrīsī's attention, and which are also described in detail.[79]

While al-Idrīsī is quite detailed in his description of the Frankish territories and their distinguishing features, he is surprisingly silent on the subject of the Franks themselves. Unlike al-Masʿūdī and other writers, for whom the "characteristics" of the Franks and the lands they inhabited were of great interest, al-Idrīsī appears reluctant to delve into a discussion of the defining "traits" of the Franks relative to other ethnic/racial groups. On the rare occasions in which he does refer to the characteristics of the Franks, the attribute he mentions most often is that of courage. In his description of Nevers, he writes "in it are brave men" (p. 742). In a similar vein, when writing of one of the German provinces, he informs the reader "its people are brave in war and they possess a readiness and willingness [to fight]" (p. 874). However, such references are few and far between; al-Idrīsī appears far more interested in the geography of Western Europe than in its inhabitants, a fact clearly reflected in *Nuzhat al-mushtāq*.

As a general rule, individual Franks (and to a larger extent, individual Europeans) receive scant attention within the pages of *Nuzhat al-mushtāq*. When al-Idrīsī does make mention of an individual, the individual concerned is most likely a sovereign, and the reference is in regard to the principalities that constitute his kingdom. However, there is one instance in which individual Franks receive a great deal of attention (relative to the other nameless European figures that appear in the text). These individuals are Roger, the "son of Tancred" (p. 589), who is identified as the leader of the Norman conquest of Muslim Sicily in the mid-eleventh century (p. 589), and his descendants (in particular, Roger II) (pp. 589–90). Regarding Roger, "son of Tancred," al-Idrīsī is effusive in his praise of the Norman king, despite his role in wresting control of the island kingdom from Muslims, a stance that certainly reflects the fact that the work was commissioned by Roger II. Al-Idrīsī introduces the conqueror of Sicily as "the gallant man, the best [of men], the great, the powerful, the consecrated, the glorious Roger, son of Tancred, the flower of the kings of the Franks" (p. 589); the description identifies him as a man worthy of the distinction of having conquered a nation that is described in the preceding section as "unique in time, virtuous and excellent and distinguished among the nations by [its] nobility" (p. 588). Al-Idrīsī relates that the conquest itself was a long, drawn-out affair that began in the year 453 of the Muslim calendar,[80] and continued over a period of thirty years (p. 589). Moreover, in recounting the Norman conquest of Sicily, al-Idrīsī takes pains to call attention to the manner in which Roger "son of Tancred" dealt with the newly conquered inhabitants, granting them the free exercise of their religious beliefs, the ability to maintain the observance of Religious Law, and the security of their possessions, both in the present and for future generations (p. 589).

In his description of the arrangement between Roger and his new Muslim subjects, al-Idrīsī highlights one of the distinguishing features of Norman Sicily relative to other European nations led by Christian kings: its tolerance of religious diversity. Indeed, the tolerance of the Norman kings of Sicily was the stuff of legend among Muslim writers through the time of Frederick II of Sicily and his son Manfred in the thirteenth century.[81] However, in describing the agreement between the Norman kings and their Muslim subjects as guaranteeing them the unencumbered practice of their religion, al-Idrīsī leaves the reader with an image of the position of the Muslims in Sicily that is decidedly more positive than what is presented by another famous Muslim, Ibn Jubayr, in his account of his visit to the island kingdom some thirty years later.

In his description of the Muslims' position in Sicily, al-Idrīsī's status as a guest of Roger II appears to have been a relevant factor, particularly when his account is compared to that of Ibn Jubayr, who visited Sicily, not as a guest of the king, but as an independent traveler. In his famous account of his travels, the Granadan Ibn Jubayr also remarks on the arrangement between the Norman rulers and their Muslim subjects, but paints a far darker picture of the position of the Muslims in the kingdom, and the future of their religion on the island. Ibn Jubayr writes of an atmosphere in which the free practice of Islam is incrementally encroached upon, and in which the Muslim character of the kingdom is being undermined. Moreover, Ibn Jubayr presents a far less tolerant image of the rulers themselves, as he recounts interviews with Muslim members of the royal court who are constrained to practice their faith in secret.[82] Writing for a Muslim audience, Ibn Jubayr was not limited in his discussion of the topic in any fashion, as was al-Idrīsī, who was writing for the king of Sicily. Despite the reputation of the Norman kings of Sicily for their tolerance, al-Idrīsī may have been conscious of the implicit restrictions on the scope of his observations, particularly regarding the political and religious situation in Sicily. However, such an issue would not be a concern for the famous scholar who would follow in his footsteps two centuries later.

Unlike al-Mas'ūdī and al-Idrīsī, Ibn Khaldūn is not widely known for his contributions to the subject of geography. As a historian and sociologist, Abū Zayd 'Abd al-Rahman ibn Muhammad ibn Khaldūn Walī al-Dīn al-Tunisi al-Hadrami al-Ishbili al-Maliki, or Ibn Khaldūn (1332–1406 C.E.) as he came to be known to later generations, is most commonly associated with, and effusively praised for, his most famous work, the *Muqaddimah*.[83] Among the many contributors to the legacy of medieval Islamic scholarship, Ibn Khaldūn has come to be regarded as one of the truly original thinkers for his approach toward history, treating it as a science rather than a mere narrative, and he is regarded by many as a "founding father" of the discipline of sociology.[84] However, comparatively little attention has been given to Ibn Khaldūn's discussion of world geography, despite the amount of attention it receives in the *Muqaddimah*. It may be that his ideas relating to race/ethnicity, his writings on geography, climate, and their influence on human beings, and even his conception of what constitutes religious knowledge, have been overshadowed by his analysis of the historical phenomenon of the rise and fall of civilizations. As the beneficiary of the wealth of knowledge, theoretical and practical, left by writers such as al-Khwārizmī, al-Mas'ūdī, and al-Idrīsī, the information provided by the various Muslim accounts of the Crusades, especially as it related to the behavior and character of the Crusaders, and an additional century of contact with Western Europe through trade and diplomacy, Ibn Khaldūn was ideally situated to draw from these sources to produce a more nuanced representation of Europe and its inhabitants.

In composing the *Muqaddimah*, Ibn Khaldūn drew from a variety of sources, Muslim and non-Muslim, and his diligence in identifying his sources separates him from many other medieval Muslim historians.[85] For geography and cartography, Ibn Khaldūn relied heavily on al-Idrīsī's *Nuzhat al-mushtāq*, using it as a primary point of reference for the sections in both the *Kitāb al-'ibar* and its preface, the *Muqaddimah*, which deals with questions relating to geography and cartography.[86] Commenting on the value of al-Idrīsī's work, Ibn Khaldūn expresses his confidence in the comprehensive nature of the *Nuzhat al-mushtāq* in clear terms:

> (All) this [information regarding the Nile, Euphrates, Tigris and Oxus rivers][87] was mentioned by Ptolemy in his work and by the Sharīf (al-Idrīsī) in the *Book of Roger*. All the mountains, seas, and rivers to be found in the cultivated part of the earth are depicted on maps and exhaustively treated in geography. We do not have to go any further into it.
>
> (p. 103)

After a brief discussion of the limits of the habitable world, Ibn Khaldūn presents a map of the earth, which, he informs the reader, was drawn "as was done by the author of the *Book of Roger*" (p. 109). Ibn Khaldūn depends upon the *Nuzhat al-mushtāq* to a great extent, despite both his harsh criticism of past writers for some of the inaccuracies found in their works, and the limitations of al-Idrīsī's work, particularly in its depictions of the nations of the East, a fact that is attested to both through his own admission and by the numerous similarities between the map he provides in *Kitāb al-'ibar* and al-Idrīsī's famous circular world map.[88]

While al-Idrīsī figures prominently in the *Muqaddimah* as a source for geographical information, al-Mas'ūdī enjoys a similar position as a historical source. No other historian is quoted as often as al-Mas'ūdī,[89] whose works, particularly the *Murūj* (and to a lesser extent, the *Tanbīh*) are given more attention than any other historical sources in *Kitāb al-'ibar*. While al-Mas'ūdī is often quoted in conjunction with other Muslim historians to either illustrate the variety of opinions regarding issues in which there are conflicting accounts or to show that there is consensus,[90] he also receives particular attention above and beyond what is given to other Muslim historians from Ibn Khaldūn, who does not hesitate to praise or criticize him, depending on the circumstances. At one point, Ibn Khaldūn informs his audience that, "It is well known to competent persons and reliable experts that the works of al-Mas'ūdī and al-Wāqidī are suspect and objectionable in certain respects" (p. 8), referencing issues regarding the veracity of some of al-Mas'ūdī's statements, and his status as a Shī'a in the eyes of Sunnī theologians (p. 8, n.16).

In another instance, he acknowledges the fact that al-Mas'ūdī's travels enabled him to provide a detailed account of many of the nations of the world, but then remarks that his assessment of the conditions of the lands of the Berbers is "incomplete" (p. 65). However, Ibn Khaldūn's sharp criticism of al-Mas'ūdī is tempered by his enthusiasm in his praise of the tenth-century writer. In commenting upon the *Murūj*, Ibn Khaldūn writes:

> In this work, al-Mas'ūdī commented upon the conditions of nations and regions in the West and in the East during his period (which was) the three hundred and thirties [the nine hundred and forties]. He mentioned their sects and customs. He described the various countries, mountains, oceans, provinces, and dynasties. He distinguished between Arabic and non-Arabic groups. His book, thus, became the basic reference work for historians, their principal source for verifying historical information.
>
> (pp. 63–4)

It is al-Mas'ūdī's attention to the non-Islamic and pre-Islamic world that is of particular value to Ibn Khaldūn, who quotes al-Mas'ūdī in reference to religions such as Zoroastrianism and Avesta, as well as to Jewish history, Christianity, and many other religions and movements of note.[91] In addition, al-Mas'ūdī's approach toward history appears to have influenced Ibn Khaldūn in the formation of his conception of history as a science.[92] Al-Mas'ūdī's comprehensive approach toward history and his openness toward non-Islamic and pre-Islamic peoples and cultures were also sources of inspiration for Ibn Khaldūn, whose own work, while focusing primarily on the history of the Berbers of North Africa, eventually expanded to address many of the other nations and peoples of the world, Muslim and non-Muslim, although not nearly to the same degree as either the *Murūj* or *Tanbīh*.[93] Ibn Khaldūn affirms the value of al-Mas'ūdī's work in the *Muqaddimah* when he discusses the need for historians of his time to emulate the tenth-century scholar in his approach toward history:

> When there is a general change of conditions, it is as if the entire creation had changed and the whole world been altered, as if it were a new and repeated creation, a world brought into existence anew. Therefore, there is need at this time that someone should systematically set down the situation of the world among all regions and races, as well as the customs and sectarian beliefs that have changed for their adherents, doing for this age what al-Mas'ūdī did for his. This should be a model for future historians to follow.
>
> (p. 65)

For Ibn Khaldūn, al-Mas'ūdī's universal outlook is worthy of emulation, and more importantly, is necessary for an accurate understanding of the contemporary world. Al-Mas'ūdī's approach of taking into consideration both internal factors (history and culture) and external factors (environment) in order to better understand groups and nations informed Ibn Khaldūn's writing, in which this approach was developed and articulated in a more profound manner. In so doing, Ibn Khaldūn demonstrates his ability to integrate ideas and information in order to inform and reinforce his perspective, employing it in many different areas, including that of his discussion of the effects of climate on human character, particularly as it applies to the peoples of the intemperate zones, among whom Europeans figured prominently.

In accordance with the opinions of Ptolemy and al-Idrīsī, Ibn Khaldūn describes the earth as being divided into seven habitable zones (p. 97). According to Ibn Khaldūn, only the third, fourth, and fifth zones are truly conducive to the development of civilized societies, as they are temperate, an ideal balance of heat and cold (p. 167). The peoples of the temperate zones include the inhabitants of Morocco, Syria, Iraq, Western India, China, Spain, and the Galicians (p. 168). Of them he writes:

> The human inhabitants of these zones are more temperate (well-proportioned) in their bodies, color, character qualities, and (general) conditions. They are found to be extremely moderate in their dwellings, clothing, foodstuffs, and crafts ... They rival each other in production of the very best tools and implements ... They avoid intemperance quite generally in all their conditions.
>
> (pp. 167–8)

In contrast to their more refined neighbors, the inhabitants of the first and second zones, as well as those of the sixth and seventh zones, are marked by intemperance, due to the effects of excessive heat in the former case and excesses of cold in the latter (pp. 168–9). Although for Ibn Khaldūn the pernicious effects of heat on human character and civilization are more profound than that of cold,[94] the inhabitants of the four intemperate zones are nonetheless lumped together in his analysis of the regions. The peoples of the sixth and seventh zones include the Slavs, the English, the Germans, and the Turks, among others (pp. 158–66). Like their counterparts in the first and second zones (Sub-Saharan Africa), the conditions of the Northern and Western Europeans are "remote from those of human beings and close to those of wild animals" (p. 169). Among the Europeans, the Slavs in particular are described as eschewing human contact, as their distance from a temperate climate results in a disposition that is more animal in nature, which consequently separates them from humans (pp. 168–9). In describing the peoples of the far North in these terms, Ibn Khaldūn reflects the perspective of not only Muslim scholars like al-Mas'ūdī, but also of classical scholars like Aristotle, who himself characterized northern peoples as more impulsive and less intelligent than the peoples of the South.[95]

Ibn Khaldūn also describes the peoples of the intemperate regions as markedly different from their temperate counterparts in their apprehension of religion and religious concepts. For Ibn Khaldūn, the temperate zones are the seats of religion and religious scholarship, while the intemperate zones are devoid of religion. Of the people of the intemperate zones, Ibn Khaldūn writes:

> They are ignorant of prophecy and do not have a religious law, except for the small minority that lives near the temperate regions ... in the north, there are those Slav, European Christian [Frank], and Turkish nations that have adopted Christianity. All the other inhabitants of the intemperate zones in the south and in the north are ignorant of all religion. (Religious) scholarship is lacking among them.
> (p. 169)

In adopting this position, Ibn Khaldūn hearkens back to the works of al-Masʿūdī and his theory that the climate of the intemperate regions affects the very constitution of its inhabitants in a way that results in flaws in their religious character, along with their inability to display the other attributes of civilization in evidence among the peoples of the temperate zones.

The peoples of the intemperate zones are also distinct from their counterparts in the temperate zones in physical appearance. For Ibn Khaldūn, the fourth zone in particular is the most temperate of the zones, more so than the third and fifth zones, which are temperate, but border the intemperate second and sixth zones, respectively (pp. 170–1). In describing the inhabitants of the fourth zone, he writes: "The physique and character of its inhabitants are temperate to the (high) degree necessitated by the composition of the air in which they live" (p. 171). This same principal holds true for the inhabitants of the intemperate zones. For the peoples of the first and second zones, the intemperate South, the overabundance of heat results in black skin (p. 170). For Europeans, the inhabitants of the sixth and seventh zones of the intemperate North, Ibn Khaldūn imagines a similar phenomenon at work, albeit with different results:

> Something similar happens in the corresponding zones to the north, the seventh and sixth zones. There, a white color (of skin) is common among the inhabitants, likewise the result of the composition of the air in which they live, and which comes about under the influence of the excessive cold in the north. The sun is always on the horizon within the visual field (of the human observer), or close to it. It never ascends to the zenith, nor even (gets) close to it. The heat, therefore, is weak in this region, and the cold severe in (almost) all seasons. In consequence, the color of the inhabitants is white, and they tend to have little body hair. Further consequences of the excessive cold are blue eyes, freckled skin, and blond hair.
> (p. 170)[96]

Such physical attributes were due entirely to the environment of the zone in which one lived; movement from one zone to another would result in a gradual adjustment toward the physical characteristics peculiar to the new zone, particularly in the case of one's descendants (p. 171).

Writing in the fourteenth century, Ibn Khaldūn was part of a world different from that of al-Idrīsī, and far different from that of al-Mas'ūdī. The 'Abbāsid Caliphate, which for al-Mas'ūdī in the tenth century was the pre-eminent military and political power, and for al-Idrīsī in the twelfth century was a venerable institution deserving of at least nominal respect, had been destroyed by Ibn Khaldūn's time, extinguished during the Mongol conquests of the thirteenth century. Likewise, the Mediterranean Sea, which during al-Mas'ūdī's time had been almost the exclusive preserve of the Muslim powers, and during al-Idrīsī's day was still largely controlled by Muslim interests, was in the time of Ibn Khaldūn a silent witness to the gradual, inexorable advance of European power and influence, in this instance due largely to their naval expertise. Ibn Khaldūn speaks to this new reality in a discussion concerning the differences in prosperity that exist between the various nations of the world, writing: "At this time, we can observe the condition of the merchants of the Christian nations who come to the Muslims in the Maghrib [Morocco]. Their prosperity and affluence cannot be fully described because it is so great."[97] This is a tacit acknowledgement of the role played by Western merchants, particularly merchants from Venice, Genoa and Pisa, who had played a significant role in the establishment of the Crusader States through their naval support and the conveyance of supplies, and who in the aftermath of the Crusades had maintained strong commercial ties to the regional Muslim powers.[98]

Ibn Khaldūn's comments about the changing role of Western Europe on the world stage are not limited to the commercial or military arena. In one of the most interesting digressions in the *Muqaddimah*, he refers to stories of burgeoning scholarship in the nations of Western Europe:

> We further hear now that the philosophical sciences are greatly cultivated in the land of Rome and along the adjacent northern shore of the country of the European Christians. They are said to be studied there again and to be taught in numerous classes. Existing systematic expositions of them are said to be comprehensive, the people who know them numerous, and the students of them very many.[99]

Thus, Ibn Khaldūn provides an instance in which reference is made to the growth of scholarship in Western Europe in a medieval Muslim work, and in a relatively objective manner. Taken at face value, this passage seems to indicate that civilization is even possible in the intemperate sixth and seventh zones. However, even in light of this new information, Ibn Khaldūn is not able to mask his incredulity regarding the possibility of an advance of scholarship in the intemperate North. Upon concluding his account of these reports of European scholarship, he attaches both the proviso that "God knows better what exists there,"[100] and reinforces it with a passage from the Qur'ān: "He creates whatever He wishes, and His is the choice."[101] These two passages serve as indications of the fact that he cannot confirm the authenticity of the account in question, but that it is possible, as God, in His infinite power, is capable of transforming even the Europeans into scholars.

In the *Muqaddimah*, Ibn Khaldūn offers a glimpse at the latter stages of the evolution of the medieval Mediterranean Muslim worldview, in this instance as it relates to European Christians. The *Muqaddimah* is clearly grounded in the works of past Muslim scholars, as there are frequent references to the works of al-Mas'ūdī and al-Idrīsī, among others; and like many of the works of his predecessors, it also draws from non-Muslim sources. However, Ibn Khaldūn adopts a stance that is uniquely his own, examining many of the ideas of his predecessors in the light of historical evidence, anecdotal evidence and his own theories concerning human nature to craft what he intends to be a more informed view of the Muslim and non-Muslim world around him. He is not always able to transcend the misconceptions espoused by his predecessors, but he is able to cast a critical eye on many of the widely held ideas of his time that had escaped prior scrutiny, while transmitting, in a general sense, the greater body of knowledge about the various regions of the then known world and the peoples who inhabited them.

The medieval Muslim understanding of Western Europe both prior to and during the period of the Crusades was one that was influenced by the lack of sufficient, accurate information on the area and its inhabitants. The remoteness of the centers of Western Europe from the centers of 'Abbāsid power relegated Europeans to the periphery of the collective medieval Muslim consciousness. For Eastern Mediterranean Muslims, the general inaccessibility of Western European sources due to the language barrier combined with military, political, and religious tensions effectively prevented valuable information about their Western counterparts from being available. In lieu of this vital, accurate information, Muslim writers turned to the accounts of their Muslim predecessors to construct a picture of Western Europe and its inhabitants. The result of such a compromise was a caricature of Western Europe and its peoples that was not unlike the Western European Christian image of Muslims in its use of stereotypes and its exaggerated nature. The accounts of Muslim writers who had come in contact with Western Europeans in the course of their travels did little to dispel these commonly held stereotypes, but rather served to reinforce them through their depictions of Western Europeans as unclean, uncouth, and generally unfit for the company of Muslims.

In the end, it was left to an unprecedented phenomenon to generate a greater awareness of Western Europe and its peoples among the Muslims.

58 Al-iFranj: *Medieval Muslim perceptions*

As a distant, vaguely defined enemy, the Western European had failed to make a lasting impression on the Muslim collective consciousness during the first three centuries of Muslim civilizations. However, this condition was destined to change irrevocably; Western Europeans would soon become a very real threat against which the human and material resources of substantial parts of the Muslim world would be marshaled. This new development would radically reshape both the immediate and distant future for both regions, and would produce a dialectic between the nations and peoples that comprise the Muslim Near East and those that constitute Western Europe and its nearest relations that informs the discourse to the present day. This new, momentous change was the advent of the Crusades.

Notes

1 Bernard Lewis, V.L. Ménage, Ch. Pellat, and J. Schacht (Eds.), "*Djughrāfiyā*," ["Geography"] *The Encyclopaedia of Islam, Volume III: C-G* (Leiden: E.J. Brill, 1965) 575–6.
2 Josef W. Meri (Ed.), "Geography," *Medieval Islamic Civilization: An Encyclopedia, Volume 1: A-K* (New York: Routledge, 2006) 284.
3 Lewis, Ménage, Pellat, and Schacht (Eds.), "*Djughrāfiyā*," 576.
4 Ibid.
5 Ibid, 577.
6 One such Greek concept was that of the "climes," which was similar to the Persian concept of the *kishwars*. The two concepts were often used in conjunction with one another, at times in a confused, haphazard manner. Meri (Ed.), "Geography," 284–5.
7 Lewis, Ménage, Pellat, and Schacht (Eds.), "*Djughrāfiyā*," 578.
8 Ibid.
9 Carole Hillenbrand, *The Crusades: Islamic Perspectives* (New York: Routledge, 1999) 270.
10 Ibid.
11 Lewis, Ménage, Pellat, and Schacht (Eds.), "*Djughrāfiyā*," 577.
12 Akhtar Husain Siddiqi, "Muslim Geographic Thought and the Influence of Greek Philosophy," *GeoJournal* 37.1, Ed. Wolf Tietze (Boston: Kluwer Academic, 1995) 10.
13 Bernard Lewis, V.L. Ménage, Ch. Pellat, and J. Schacht (Eds.), "Ibn Khurradādhbih," *The Encyclopaedia of Islam, Volume III: H-IRAM* (Leiden: E.J. Brill, 1971) 839. Also see Meri (Ed.), "Geography," 285.
14 Bernard Lewis, V.L. Ménage, Ch. Pellat, and J. Schacht (Eds.), "'Adjā'ib," *The Encyclopaedia of Islam, Volume III: A-B* (Leiden: E.J. Brill, 1960) 203.
15 Meri (Ed.), "Geography," 286.
16 Lewis, Ménage, Pellat, and Schacht (Eds.), "Adjā'ib," 203.
17 Ibid, 203–4.
18 The Byzantine Empire stood as the one exception; as northern neighbors and one of the primary enemies of the 'Abbāsid Caliphate, the *Rūm* (as they were known to their Muslim neighbors) were the objects of a great deal of attention.
19 Meri (Ed.), "Geography," 286.
20 For example, the term *Saqāliba* ("Slav") was liberally applied to various groups within Northern Europe that possessed fair hair and a ruddy complexion. See Bernard Lewis, V.L. Ménage, Ch. Pellat, and J. Schacht (Eds.), "Sakāliba," *The Encyclopaedia of Islam, Volume III: NED-SAM* (Leiden: E.J. Brill, 1995) 872.

Al-iFranj: *Medieval Muslim perceptions* 59

21 Nadia Maria El-Cheikh, "Byzantium Through the Islamic Prism from the Twelfth to the Thirteenth Century," *The Crusades from the Perspective of Byzantium and the Muslim World*, Eds Angeliki E. Laiou and Roy Parviz Mottahedeh (Washington, DC: Dumbarton Oaks, 2001) 56.
22 Bernard Lewis, V.L. Ménage, Ch. Pellat, and J. Schacht (Eds.), "IFrandj," *The Encyclopaedia of Islam, Volume III: H-IRAM* (Leiden: E.J. Brill, 1971) 1044.
23 Ibid.
24 Ibid.
25 Ahmad M.H. Shboul, *Al-Masʿūdī & His World: A Muslim Humanist and His Interest in Non-Muslims* (London: Ithaca, 1979) xv.
26 Ibid, 56.
27 Ibid, 60–8.
28 It has been proven that al-Masʿūdī was Shīʿite, although there is some debate as to whether he was an Ismāʿīlī or a Twelver (Imāmite) Shīʿite. The majority holds that he was a Twelver Shīʿite. Ibid, 39–40.
29 Ibid, 56–8.
30 Ibid, 56.
31 Although both the *Murūj al-Dhahab wa 'l Maʾādin al-Jawhar* and *Kitāb al-Tanbīh wa 'l-Ishrāf* will be discussed in the context of al-Masʿūdī's sources of information, the *Murūj al-Dhahab wa 'l Maʾādin al-Jawhar* will be the primary focus of the subsequent portions of this section. Also, the *Murūj al-Dhahab wa 'l Maʾādin al-Jawhar* will be referred to by the abbreviation *Murūj*, while the *Kitāb al-Tanbīh wa 'l-Ishrāf* will be referred to by the abbreviation *Tanbīh*.
32 S. Maqbul Ahmad, "Al-Masʿūdī's Contributions to Medieval Arab Geography," *Islamic Culture* 27 (1953): 66.
33 S. Maqbul Ahmad, "Al-Masʿūdī's Contributions to Medieval Arab Geography: Some Sources of His Knowledge," *Islamic Culture* 28 (1954): 275.
34 Ahmad, "Al-Masʿūdī's Contributions to Medieval Arab Geography," 67.
35 Ibid, 68.
36 Ahmad, "Al-Masʿūdī's Contributions to Medieval Arab Geography: Some Sources of His Knowledge," 277–9.
37 Ahmad, "Al-Masʿūdī's Contributions to Medieval Arab Geography," 70.
38 Ibid, 71.
39 Ibid, 72–3. Al-Masʿūdī used the information regarding the earth's circumference, diameter, and shape in the works of the aforementioned Muslim scholars in conjunction with the information found in the works of Ptolemy.
40 Ibid, 75–7. Al-Masʿūdī's chief criticism of the Muslim geographers was that, like al-Jāhiz, their works were not based on personal experience and observation through travel, and as such could not be viewed as authoritative.
41 Ahmad, "Al-Masʿūdī's Contributions to Medieval Arab Geography: Some Sources of His Knowledge," 279–80.
42 Ibid, 280.
43 Ahmad, "Al-Masʿūdī's Contributions to Medieval Arab Geography," 74.
44 Ahmad, "Al-Masʿūdī's Contributions to Medieval Arab Geography: Some Sources of His Knowledge," 281.
45 Shboul, *Al-Masʿūdī & His World*, 178.
46 In the opening passage of the *Murūj*, al-Masʿūdī states:

> For there can be no comparison between one who lingers among his own kinsmen and is satisfied with whatever information reaches him about his part of the world, and another who spends a lifetime in travelling the world, carried to and fro by his journeys, extracting every fine nugget from its mine and every valuable object from its place of seclusion. *Murūj*, Sec. 7.

English translation from Tarif Khalidi, *Islamic Historiography: The Histories of Mas'ūdī* (Albany: State U of New York, 1975) 1–2.
47 Khalidi, *Islamic Historiography*, xiii.; Shboul, *Al-Mas'ūdī & His World*, 5, 16.
48 Shboul, *Al-Mas'ūdī & His World*, 5.
49 Hillenbrand, *The Crusades*, 270.
50 Ibid.
51 Al-Mas'ūdī', *Murūj al-Dhahab wa Ma'ādin al-Jawhar*, Vol. 2 (Beirut: Dār al-Kutub al-'Ilmiyyah, 1990) 36. The following is my translation of the original text, pages 36–9. Subsequent citations will appear parenthetically.
52 A *ratl* appears to have been an unspecified type of Frankish currency.
53 Shboul, *Al-Mas'ūdī & His World*, 191.
54 Ibid.
55 *Kitāb al-Tanbīh wa 'l-Ishrāf*, 23–4. Trans. S.M. Ziauddin Alavi, "Al-Mas'ūdī's Conception of the Relationship between Man and Environment," *Al-Mas'ūdī Millenary Commemoration Volume*, Ed. S. Maqbul Ahmad and A. Rahman (Calcutta: Little Flower, 1960) 93–7. 95.
56 Khalidi, *Islamic Historiography*, xvii.
57 In particular, this idea played an important role in Ibn Khaldūn's approach to the study of history.
58 For example, as a result of his experiences on the Caspian Sea, his interviews with merchants and sailors, and his knowledge of a certain Russian expedition that had traveled along the Caspian en route to raiding a Muslim territory, al-Mas'ūdī correctly asserted that the Caspian Sea was not connected to the Black Sea, an idea which was widely held among Muslims and Europeans alike. European misconceptions regarding this supposed connection would not be corrected until the voyages of the missionary John de Plano Carpini in the thirteenth century. Mohammad Shafi, "Al-Mas'ūdī as a Geographer," *Al-Mas'ūdī Millenary Commemoration Volume*, Eds S. Maqbul Ahmad and A. Rahman (Calcutta: Little Flower, 1960) 74.
59 Abū 'Ubayd al-Bakrī, *Geografia de España: Kitāb al-Masālik wa-l-Mamālik*, Trans. Eliseo Vidal Beltran (Zaragoza: Anubar Ediciones, 1982) 9.
60 "Al-Andalus," according to al-Bakrī, "is a territory of 'Jihād' and a zone of frontier defenses – *ribats*." Ibid, 39.
61 For al-Bakrī, al-Andalus possesses the excellent qualities of Syria, Yemen, India, China, and Aden, in addition to Greek ruins and other monuments from antiquity. Ibid, 20. Subsequent citations will appear parenthetically.
62 "Alfonso, Ordoño, and Ramiro." Ibid, 21.
63 Nafis Ahmad, *Muslim Contributions to Geography* (Lahore: Ashraf, 1972) 46.
64 There has been some speculation that Roger II's hospitality was based on political calculations, as he may have been interested in installing al-Idrīsī as a puppet ruler, either in Muslim Spain (which the Sicilian king hoped to conquer), or in his holdings in North Africa. S. Maqbul Ahmad, "Cartography of al-Sharīf al-Idrīsī," *The History of Cartography, Volume II, Book One: Cartography in the Traditional Islamic and South Asian Societies*, Eds J.B. Harley and David Woodward (Chicago: U of Chicago P, 1992) 156.
65 The *Kitāb Nuzhat al-Mushtāq fī' Khtirāq al-'Āfāq* will be referred to by the abbreviated title *Nuzhat al-mushtāq* in future discussions of the work.
66 Bernard Lewis, *The Muslim Discovery of Europe* (New York: W.W. Norton, 1982) 147.
67 Ahmad, *The History of Cartography, Volume II, Book One*, 156, 158.
68 Ibid, 157.
69 Ibid, 170.
70 Ibn Khaldūn, *The Muqaddimah: An Introduction to History, Volume I*, Trans. Franz Rosenthal (New York: Pantheon Books, 1958) 103.

Al-iFranj: *Medieval Muslim perceptions* 61

71 Ahmad, *The History of Cartography, Volume II, Book One,* 171.
72 Ahmad, *The History of Cartography, Volume II, Book One,* 172; N. Ahmad, *Muslim Contributions to Geography,* 47.
73 S. Maqbul Ahmad, *India and the Neighboring Territories in the Kitāb Nuzhat al-Mushtāq fī' Khtirāq al-'Āfāq of al-Sharīf al-Idrīsī* (Leiden: E.J. Brill, 1960) 5.
74 Ibid, 6.
75 Ahmad, *The History of Cartography, Volume II, Book One,* 169–70.
76 From the mid-ninth century on, a number of Arabic translations of Ptolemy's *Geographikê Hyphêgêsis* were put forward, many of which contained additions to and corruptions of the original material. As a result, it is difficult to ascertain the identity of the translation that he used as the foundation of *Nuzhat al-mushtāq*, or its quality. Ibid, 168.
77 The Balkhī was one of the two schools of thought – the other being the older Ptolemaic school – which emerged during the early period of Muslim cartography. Two features distinguished the Balkhī school from the Ptolemaic: (1) followers of the Balkhī school limited their focus to the Muslim world, dealing primarily with regional maps within its confines; and (2) Balkhī maps lacked a mathematical basis for their latitudes and longitudes. Ibid, 156–7.
78 al-Idrīsī, *Kitab Nuzhat al Mushtaq fī' Khtiraq al Āfāq,* Vol. 2 (Cairo: Al-Thaqafa Al-Denia Bookshop, 1990) 734. The following is my translation of various portions of the original text. Subsequent citations will appear parenthetically.
79 Al-Idrīsī is always careful to distinguish between the lands of the Franks and those of the Germans, at times enumerating the provinces that constitute each kingdom. For example, he is meticulous in distinguishing between the territories that he identifies as "Frankish Burgundy" and "German Burgundy." Ibid, 742.
80 Ibid, 589. This corresponds roughly to the late 1050s C.E. The historian Ibn al-'Athīr places the actual period of conquest at 484/1091–2. Ibn al-'Athīr, *The Chronicle of Ibn al-Athīr for the Crusading Period from al-Kāmil fī'l-ta'rīkh, Part I, the Years 491–541/1097–1146: The Coming of the Franks and the Muslim Response,* Trans. D.S. Richards (Burlington: Ashgate, 2006) 13.
81 Hillenbrand, *The Crusades,* 337–41.
82 Ibn Jubayr, *The Travels of Ibn Jubayr,* Trans. R.J.C. Broadhurst (London: Camelot, 1952) 342.
83 The *Muqaddimah* ("Introduction") is in fact the preface to a larger work, the *Kitāb al-'ibar*, which focuses on the history of the Berber tribes of North Africa, with some attention to world history as well. N.J. Dawood, "Introduction," *The Muqaddimah: An Introduction to History,* Trans. Franz Rosenthal (Princeton: Princeton UP, 1969) viii–ix.
84 Róbert Simon, *Ibn Khaldūn: History as Science and the Patrimonial Empire* (Budapest: Akadémiai Kiadó, 2002) 9.
85 Walter J. Fischel, "Ibn Khaldūn and al-Mas'ūdī," *Al-Mas'ūdī Millenary Commemoration Volume,* Eds S. Maqbul Ahmad and A. Rahman (Calcutta: Aligarh Muslim University, 1960) 52.
86 Ahmad, *The History of Cartography, Volume II, Book One,* 170.
87 Ibn Khaldūn, *The Muqaddimah: An Introduction to History,* Vols. 1–3, Trans. Franz Rosenthal (New York: Pantheon, 1958) 101–3. Subsequent citations will appear parenthetically.
88 Ahmad, *The History of Cartography, Volume II, Book One,* 170.
89 Fischel, *Al-Mas'ūdī Millenary Commemoration Volume,* 54.
90 Ibid.
91 Ibid, 57.
92 Ibid.
93 Ibid, 58.

94 In an earlier section, Ibn Khaldūn explains this fact as part of his position that the northern quarter of the earth has a greater number of civilizations than the southern quarter. Ibn Khaldūn, *Muqaddimah*, 103–9.
95 Arthur H. Williamson, "Scots, Indians and Empire: The Scottish Politics of Civilization 1519–1609," *Past and Present* 150 (1996): 47.
96 In this instance, Ibn Khaldūn articulates the perceived connection between the sons of Japheth and the sons of Ham as peoples inhabiting the less favorable climes. The sons of Japheth (of whom Northern Europeans make up the greatest part) are negatively affected by the extreme cold of the northern climes (the sixth and seventh zones). Similarly, the sons of Ham (primarily Sub-Saharan Africans) are influenced by the extreme heat of the southern climes (the second and first zones). The "effects" manifest themselves in the mentalities, physiques, and cultures of the peoples in question. However, as Albertus Magnus illustrates in *Liber de natura locorum*, "extreme" climate (and its perceived negative effects) is a relative concept. After reading the opinions of an inhabitant of the fourth zone (Ibn Khaldūn) and an inhabitant of the sixth/seventh zones (Albertus Magnus), one wonders what an inhabitant of the first/second zones would have opined on the issue.
97 Khaldūn, *Muqaddimah*, Vol. 2, 281.
98 P.M. Holt, *The Age of the Crusades: The Near East from the Eleventh Century to 1517* (London: Longman Group Limited, 1986) 34, 103, 163.
99 Khaldūn, *Muqaddimah*, Vol. 3, 117–18.
100 Ibid, 118.
101 Qur'ān 28:68.

3 The medieval travel narrative and the Other in Ibn Fadlān, *The Travels of Ibn Jubayr*, and *Mandeville's Travels*

In the field of medieval geography, the travel narrative occupied an important place in the literary landscape of Western Europe and the Eastern Mediterranean/Near East, between the works within the "learned" tradition[1] and the popular works of the day (epics, vernacular romances, and *ajā'ib* literature) in which descriptions of distant places and peoples were to be found.[2] The travel narrative effectively strode the fence, offering an interested public details about distant lands and peoples that were grounded in reality to a far greater extent than what was to be found in the popular works (now recognized as works of fiction),[3] but presented in a style that was often consciously informal, and that made allowances for compromising the truth in the interests of excitement within an account.[4] Moreover, travel narratives carried an authority that rivaled, and in some ways exceeded, that of the scholars, an authority derived from the lived experience of traveling. At a time in which traveling, even in adjacent territories, was an expensive, arduous, and dangerous undertaking, the experience (real or fabricated)[5] of the writer of the travel narrative privileged the information contained therein over that of the homebound scholar.

The travel narrative should be understood within the context of the learned tradition, epics, *ajā'ib* literature, and vernacular romances, as all of the aforementioned genres exerted considerable influence. When individuals traveled, the scholars' theories informed their expectations of what and whom they would encounter, and the ways in which they interpreted what they observed. Similarly, the popular works (epics, *ajā'ib* literature, vernacular romances) influenced the production of the narratives in terms of the appearance of "marvels" – wondrous natural phenomena, strange indigenous practices, and monstrous/quasi-human groups. The picture painted by the scholar shaped the traveler's expectations and interpretation of the places and peoples he encountered in the course of his travels, while the popular works informed him as to the public's expectation of what would be included in, or added to, his account.

In the medieval Muslim world of the Mediterranean and Near East and the Christian world of Western Europe, works in the learned tradition on geography and the popular fare combined to constitute the public's impression of the world; the balance tilted in favor of the scholars or the storytellers in accordance to the area and peoples under discussion. The travel narratives serve as gauges of this balance between "fact and fiction"[6] on the part of the general public, reflecting their audience's knowledge about an area and its inhabitants, and, equally important, the type of information it expects the account to provide relative to the area in question. The narratives are almost a communal project, combining the specific experiences of the individual traveler and the cultural norms and prejudices of the society of which he is a part.

One of the earliest Muslim accounts of travel in Europe was that of the aforementioned tenth-century writer Ibn Fadlān. Born Ahmad ibn Fadlān ibn al-Abbās ibn Rāshid ibn Hammād, Ibn Fadlān is a mysterious figure; nothing is known about his life beyond his account of his participation in an embassy from the 'Abbāsid Caliph al-Muqtadir to the king of the Bulghars during the 920s.[7] The purpose of the embassy was missionary activity – to instruct the king's subjects in the tenets of Islam – and came at the request of the king, who had sent a letter to the Caliph,[8] although his motives may not have been entirely religious in nature.[9] The embassy left Baghdad on June 21, 921, and arrived at the Bulghar capital on May 12, 922, leaving after the king's subjects had received religious instruction.[10] Remarkably, neither Ibn Fadlān nor the embassy is mentioned by any other Muslim writers of the tenth century, and the only existing information about it is to be found within the account itself.[11] Ibn Fadlān's account introduced the medieval Muslim world to the peoples of Central Asia, most notably the nomadic and settled Turks, the Bulghars, and the Kazars; it also contained a description of the customs, beliefs, and manners of the Rūs, a European ethnic group, which proved to be one of the earliest extant accounts in which they are mentioned.

The primary focus of Ibn Fadlān's account is the customs, manners, and beliefs of the nomadic and settled peoples of Central Asia. However, one of the groups he was able to observe was the "*Rūs*";[12] he provided one of the earliest accounts of their culture. In his description of the Rūs, Ibn Fadlān ascribes characteristics that would become commonly associated with other European ethnic groups. He begins with a physical description of the Rūs, who are distinguished by their stature: "I have never seen people with a more developed bodily stature than they. They are as tall as date palms, blonde, and ruddy, so that they do not need to wear a tunic nor a cloak."[13] However, their striking appearance is offset by their customs and hygienic practices. There is no ambiguity concerning Ibn Fadlān's impression of Rūs hygiene: "They are the dirtiest creatures of God. They have no shame in voiding their bowels and bladder, nor do they wash themselves when polluted by emission of semen, nor do they wash their hands after eating. They are like asses who have gone astray."[14] Ibn Fadlān drives the point home with a description of a specific hygienic practice common among the Rūs, the washing of the face and head:

As a matter of duty they daily wash their faces and heads in a manner so dirty, and so unclean, as could possibly be imagined. Thus it is carried out. A slave girl brings each morning early a large vessel with water, and gives the vessel to her master, and he washes his hands and face and the hair of his head. He washes it and combs it with a comb into the bucket, then blows his nose and spits into the bucket. He holds back nothing impure, but rather lets it go into the water.

After he has done what was necessary, the girl takes the same vessel to the one who is nearest, and he does just as his neighbor has done. She carries the vessel from one to another, until all in the house have had a turn at it, and each of them has blown his nose, spat into, and washed his face and hair in the vessel.[15]

As the Rūs of Ibn Fadlān's account are idol worshippers, the description of their religious practices (including the detailed account of a Rūs funeral) were not entirely applicable to medieval Muslims' perceptions of Christian Western Europeans. However, the allegations of poor hygienic practices and overall filth leveled against the Rūs in the tenth century became a stereotype commonly associated with Western Europeans throughout the Middle Ages.

One of the most celebrated contributors to the genre of medieval Muslim travel literature was the twelfth-century Spanish traveler Ibn Jubayr. Muhammad ibn Ahmad ibn Jubayr (1145–1217 C.E.) was a native of Granada who, from February 3, 1183, to April 25, 1185, undertook a journey from Spain to the Arabian Peninsula in performance of the Hajj.[16] However, the journey to Mecca and Medina was only one part of Ibn Jubayr's itinerary; his travels took him through modern-day Iraq, the Levant, Egypt, and Sicily. During the course of his travels, Ibn Jubayr observed not only the sites of interest, but also the conditions of the inhabitants, the type of relations that existed between the various religious and ethnic/racial groups to be found, and the general atmosphere. His attention to the social and political atmosphere of the places on his itinerary is particularly valuable in that, as his travels through the Levant took place during 1183–85, he was able to witness Salāh al-Dīn's consolidation of his power in the area in real time, as well as the reaction of the local Crusaders to these developments. His comments on the political and military situation in the area offer a different perspective than that of many of the Muslim and Western sources, which generally reflect a partisan bias toward individual leaders. Moreover, as a Spanish Muslim, Ibn Jubayr brought a familiarity to the realities of living in a multi-religious society informed by his experiences in his native land, which enabled him to assess the situations in both the Levant and Sicily through the prism of Spain's unique historical circumstances. In particular, the military tension generated by the gradual, inexorable Christian re-conquest of Spain provided him with valuable insight into the nature of the conflict found in the Levant, as the two struggles were connected by the theme of religiously motivated warfare. Ibn Jubayr was in a unique position to comment not only on the situation of the Muslims living in the Levant, but also on the conditions of the Christians he found in both this region and in the other places that he visited in the course of his travels.

Despite the assertion that Ibn Jubayr was generally more moderate in his attitude toward Western Europeans than his contemporary coreligionists,[17] he nevertheless shared many of the popular medieval Muslim prejudices concerning the Franks, which periodically find their way onto the pages of his account. For example, in describing the Crusader stronghold Acre, Ibn Jubayr levels the oft-repeated Muslim charge of filth against the Frankish inhabitants, which in this instance is conflated with religious error: "Unbelief and unpiousness there burn fiercely, and pigs [Christians] and crosses abound. It stinks and is filthy, being full of refuse and excrement" (p. 318). In describing Christian Acre as being exceptionally filthy, Ibn Jubayr evokes the long-held stereotype of a lack of basic standards of cleanliness among the Franks, reinforcing it through both the image he provides of a city choked by rubbish and excrement and through references to their religious "pollution" of the city.[18] These themes of Frankish filth in both the immediate physical and spiritual sense, and the dangers of contamination that both types present to Muslims, recur throughout the course of the text, with the concerns of Ibn Jubayr becoming more pronounced as his travels bring him into closer contact with larger numbers of Christians in Frankish-controlled territories.

The theme of Western European filth is also present in Ibn Jubayr's depiction of the city of Messina, a city he finds simultaneously alluring and repugnant. Describing the city as a bustling metropolis with a thriving marketplace in which the traveler will find all of the commodities necessary for a luxuriant existence (pp. 338–9), Ibn Jubayr is nonetheless compelled to comment upon the deleterious effects of the Frankish atmosphere of the city upon residents and visitors alike:

> This city is the mart of the merchant infidels, the focus of ships from the world over, and thronging always with companies of travellers by reason of the lowness of prices. But it is cheerless because of the unbelief, no Muslim being settled there. Teeming with worshippers of the Cross, it chokes its inhabitants, and constricts them almost to strangling. It is full of smells and filth; and churlish too, for the stranger will find there no courtesy.
>
> (pp. 338–9)

In this portrait of the city, Ibn Jubayr conflates the ideas of material filth, spiritual pollution, and barbarity, which are all portrayed as being consonant with Frankish society. The city is "teeming" with Franks, who, like the abundant refuse in the city, make the city oppressive for inhabitants and travelers alike, while contributing to the material filth and odor found therein. Moreover, the Frankish presence produces an unpleasant, "cheerless" environment in Messina due to its lack of a Muslim presence, even more than the residents' lack of etiquette. The Franks have negatively impacted the physical, spiritual, and social atmosphere of Messina, as their lack of cleanliness, unbelief, and lack of manners all leave an imprint on the city that the Muslim traveler is bound to notice.

For Ibn Jubayr, Frankish lands should hold no attraction for Muslims, as the overall atmosphere in these areas is thoroughly antagonistic toward Muslim religious, physical, and cultural sensibilities. This idea is stated most emphatically in a digression during his account of his travels through Crusader-controlled Tyre, in which he shares his opinion on the subject of Muslim habitation of Frankish territories:

> There can be no excuse in the eyes of God for a Muslim to stay in any infidel country, save when passing through it while the way lies clear in Muslim lands. They will face pains and terrors such as the abasement and destitution of the capitation and more especially, amongst their base and lower orders, the hearing of what will distress the heart in the reviling of him [Muhammad] whose memory God has sanctified, and whose rank He has exalted; there is also the absence of cleanliness, the mixing with the pigs, and all the other prohibited matters too numerous to be related or enumerated. Beware, beware of entering their lands.
> (pp. 321–2)

According to Ibn Jubayr, the religious, cultural, and material realities of life in a Frankish land are wholly irreconcilable with Muslim sensibilities. The atmosphere in such lands is not just different from, but also antagonistic toward Muslim values, to say nothing of the military and political hostility that marks relations between Muslim and Western European nations, and places Muslims in Crusader-controlled territories in the unenviable position of having to witness their fellow Muslims from neighboring areas suffer as a result of the vicissitudes of war:

> Among the misfortunes that one who visits their land will see are the Muslim prisoners walking in shackles and put to painful labour like slaves. In like condition are the Muslim women prisoners, their legs in iron rings. Hearts are rent for them, but compassion avails them nothing.
> (p. 322)

Ibn Jubayr presents a grim picture of the Frankish areas of the Levant as being wholly at odds with Muslim sensibilities in the most fundamental areas of Muslim life, wholly unsuitable for Muslim habitation. For Ibn Jubayr, Frankish lands are foreign not only in immediately recognizable areas such as religion, but also in the aspects that constitute one's daily existence: the material, cultural, and social atmosphere of one's surroundings.

68   *The medieval travel narrative*

However, despite Ibn Jubayr's predisposition against the Franks, he does not hesitate to highlight areas in which their practices are superior to those of his coreligionists. For example, in his description of the conditions of the Muslim inhabitants of the area of Tibnin, he inserts an aside on the comparative state of Muslims living under Frankish rule versus those living under the dominion of their coreligionists:

> Our way lay through continuous farms and ordered settlements, whose inhabitants were Muslims living comfortably with the Franks. God protect us from such temptation. They surrender half their crops to the Franks at harvest time, and pay as well a poll-tax of one dinar and five qirat for each person. Other than that, they are not interfered with, save for a light tax on the fruits of trees. Their houses and all their effects are left to their full possession. All the coastal cities occupied by the Franks are managed in this fashion, their rural districts, the villages and farms, belonging to the Muslims. But their hearts have been seduced, for they observe how unlike them in ease and comfort are their brethren in the Muslim regions under their (Muslim) governors. This is one of the misfortunes afflicting the Muslims. The Muslim community bewails the injustice of a landlord of its own faith, and applauds the conduct of an opponent and enemy, the Frankish landlord, and is accustomed to justice from him. He who laments this state must turn to God.
>
> (pp. 316–17)

Ibn Jubayr's criticism of the failure of the local Muslim rulers to implement a system of governance that measures up to the standards of their Frankish neighbors is both an impartial appraisal of the practices of the Franks in the Levant in dealing with their Muslim subjects and an indictment of the Levantine Muslim kingdoms. In his critique, he strikes a chord somewhat similar to that of the later author of *Mandeville's Travels*[19] and Salāh al-Dīn himself, as all three individually lament the current condition of their coreligionists, observing with chagrin the fact that in each case the believers are being outstripped by the unbelievers in piety and virtuous acts.[20] However, in this instance Ibn Jubayr's observations are all the more salient in that whereas there is propagandistic value in the speech of the "sultan" of *Mandeville's Travels* and in Salāh al-Dīn's letter, Ibn Jubayr's digression appears to be purely a reaction to his personal observations and comparisons of the conditions of Muslims living in both Frankish and Muslim territories.

The disappointment registered by Ibn Jubayr in this passage points to his underlying assumptions of Muslim moral superiority, and his consternation over the failure of the existing conditions to bear out these assumptions. His critique of the injustice of the Muslim rulers in the Levant finds its parallel in the *Pseudo-Turpin Chronicle*'s[21] comments on the perceived hypocrisy of the Christian nobility in eschewing the core principles of their faith as it pertains to the less fortunate. However, in the *Pseudo-Turpin Chronicle*, it is a Saracen king, Aigalonde, who calls the inimitable Charles the Great (Charlemagne) to task. Aigalonde, who is on the verge of conversion himself (following successive defeats at the hands of King Charles), refuses baptism upon witnessing the treatment of the pious poor in the Christian camp. His emphasis on the intra-religious injustice suffered by the vulnerable at the hands of their coreligionists is reminiscent of Ibn Jubayr in tone and content:

> Þese þat sitte aboute þe beth wele icloþed; þe ette gode metis and drinke gode drinkis. But þose þat þou calliste þi goddis messengeris bethe euylle icloþed and fare euylle; þey sitte aferre and litille made of. He seruythe euylle his lorde þat dothe so litille worship to his seruanttis; and grete vnreuerence and shame he dothe to his god þat þus dothe to his meynye. Þi law3e þat þou seydiste whas [gode], now þou shewyste to me þe contrary, þat 'it' is false.[22]

The denunciation of Christian hypocrisy by a Saracen is intended to elicit a degree of collective soul-searching for the Christian audience of *The Pseudo-Turpin Chronicle*. Similarly, Ibn Jubayr's critique of the Levantine Muslim nobility obliges his Muslim audience to acknowledge the fact that for most Muslims in the region, justice can only be found with the Christian rulers. In presenting an uncomfortable truth, believers are not always superior to non-believers in their actions, both Ibn Jubayr and the *Turpin* writer(s) impose an introspective moment on their audiences. However, the *Pseudo-Turpin Chronicle* utilizes the critique to model the desired rededication to core religious values through the actions of Charles, who immediately acts to improve the condition of the pious poor through royal edict.[23] In the end, the type of spiritual awakening that is so atypical amongst unjust rulers in reality can only be accomplished within the context of a romance.

The aforementioned example notwithstanding, Ibn Jubayr's descriptions of Frankish lands and their inhabitants confirm and reinforce contemporary medieval Muslim perceptions of Western Europeans. Through his descriptions of both Crusader territories in Syria and Sicilian cities with a significant Frankish presence, the reader is left with an impression of material and spiritual corruption as hallmarks of Western European society.

However, even in the instances in which one encounters Franks like the aforementioned rulers of Tibnin, Ibn Jubayr's characterization of them is decidedly negative. For Ibn Jubayr, the situation in Sicily, which appears to be one of peaceful coexistence between Muslim subjects and their Norman overlords, carries an implicit threat for the future prospects of Muslim Sicilians, and the conciliatory behavior of the Sicilian Franks is regarded as a dangerous temptation for the native Muslims (p. 345). Living on the frontiers of the Muslim and Christian worlds, Ibn Jubayr is deeply concerned with the issue of Western European expansion, and likely saw parallels between the Norman conquest of Sicily, the ongoing conflict in his native

70 *The medieval travel narrative*

Spain, and the Crusader States. As such, Ibn Jubayr's position as an individual living in a multi-religious society is tempered by the military and political tension accompanying the Christian re-conquest of Spain, which may have contributed to his negative view of Franks in general, a view that is articulated in his portrayal of the Franks he observed and encountered during the course of his remarkable two-year journey.

Of the numerous works that comprise the genre of medieval travel literature, perhaps the most famous "English"[24] account is *Mandeville's Travels*. With an itinerary that included the Levant, India (including the realm of Prester John), Ethiopia, and the kingdom of the Mongol Khan, the *Mandeville* writer purports to describe the ethnography, topography, and relevant history of many of the areas of interest in what was the known world outside of Europe. Throughout the account, the *Mandeville* writer's focus in recounting his alleged experiences is to engage his audience; he only discusses aspects of his travels that would be common to any visitor from abroad, and the reader is never afforded any insight into the ways in which the author could theoretically have been personally affected by his experiences.[25] At various points within the text, the author even engages in a discussion of issues related to geography, asserting the sphericity and circumnavigability of the earth, as well as his opinion that it is habitable in all places. He contends that the Antipodes exist, are inhabited and are reachable, and also discusses the climates of the various areas he has visited, and the effect that the climate of each land has on the activities and customs of its indigenous population.[26] Moreover, the writer's inclusion of the fantastic, in particular as it relates to monstrous races and exoticized cultural practices (which are often placed alongside information that is more or less accurate), adds to the work's value in representing medieval Western Europeans' understanding of the world beyond their borders, a fact that is further reinforced by the work's popularity in medieval Europe.[27]

The text is an excellent example of the medieval travel narrative. The primary focus of the narrative is on the realm of the Great Khan of China, the various places of interest for Christians in the Near East, and India and the kingdom of Prester John. However, Saracens make periodic appearances throughout the text, and a chapter is dedicated to their beliefs and customs. The *Mandeville* writer first focuses his attention on Saracens in the chapter in which he provides an account of the "Tower of Babylon" in Cairo and of the names of the previous sultans. Before providing the aforementioned account, he presents the reader with his own credentials as one familiar with the Saracen world, and the sultan of Cairo in particular:

> I oughte right wel to knowen it for I dueled with him as soudyour in his werres a gret while ayen the Bedoynes. And he wolde haue maryed me fulle highly to a gret princes doughter yif I wolde han forsaken my lawe and my beleue, but I thanke God I had no wille to don it for no thing that he behighte me.
>
> (p. 24)

Having established his position as an authority, the *Mandeville* writer continues, enumerating the five kingdoms over which the sultan holds sway: Egypt, Jerusalem, Syria, Aleppo, and Arabia (p. 25). The author also includes an account of the previous sultans and their political fortunes, a description of the current sultan and the political and military power he wields, and a description of the "Tower of Babylon" – which he distinguishes from the Biblical Tower of Babel (p. 28) – before rounding it out with a description of Egypt, the Arabian Peninsula, and the area that is modern-day Iraq. However, the focus of the account is on the environment of Cairo and the surrounding areas. The description of the "Sultan" foreshadows coming descriptions of the Great Khan, Prester John, and even the Emperor of Persia, particularly in the attention paid to the lands in the sultan's possession, the scope of his military and political power and manifestations of this power, and the history of his predecessors. Saracens are very much in the background in this chapter, with elements of Saracen culture factoring into the account insomuch as they affect the overall environment of the areas under discussion. While the *Mandeville* writer does provide a great deal of information in the chapter (including an interesting and accurate description of the Arabian Peninsula),[28] Saracens and Saracen culture are of not of primary importance at this point in the account.

If Saracens appear to be relegated to the background in the earlier chapters of the work, it is due mainly to the *Mandeville* writer's focus on an aspect of the journey that would have been of far greater importance to his audience: the relevance of the areas to the accounts in the Old and New Testaments, and specific landmarks of interest along the way. This section of the account is dedicated to the journey to Jerusalem and the areas of Syria and Palestine; his attention is on a narrative that predates the Arab expansion and the subsequent emergence of an Arab culture in the region by many centuries. This part of the account carries strong religious overtones, and because the current inhabitants cannot participate in the discourse as coreligionists, their presence in the narrative is minimized.

When he does focus his attention on Saracens, it is evident that for the *Mandeville* writer, like Bacon and other medieval theologians, the defining characteristic of the Saracens is their religion. While there are numerous references to Saracens throughout his description of Jerusalem and the surrounding lands, the only instances in which there is a detailed discussion regarding Saracens and Saracen culture involve matters of religious belief and practice. In this there is but one exception, although it is somewhat familiar in its nature. In Chapter XXIV, the *Mandeville* writer provides a genealogical survey of the Tartars in which, among others, Saracens are named:

> Yee shulle vndirstonde that alle the world was destroyed be Noes Flood saf only Noe and his wif and his children. Noe had iii. sones, Sem, Cham, and Iapheth. This Cam was he that saugh his fadres preuy

members naked whan he slepte and scorned hem and schewed hem with his finger to his bretheren in scornynge wise, and therefore he was cursed of God; and Iapheth turned his face awey and couered hem. Theise iii. bretheren had cesoun in alle the lond. And this Cham for his crueltee toke the gretter and the beste partie toward the est, that is clept Asye. And Sem toke Affryk. And Iapheth toke Europe . . .

And of the generacoun of Sem ben comen the Sarrazines. And of the generacoun of Iapheth is comen the peple of Israel and [vs] though that wee duellen in Europe . . . Natheless the soothe is this: that the Tartarynes and thei that duellen in the gret Asye, thei camen of Cham. But the emperour of Chatay clepeth him not Cham bu[t] Can, and I schalle telle you how.

(pp. 160–1)

This passage is singular in its divergence from the general narrative in which Africans (as well as Arabs) are linked to Ham, and thus God's curse. Here, it is the people of Asia, and in particular the Tartars, who are identified as the progeny of Ham, and as such, the inheritors of the curse, while the Saracens are linked to the respectable Shem. However, even in this the *Mandeville* writer does not stray too far from the general narrative; while Arabs are not linked to Ham, they are linked to Africans through descent from Shem. While the reason for this dramatic shift in the *Mandeville* writer's narrative, wherein the people of Asia are identified as the descendants of Ham, is not wholly apparent, it is possible that it is a reflection of the developments of the thirteenth century, in which the Mongols burst upon the world's stage in dramatic fashion, establishing themselves as perhaps the preeminent threat to Western Europe, and recalling the prophesied calamities that were to accompany the end of the world. In this instance, the author may have followed in the footsteps of the scholars along a familiar path in attempting to situate the newest threat within the framework of the Bible.

However, when the topic of Saracens is raised, the main focus of the author is on Saracen beliefs and practices. Within this context there are several general themes: Saracen beliefs proper, Saracen conceptions of Jesus (and of the amenability of these beliefs to Christianity), and a "biography" of the Prophet. Of their beliefs, the *Mandeville* writer offers a pithy summation in describing the contents of the *Alkaron*:[29] "in the whiche boke among other thinges is written, as I haue often tyme seen and radd, that the gode schulle gon to Paradys and the euele to Helle. And that beleeuen alle Sarazines" (p. 96). The *Mandeville* writer also enumerates the bounties of paradise in accordance with Saracen teachings, describing paradise as a veritable garden of delight in which can be found fruits regardless of season, rivers of milk, honey, sweet water, and wine, houses made of precious stones and precious metals, and maidens who will remain thus in perpetuity (p. 96). The author also makes a distinction between belief and practice in the area of marriage that, while incorrect in its characterization of the law in question, does make a distinction between popular practice and doctrine: "Also

Machomet commanded in his Alkaron that euery man scholde haue ii. wyfes or iii. or iiii., but now thei taken vnto ix. and of lemmannes als manye as he may susteyne" (p. 99). This distinction on the part of the author is all the more remarkable, inasmuch that without this distinction the Saracen faith itself might be perceived in an even less favorable light.

Generally speaking, the *Mandeville* writer's approach in explaining the beliefs of the Saracens is objective (relative to the writings of many of his contemporaries and predecessors in the West), and at times even sympathetic. Here, for example, is his version of the type of explanation a Saracen might provide of his religion:

> And yif ony man aske hem what is here beleeue, thei answeren thus and in this forme: "Wee beleuen God formyour of Heuene and of erthe and of alle othere thinges that He made, and withouten Him is no thing made. And we beleuen of th[e D]ay of Doom, and that euery man schalle haue his meryte after he hath disserued. And we beleue it for soth alle that God hath seyd be the mouthes of his prophetes."
>
> (p. 99)

In this explanation via an imagined Saracen, he approximates the religion of the Eastern Mediterranean Muslims in a far more accurate manner than many of his contemporaries.

In describing the religion of the Saracens, the author also devotes a considerable amount of time to the Muslim depiction of Jesus, emphasizing the ways in which the Saracen religion is amenable to Christianity. The *Mandeville* writer informs his audience that Saracens believe in the Virgin birth (p. 99), and in the miracles commonly associated with Jesus (p. 97), along with an additional miracle, that of Jesus speaking to Mary as an infant (p. 97). The reader also learns of the Saracen belief in Mary's suffering during childbirth (p. 97), as well as a legend pertaining to her alleged fears that the angel Gabriel was really a local necromancer in disguise, and the story behind this particular individual (p. 97). Moreover, according to the *Mandeville* writer, Saracens hold Jesus in higher regard than the other prophets:

> And amonges alle prophetes Ihesu was the most excellent and the most worthi next God, and that He made the gospelles, in the whiche is gode doctryne and helefulle, fulle of claritee and sothfastness and trewe prechinge to hem that beleeuen in God . . .
>
> (p. 97)[30]

> And thei seyn also that Abraham was frend to God; and Moyses was familier spekere with God; and Ihesu Crist was the word and the spirit of God; and that Machomete was messager of God. And thei seyn that of theise iiii. Ihesu was the most worthi and the most excellent and the most gret . . .
>
> (pp. 99–100)

Furthermore, the author assures his audience that Saracens still display the utmost respect for the Bible:

> And whan thei mowe holden the boke of the gospelles of oure lord writen, and namely *Missus est angelus Gabriel*, that gospelle thei seyn, tho that ben lettred, often tymes in here orisouns, and thei kissen it and worschipen it with gret deuocoun.
>
> (p. 98)

For the *Mandeville* writer Saracens are, if not entirely Christian, at least near to Christians in many respects.

However, the differences in doctrine regarding the role of Jesus remain, and in this matter the *Mandeville* writer is not silent, providing a summation of the Saracen position on the controversy:

> For He was neuere crucyfyed, as thei seyn, but that God made Him to stye vp to Him withouten deth and withouten anoye. But He Transfigured His lykness into Iudas Scarioth, and him crucifyeden the Iewes and wenden that it had ben Ihesu Crist, but Ihesu steygh to Heuene alle quyk ... And thei seyn yit that, and He had been crucyfyed, that God had don ayen His rightwisness for to suffer Ihesu Crist that was innocent to ben put vpon the cros withouten gylt. And in this article thei seyn that wee faylen and that the gret rightwisness of God ne myghte not suffer so gret a wrong.
>
> (p. 98)

Having explained the Saracen position regarding the Crucifixion, the author then presents a Christian corrective:

> And in this fayleth here feyth. For thei knoulechen wel that the werkes of Ihesu Crist ben gode and His wordes and His dedes and His doctryne be His gospelles weren trewe and His miracles also trewe; and the blessede virgine Marie is good and holy mayden before and after the birthe of Ihesu Crist; and alle tho that beleuen perfitely in God schul ben saued.
>
> (p. 98)

The *Mandeville* writer adopts a similar approach in explaining the Saracen position in rejecting the Christian concept of the Trinity, but here he attributes it to silence on the concept within the *Alkaron* and a general lack of understanding on the part of the Saracens (p. 99). In the end, the *Mandeville* writer's judgment on the Saracens' faith is thus:

> thei han many gode articles of oure feyth, alle be it that thei have no parfite lawe and feyth as Cristene men han ... for thei han the gospelles

and the prophecyes and the Byble writen in here langage; wherfore thei conen meche of Holy Writ but thei vnderstonde it not but after the letter.

(p. 100)

However, he assures his audience that in general the Saracens are, because of their proximity to Christians in articles of faith, "lightly conuerted, and namely tho that vnderstonden the scriptures and the prophecyes" (p. 100).

The overall objectivity of the *Mandeville* writer (relative to other Western writers) even extends to his "biography" of the Prophet. While in the main the "biography" is fictitious,[31] the account is nonetheless devoid of much of the vitriol that often accompanies Western "biographies," and even relates the legend of a miracle said to have taken place during the Prophet's youth (p. 102). Moreover, within the "biography," the *Mandeville* writer includes some interesting genealogical information regarding the different groups of Saracens:

> This Machomete regned in Arabye the year . . . vi [c.] and x. and was of the generacoun of Ysmael, that was Abrahames sone that he gat vpon Agar his chamberere. And therfore ther ben Sarazines that ben clept Ismaelytenes, and some Agaryenes of Agar, and the othere properly ben clept Sarrazines of Sarra; and summe ben clept Moabytes, and summe Amonytes, for the ii. Sones of Loth, Moab and Amon, that he begat on his doughtres that weren afterward grete erthely princes.
>
> (pp. 102–3)

It is interesting to note that within the context of this "biography," the *Mandeville* writer refrains from passing judgment, perhaps trusting the contents of the account to speak in his stead.

Within his account of his travels in Muslim kingdoms, the *Mandeville* writer reserves his harshest criticism for his fellow Christians in Europe, delivering it in a circuitous manner. His critique comes in the form of an outburst on the part of a sultan during the course of a private conversation recorded by the *Mandeville* writer. The sultan inquires after the manner in which Christian sovereigns govern their countries, and when his guest responds that they govern justly, the sultan corrects him, laying the sins of his fellow Christians before him:

> For yee Cristene men ne recche right noght how vntrewely ye seruen God. Yee scholde yeuen ensample to the lewed peple for to do wel, and yee yeuen ensample to don euylle . . . And also the Cristene men enforcen hem in alle maneres that thei mowen for to fighten and for to desceyuen that on that other . . . Thei scholden ben simple, meke, and fulle of almesdede as Ihesu was, in whom thei trowe; but thei ben alle the contrarie and euere enclyned to the euylle and to don euylle . . . And

non of hem holdeth feyth to another, but thei defoulen here lawe that
Ihesu Crist betook hem to kepe for here saluacoun.

(pp. 100–1)

Moreover, through the words of the sultan, the *Mandeville* writer attributes Christian military reverses to the rampant immorality of the Christian world:

And thus for here synnes han thei lost alle this lond that wee holden. For for hire synnes God hath taken hem into our hondes, nought only be strengthe of oureself but for here synnes. For wee knowen wel in verry soth that whan yee seruen God, God wil helpe you, and whan He is with you, no man may ben ayenst you.

(p. 101)

The fact that he, a Christian, is receiving this admonition from a Saracen, one who, in the words of the *Mandeville* writer has "no parfite lawe and feyth as Cristene men han" (p. 100), is not lost on him (pp. 101–2), and he leaves his audience to ponder the implications of the sultan's words.

The *Mandeville* writer's relative objectivity in his description of Saracens and their religion notwithstanding, his religious perspective is apparent throughout, whether articulated directly or indirectly through a Saracen proxy. Despite the present strength of the Saracens, the author assures the audience that Saracens know by their own prophecies that "the lawe of Machomete schalle faylen as the lawe of the Iewes dide, and that the lawe of Cristene peple schalle laste to the Day of Doom" (pp. 98–9). Moreover, the very same sultan who berates Christians for their immorality promises the author and the audience, on the strength of Saracen prophecies, "that Cristene men schulle wynnen ayen this lond out of oure hondes whan thei seruen God more deuoutly" (p. 101). The criticism of the *Mandeville* writer – direct and indirect – is intended to motivate European Christians to emulate the Saracens in their adherence to their faith through their actions.

For the Sarazines ben gode and feythfulle, and thei kepen entirely the commandment of the holy book Alkaron that God sente hem be His messenger Machomet, to the whiche, as thei seyn, seynt Gabrielle the aungel often tyme tolde the wille of God.

(p. 102)

However, this use of Saracens as "virtuous pagans" has its limits, which become apparent during the *Mandeville* writer's discussion of Christian conversion to Islam. For him, there can be only three explanations for such instances of conversion: poverty, ignorance, or evil (p. 103). Even as he explains the beliefs and customs of the Saracens, the *Mandeville* writer remains cognizant of the inherent danger of his actions, of expounding upon the tenets of a religion that is perceived as being in competition with Christianity, particularly as he is portraying it in a relatively objective manner.

The works of Ibn Fadlān, Ibn Jubayr, and the *Mandeville* writer reflect both the experiences of the individual traveler abroad (with the exception of the *Mandeville* writer) and the expectations of the audience. In so doing, these works demonstrate the ways in which medieval travel narratives served as a form of popular scholarship, providing information about distant lands and peoples in a manner that resonated with a lay audience. The presentation of the travel accounts as narratives resonated with audiences with an affinity for epics, romances, and "marvel" (*ajā'ib*) literature. Moreover, the details of the writers' travels were sufficient to stir the imagination of readers for whom travel in and of itself was an adventure. But most important of all, medieval travel narratives enabled the writers' audiences to gaze upon the world beyond the confines of their society, to participate in the experience of traveling and all of the vicissitudes that accompanied such an undertaking in the Middle Ages. This last aspect helps explain the popularity of the medieval travel narrative as a genre, and the continued popularity of many of these works, even to the present day.

Notes

1 The term "learned" tradition refers to the scholastic tradition largely derived from Greek and Latin sources in medieval Western Europe, and Greek, Indian, and Persian sources in the medieval Muslim world.
2 During the medieval period, the *chansons de geste* were accepted as largely accurate historical accounts. An example of the credibility attached to these accounts can be found in the chronicler Ambroise's reference to the *chansons de geste* as historical evidence in support of his claims regarding the political situation in the crusader camp during the Third Crusade. The reference in question can be found in the discussion of Western chronicles of the crusades found in Chapter 6.
3 The extent to which an individual presented a wholly factual account was often a reflection of the extent of his actual travel experience relative to the places in question. However, even in the case of seasoned travelers, the temptation to add "details" about mythical places and peoples often proved too great to resist.
4 It should be noted that even the Classical/Late Antique and medieval authorities included spurious accounts within their works. This tendency among the scholars was most pronounced in their discussion of places and peoples on the periphery of the then-known world, such as the "monsters" in Sub-Saharan Africa and India, or the "natives" in the islands of Southeast Asia and the Pacific Rim. See Chapter 1 for a discussion of this phenomenon as it relates to Sub-Saharan Africa and India in the works of some of the Late Antique and medieval geographers (Isidore of Seville in particular).
5 For example, *Mandeville's Travels* (which is discussed in detail in this chapter) makes a claim to authority based upon the writer's alleged experiences abroad. The work is now recognized as the production of a writer or writers who did not undertake the voyages outlined in the work, but rather compiled information from other sources and invented the remainder (e.g., Mandeville's conversation with the "sultan"). However, the claim of having traveled was often sufficient for medieval audiences; in the case of *Mandeville's Travels*, it became one of the most popular works within the genre in Western Europe.

78 The medieval travel narrative

6   The binary distinction between fact and fiction is problematic relative to a discussion of the portrayal of the known (and unknown) world in medieval works of literature, as monstrous races and other "marvels" were widely accepted facts within both the medieval Latin West and the Muslim world.
7   Bernard Lewis, V.L. Ménage, Ch. Pellat, and J. Schacht (Eds), "Ibn Fadlān," *The Encyclopaedia of Islam, Volume III: H-IRAM* (Leiden: E.J. Brill, 1971) 759.
8   Ibid.
9   The Bulghar king, identified as Almish ibn Shilki in the account, held sway over a kingdom comprised of both pagan tribes and tribes that had recently converted to Islam, and may have wanted to establish a monotheistic state religion in order to consolidate his power. In addition, he was a client of the Khazars, and may have sought to establish an alliance with the Caliph, who was hostile to the Khazars, to free himself from subservience to them. Richard Frye, *Ibn Fadlan's Journey to Russia: A Tenth-Century Traveler from Baghdad to the Volga River* (Princeton: Markus Wiener, 2005) 9. (A translation of the account can be found in this work.)
10 Lewis, Ménage, Pellat, and Schacht (Eds), "Ibn Fadlān," 759.
11 Ibid. Ibn Fadlān's experiences in Eastern Europe were largely overlooked by his contemporaries. However, in recent years there has been some interest in them; they were the basis for the film, *The Thirteenth Knight*.
12 There is some debate over whether the "*Rūs*" were in fact Swedish Vikings or a group of Slav and Viking traders. Frye, *Ibn Fadlan's Journey to Russia*, ix.
13 Ibid, 63.
14 Ibid, 64.
15 Ibid, 65.
16 Ibn Jubayr, *The Travels of Ibn Jubayr: Being the Chronicle of a Medieval Spanish Moor Concerning His Journey to the Egypt of Saladin, the Holy Cities of Arabia, Baghdad the City of the Caliphs, the Latin Kingdom of Jerusalem, and the Norman Kingdom of Sicily*, Trans. R.J.C. Broadhurst (London: Camelot, 1952) 15–16.
17 Jubayr, "Introduction," *The Travels of Ibn Jubayr*, 19. Subsequent citations will appear parenthetically.
18 "The Franks ravished it from Muslim hands . . . and the eyes of Islam were swollen with weeping for it; it was one of its griefs. Mosques became churches and minarets bell-towers" Ibid, 318.
19 *Mandeville's Travels*, and a Saracen critique of Christian European kings, is the subject of the upcoming section.
20 For Salāh al-Dīn's critique of Muslim support of the Counter Crusade, see the excerpt of Abu Shama's reproduction of the Sultan's letter exhorting the faithful to action in Chapter 7.
21 The *Historia Karoli Magni et Rotholandi*, or *Pseudo-Turpin Chronicle* (so named for its specious attribution to Charlemagne's archbishop, Turpin of Reims), enjoyed great popularity during the Middle Ages. Several hundred Latin and vernacular manuscripts remain of this classic of the mid-twelfth century. Ian Short (Ed.), *The Anglo-Norman Pseudo-Turpin Chronicle of William de Briane* (Oxford: Anglo-Norman Text Society, 1973) 1.
22 Stephen H.A. Shepherd (Ed.), *Turpines Story: A Middle English Translation of the Pseudo-Turpin Chronicle* (Oxford: Oxford UP, 2004) 21. ll. 635–41.
23 "[W]an Charlis perseyuyd þat Aigalonde wolde no3t be baptizide for he saw how vngodely þe pore peple of God was itretid, he lete ordeyne þat alle þe pore peple þat ware in þe hooste shode be honestly cloþid, and fro þensforth þey had sufficiently mette and drinke ry3t inow" (Ibid, ll. 644–8).
24 While the experiences recounted in *Mandeville's Travels* are attributed to Sir John Mandeville, a knight from St. Albans, the evidence suggests the work was

originally composed by an unknown Benedictine author in northern France in the late 1350s; the copy from which the Insular Version is derived likely arrived in England in the mid-1360s. M.C. Seymour (Ed.), "Introduction" and "Commentary," *The Defective Version of Mandeville's Travels* (Oxford: Oxford UP, 2002) xi, 173.
25 C. David Benson, "Public Writing: Mandeville's Travels and The Book of Margery Kempe," *Public Piers Plowman* (University Park: Pennsylvania State UP, 2004) 116.
26 Rosemary Tzanaki, *Mandeville's Medieval Audiences* (Burlington: Ashgate, 2003) 91–3.
27 Over 250 manuscripts of the text have survived to the present day. M.C. Seymour (Ed.), *Mandeville's Travels* (Oxford: Clarendon, 1967) xiii. Subsequent citations will appear parenthetically.
28 "And wyteth wel that the rewme of Arabye is a fulle gret contree. But therein is ouermoche desert, and no man may dwelle there in that desert for defaute of water. For that lond is alle grauelly and fulle of sond, and it is drye and nothing fructuous because that it hath no moisture, and therefore is there so moche desert. And yif it hadde ryueres and welles and the lond also were as it is in other parties, it scholde ben als fulle of peple and als fulle enhabyted with folk as in other places, for there is fulle gret multitude of peple where as the lond is enhabyted.

Arabye dureth fro the endes of the reme of Caldee vnto the laste ende of Affryk and marcheth to the lond of Ydumee toward the ende of Botron." (p. 29)
29 The Qur'ān; his familiarity with the Arabic word *mushaf* (*Meshaf* in the text), which refers to a copy of the Qur'ān is impressive, as is his knowledge of the word *haram* (*Harme* in the text), as indicative of an attribute of the Qur'ān as holy, or sacred. Ibid, 96. Also, cf. Hans Wehr's *Dictionary of Modern Written Arabic (Arabic-English)*, 4th ed., Ed. J. Milton Cowan (Ithaca: Spoken Language Services, 1994) 201, 589–90, for definitions of *haram* and *mushaf*, respectively.
30 This passage is a summation of the Qur'ān's account of Jesus and his ministry.
31 The "biography" includes accounts of the Prophet as an astronomer and governor of Khurasan, being afflicted with epilepsy, and an account connecting the prohibition of alcohol to the murder of a hermit by his companions while he was in a drunken stupor. *Mandeville's Travels*, 102–3.

4 The lesser evils
Familiar Saracens and Saracen Converts

For medieval European scholars, the image of the Muslim was informed by Classical, Late Antique, and medieval works of geography (and what would now be categorized as ethnography); the image of the Muslim in the popular imagination was a reflection of societal concepts of abnormality. In the popular discourse, the Muslim was the embodiment of the greatest threats to the Western European cultural fabric, and Muslim society became the location of abhorrent ideas and phenomena. The identification of such perceived threats with a foreign society carried with it the implication that such concerns were not native to Western European society, and thus could be excised from European society without affecting its fundamental nature. Moreover, it enabled both writer and audience to avoid unpleasant questions about the nature of their society.[1]

However, the conflation of "Muslim," or rather "Saracen," and "foreign" raises other questions. If the designation "Muslim/Saracen" carries with it the connotation of the foreign, what is one to make of Spain, Portugal, and Sicily, areas that had significant Muslim populations (and for a time Muslim rulers) throughout the Middle Ages? Were they a part of medieval Europe (in the manner of France or Germany) or a part of the Muslim world? If they were a part of Europe, what was the status of the Muslims therein? Were they also Europeans,[2] or were they an Other by virtue of their Muslim-ness? To what degree could a Muslim be a European, and to what extent could a European kingdom contain Muslims? The Muslim characters of the medieval romances were often the sites of contestation for such questions of identity.

The question of Muslim identity was the subject of considerable speculation and debate among medieval European scholars,[3] who had already begun the process of demarcating the boundaries of European-ness vis-à-vis Muslims, a process that had been active relative to the position of Jews within the polity from the point at which a Christian state first came into existence. In the context of the medieval romance cycles, the question of identity was complicated as a result of the de facto use of a hierarchy/spectrum of racial difference, in which Saracen characters could be portrayed as (a) approximating European phenotypic and cultural norms; (b) similar in many respects to their European counterparts in terms of shared cultural norms, but yet fundamentally different in crucial, defining areas; or (c) greatly removed from European standards of beauty and culture.[4] In this hierarchy of racialized difference, Saracen characters exhibit their Saracen-ness through both their physical appearance and their demeanor throughout the course of the story, identifying themselves as monstrously Saracen, avowedly Saracen, or in rare instances, as crypto-Europeans/soon-to-be-converted Saracens.

However, at times the stories themselves complicate this hierarchical structure with issues of cultural (as opposed to phenotypical/"racial") Saracen-ness, which tend to distinguish between Saracens who are *almost* European and Saracens who are in fact crypto-Europeans. In the romances, crypto-European Saracens are generally at some stage in the process of converting to Christianity, the implication being that the conversion will complete the process, and the Saracen will then *become* European. In such cases, concepts of cultural, religious and racial/ethnic Saracen-ness are conflated, and the reader is left to determine for her/himself where the cultural and ethnic/racial boundaries demarcating Saracen and European/Christian identity lie, and to what extent characters can *choose* to be Saracen or European, or, for that matter, what it *means* to be Saracen or European. Within the context of the medieval romances, Saracen is often a vaguely defined term, the meanings of which tend to be implicit rather than clearly articulated, and informed by certain well-known markers of Saracen-ness in all but the cases of the Saracen "monsters."

The ambiguity of Saracen as a marker of identity becomes especially problematic when one attempts to delineate boundaries between it and other identities. This is particularly true for the historical Muslims (upon whom the Saracen construct was ostensibly based) in their relationship relative to others, especially groups that were identified as European/Christian. In discussions of the relationships between Muslims/Islam and Europe/the West, whether in the medieval, Early Modern, or present period, scholars often employ the binary of Muslims and Europeans/Westerners. This binary is problematic; it implies that the two terms – Muslim and European/Westerner – are mutually exclusive at an essential level; that is to say, a Muslim cannot be a Westerner, and a Westerner cannot be a Muslim. This binary formula conflates ethnic/racial, cultural, geographic and religious differences in the two terms, one of which is indicative of an individual who subscribes to a particular religion and the other which describes an individual who lives in a particular part of the world.[5] It is only the conflation of the two terms in this manner that enables the binary to be effective. Thus to the term "Muslim" are added the markers of race (non-white), culture (Arab/Middle Eastern, etc.), and geography (Eastern/Southern). In a similar fashion, the term "Western" gains markers of race (white), culture (European/"American"),[6] and religion (Christian). These conflations have enabled the Muslim–Western binary to operate effectively in some shape, form, or fashion as a mode of discourse from the medieval period to the present.[7]

However, when applied to the medieval period, this binary conveniently overlooks the reality of Muslims living in Europe, and in some cases, of Muslims ruling in Europe. For much of the Middle Ages, Muslims ruled substantial portions of present-day Spain and Portugal, and lived in large numbers in Sicily. Moreover, the Muslims in question were not only the descendants of Berber, Arab, and West African conquerors. Particularly in the cases of Spain and Portugal, most of the Muslims were the descendants of native Spaniards and Portuguese who had converted to Islam.[8] The reality of Muslims in the Iberian Peninsula was an issue for Christian rulers through the early seventeenth century.[9] Similarly, Christian rulers of Sicily dealt with the issue of Muslim subjects (after the Christian re-conquest of Sicily in the eleventh century) for a significant portion of the Middle Ages. So what is to be made of these Muslims, many of whom were indigenous Europeans? Were they Europeans? By all accounts, they did not identify with the Latin-Christian cultural outlook (that was the foundation of "European" identity at the time) to the same extent as Christian Europeans,[10] but they remained culturally distinct from Muslims in North Africa and the Middle East.[11] To simply imply that their being Muslim negated their European-ness ignores issues of culture, history, and race/ethnicity that were at play at the time, and oversimplifies the complexity of the situation in substantial portions of Southern Europe. In order to make sense of this question, one must look to the ways in which it was addressed during the time(s) in question.

The most pertinent question was whether Muslim kingdoms within the confines of historically European lands – territories that had once been part of the Western portion of the Roman Empire, and were the heirs of a Latin, Christian civilization – were to be regarded as foreign Muslim lands, in the manner of Muslim territories in North Africa and beyond. In the particular case of the Muslim kingdoms in Europe, conquest (or re-conquest) was identified as an achievable goal,[12] as it was for the non-Christian kingdoms in what is now Central and Eastern Europe.

However, the issue of Muslim populations in newly (re)conquered areas such as Sicily, Toledo, or Cordoba, or of smaller Muslim populations under Christian European rule was more complicated, and scholars and members of the ruling elite looked to the example of another non-Christian group for answers relating to Muslims' status and identity within Europe. As non-Christians, Jews had historically been *the* alien presence within the body of Christendom, maintaining an alternative, clearly monotheist religion within the heart of the nations of Western Europe. From the earliest days of a Christian state, consensus had been that Jewish communities should be allowed to exist within Christian societies in recognition of their roles as hostile witnesses of Christ;[13] these communities were to be kept in a state of degradation, so that through observation Christians could be provided with an object lesson on the dangers of disbelief.[14] However, the existence of Jewish communities within medieval Western Europe did not make Jews, individually or collectively, *European*. Rather, Jews constituted an Other located within Christian Europe, a group distinguished primarily by theological difference.[15] Because of their unique role in salvation history, the presence of Jewish communities was a necessity, as the idea of the Jew played an important part in Christian identity. Yet, paradoxically, the idea of what these communities represented, the denial of the aspects of the salvation story central to Christianity, the assertion of an alternative theological discourse which claimed ownership of the authoritative, authentic reading of the sacred texts, was dangerous and disturbing to Christian authorities in medieval Western Europe. As such, Jews living in medieval Western Europe were the enemies within, an existential necessity yet simultaneously an existential threat, always proximate, but always the Other.

Jews were conceived of as the religious Other by European Christians for religious reasons that inextricably linked yet divided the two communities, and as such were viewed as an internal threat. However, Muslims, whether within or outside of Europe, were viewed as an external Other: a religious, military, and political threat.[16] This classification of Muslims as an external threat carried important implications for the medieval conception of Europe, and what did and did not count as European territory. As the internal Other, Jews were not as legitimately European; however, the presence of a Jewish community did not bring into question the European-ness of a territory. On the other hand, Muslims represented an external threat that was capable of changing fundamental aspects of a society. As individuals, Muslims represented the potential of a powerful, confident Muslim world, which made them a threat in a manner different from that posed by Jewish communities. In areas of Europe with a substantial Muslim presence or Muslim rulers, fundamental aspects of medieval Western European identity – religion, language, and culture – had been replaced and/or abandoned. Thus, as the external Other, it necessarily followed that Muslim spaces were excluded from medieval conceptions of Europe as well. Muslim-controlled areas were not part of Europe; in medieval Spain, many of the terms employed by Christians to denote concepts of a frontier relate to borders between Muslim and Christian territories.[17] The term *Reconquista* is in itself instructive in this regard, as territories had to be re-conquered – taken from Muslim control and reassigned to Christian control – before they could be properly identified as parts of Spain.[18] The cases of Sicily and Portugal demonstrate a similar perspective at work; areas became European to the extent that Muslim military, political, and cultural power and influence was curtailed, diminished, and eventually eliminated. Europe was Europe to the extent that it was free of Muslim presence and influence. Like their Jewish counterparts, Muslims in Europe were not Europeans *because* of their identity as Muslims. However, they were unique in that they also had the potential to radically alter the very European-ness of the areas they inhabited, to make Europe itself non-European.

Familiar Saracens

In the romances, issues of identity, particularly as it pertained to Muslims and other non-Christians, were often articulated and resolved through the use of certain Saracen character "types." These characters embodied certain perceived aspects of Muslim identity and its proximity to or distance from Christian, European identity. These characters can be categorized into three groups: Foreign Saracens (Saracen characters that differ dramatically from the Christian characters ethnically/racially and culturally as well as being non-Christian; the myriad examples of Saracen monsters fall under this category); Familiar Saracens (Saracens that are largely similar to their Christian counterparts in all areas, differing only but *crucially* in their status as non-Christians); and Saracen Converts (Saracens who are virtually Christian/European, and who, in the course of the work in question, will convert and join the Christians in opposing the Saracens).

Of the three character types, it is the Familiar Saracen that best exemplifies the inherent complexity of Muslim identity within medieval Europe. The Familiar Saracen is the literary embodiment of the proximate Muslim Other, a character who, by the description provided within the work in question, is not distinguished from his Christian counterparts by physical features indicative of ethnic/racial difference. Unlike the Saracen monsters (who are a common feature of medieval romances), Familiar Saracens are not bestial in appearance, nor do they exhibit markers of racial difference (e.g., dark/black complexion). Familiar Saracens are not separated from Christians by geographical distance; they are not from remote places such as India or Ethiopia. Moreover, the cultural norms of the Familiar Saracens tend to resemble those of the Christian heroes. In the romances, values such as loyalty, hospitality, and courtesy are clearly shared by Christians and Familiar Saracens in equal measure. The Familiar Saracen does not engage in "Saracen rituals" (e.g., invoking Saracen "deities"). In short, there is nothing distinctly *Saracen* about such characters to which an audience can point that alienates them from the Christian characters.

Of the few examples of the Familiar Saracen that are to be found, the Saracen king Clarell, in *The Romance of Duke Rowland and of Sir Ottuell of Spayne* (and his model Clariel in *Otinel*), serves as an apt representative. Clarell first appears in the text in the context of a skirmish between Ogier, Oliver, and Roland (three of King Charles' renowned Twelve Peers) and Clarell and three other Saracen kings. In the ensuing melee, Clarell's companions are killed, but he pleads for his life and is spared.[19] His status as a defeated Saracen king notwithstanding, Clarell is described as follows: "when his visage was alle bare/ A fayrere knyghte saw þay neuer are" (ll. 853–4). In effect, soon after his initial appearance in the text, he is distinguished from his Saracen companions and compared favorably to all knights, Saracen and Christian.

Beyond appearances, Clarell also proves to be a man of his word. Soon after he is captured, Ogier, Oliver, and Roland are ambushed. Ogier advises that they release their prisoner as he will be a burden to them; as a prisoner under their protection they are bound not to harm him, but yet must engage the other Saracens now before them (ll. 865–70). As a knight, Clarell recognizes the act as a sign of nobility, particularly in light of the situation at hand: "this was a worde of gentill blode/ to speke thus for thi foo" (ll. 872–3). But beyond his acknowledgment of the act, Clarell demonstrates that he lives by a similar code through his subsequent actions. Having been released by the three Peers, he absents himself from the coming battle, despite the fact that as a Saracen, he would benefit from an enormous numerical advantage against the same knights who had recently killed his companions and captured him (ll. 874–6). Then, when Ogier is captured during the course of the ensuing battle, Clarell returns the favor, intervening to save the Christian knight (ll. 944–8). Moreover, when another Saracen challenges Ogier's right, as a Christian, to a Saracen's protection, Clarell asserts the right of his prisoner in both word and deed, reaffirming Ogier's status as a prisoner, and killing the Saracen (ll. 949–54). In extending his protection to the captured Ogier, Clarell demonstrates his willingness to act in defense of his captive, even in opposition to a fellow Saracen.

The similarities between the Saracen Clarell and his Christian adversaries are also obvious in the depiction of Clarell's paramour and her interactions with Ogier. Having sent the captured Ogier to his lady's pavilion, the reader now catches a first glimpse of his lover, Alphayne, who is described as "white als fame," (l. 967), a characteristic generally associated with Christian princesses[20] and Saracen princesses who convert. In her treatment of Ogier, Alphayne's actions are reminiscent of those of King Charles' daughter Belesant in her role of hostess to the Saracen Ottuell prior to his duel with Roland.[21] Both Belesant and Alphayne are aware of their duties to the knight who has been placed in their care, and both appear to be comfortable in their guest's presence, displaying a willingness to discuss all topics, whether it is Belesant's maidens advising Ottuell to beware of Roland's sword (ll. 427–32) or Alphayne marveling at the ability of three knights to be the cause of discomfort to so many Saracens, including her lover, and attending to Ogier's wounds (ll. 982–4; 991–6). Not only does the Saracen Clarell resemble the Christian Peers in appearance and comportment on the field of battle, the similarities even extend to his lover and her behavior.

Yet despite the obvious similarities, such Saracens *are* different from their Christian counterparts in the romances, and precisely *because* they are Saracen. Such characters are never described as being racially or culturally alien from European Christians; one never reads of such characters engaging in non-Christian practices. However, by virtue of their identification *as* Saracens, it is implied that they are in *some* way different, even if they are not as racially, culturally and religiously distinct from the European Christian characters as are many of the other Saracens.

In the romances, the term *Saracen* serves as a site of ambiguity and alterity; it is a term in which notions of race, culture, religion, and geography are conflated to the point that despite the lack of evidence of phenotypic or cultural difference on the parts of Familiar Saracens, their Saracen-ness is reinforced by their being Saracen. Saracen is a descriptor that is self-referential, and thus does not need to be qualified by information detailing what it *means* to be Saracen. Such Saracens are Saracens precisely *because* they are Saracens. For the Familiar Saracen, Saracen-ness is something akin to a virulent, potentially contagious, yet latent disease. To all outward appearances, such characters are largely indistinguishable from their Christian counterparts. However, at key moments, they are prone to have an "outbreak" in which the symptoms of their Saracen-ness manifest themselves. At that point, the Familiar Saracen becomes a danger to the Christian characters, and must be quarantined from the Christian characters and readers, often in a violent manner.

In the case of Clarell, despite his proximity to his Christian counterparts, he remains a Saracen, and thus, the enemy. In an ironic turn of events, Clarell is exposed as undeniably, unrepentantly Saracen in his interactions with the Saracen Convert Ottuell (with whom he later engages in a duel in which each combatant champions his religion). It is Clarell's reaction to the news of Ottuell's conversion that reaffirms his Saracen-ness, and distances him from the Christian characters and the audience, as his response to the news is both a repudiation of Christians and an affirmation of his identity as a Saracen. Clarell's initial response speaks to his identity as a Saracen and his loyalty to the collective Saracen cause; he expresses both wonder and dismay at the loss of a knight of Ottuell's caliber from the Saracen ranks, and then advises him to recant:

> alas,
> Now is this a wikkede case,
> & þou so noble a knyghte.
> Whi dwelles þou there amonges thi fase?
> Foully there thou wichede was,
> & whi es this dede thus dighte?
> I rede þat þou conuerte the in hye,
> & then sall saughtyll with thyn Eme sir Garcy,
> & forsake not thy lawe.
> (ll. 1,147–55)

Clarell's reaction clearly identifies him as unmistakably, and in the context of the romance, unforgivably Saracen, and in so doing, negates the audience's accumulated good will toward him as a Familiar Saracen. Next to the Saracen Convert, his behavior demonstrates that in the designation Familiar Saracen, *Saracen* is the salient term. Despite his many positive attributes, there is no middle ground for the Familiar Saracen vis-à-vis the Saracen-Christian conflict. The Familiar Saracen must either move closer to the world of the storyteller and his audience by converting and aligning permanently with them, or occupy a position adjacent to that of the Foreign Saracen.

In the end, Clarell dies by Ottuell's hand, revealing his fatal flaw as a Familiar Saracen: despite his proximity to his Christian adversaries, he is both unwilling and unable to take the final step and *become* Christian. As such, he becomes an artifact from the convert Ottuell's past, an embodiment of the last stage in the individual process of evolution from Saracen to Christian. It is perhaps fitting that he meets his end at the hands of his more advanced relative on the evolutionary chart, the Saracen Convert.

In Clarell, the text presents the positive and negative aspects of the Familiar Saracen as they relate to the narrative of Christian triumph that lies at the heart of the medieval romances. The notion of the Familiar Saracen is simultaneously comforting in the fact that his behavior and values point toward the existence of universally held concepts of normative behavior and values, and yet problematic in his insistence on remaining Saracen, and implicitly legitimizing a religious and cultural perspective that is decidedly and defiantly non-Christian. It is precisely because the Familiar Saracen remains *Saracen* that he must meet the fate of all unconverted Saracens: in and of itself, his existence constitutes a threat. While the Familiar Saracen is a respectable, and in some ways, admirable figure, there is no room in the text for two valid cultural/religious realities. In this sense, the Familiar Saracen poses more of a threat than the Foreign Saracen, for while the latter can be read as something of a monster, the Familiar Saracen is an enemy with a plausible argument: an alternative, fundamentally different identity that nevertheless appears to result in a moral and social system not unlike that found in the audience's Christian, European society. Thus, the only feasible end for the Familiar Saracen is the fate of the Foreign Saracen. The nature of the romances dictates that as a Saracen, his views are invalid, and must be negated, usually through the use of force. This character may meet his end in a less extreme or humiliating manner than the Foreign Saracen, but his voice must be silenced within the text, as it raises questions that cannot be answered within the context of the narrative offered by the medieval romances.

In the context of the romances, the Familiar Saracen does not offer a positive outcome to the storyteller or audience. He or she is an admirable figure, in whom the audience may recognize some of the qualities of the Christian heroes. However, in so doing, the Familiar Saracen comes to inhabit an uncomfortable space in medieval popular fiction. He is not a wholly foreign, evil character upon which the writer and audience can project anger, and not a figure from whose ultimate defeat and demise they can derive satisfaction; in many ways, the Familiar Saracen is heroic. Yet, for all of the similarities between the behavior and customs of the Familiar Saracen and his or her Christian adversaries, the Familiar Saracen will never take the next step and join the ranks of the Saracen Converts. Rather, the Familiar Saracen remains familiar *yet* Saracen; by his very existence he raises uncomfortable questions about the true nature of the

Other and the true distance culturally, morally, and socially between the Christian and the Other. Moreover, by virtue of his existence, the Familiar Saracen presents the unsettling possibility that qualities like chivalry and honor can exist outside of a Christian European context, and need not be informed by it. It is perhaps because of the Familiar Saracen's implicit rejection of fundamental aspects of Christian European-ness in such an unsettling manner that this character is rarely found within the context of the romances.

The demise of the Familiar Saracen in medieval romances reinforces the concepts of Saracen-ness and Christian European-ness that his appearance may have complicated. Issues of Saracen-Christian proximity raised by the Familiar Saracens' appearance and behavior are resolved, first by the Familiar Saracen himself within the text, and then by his enemies. The Familiar Saracen legitimizes the Saracen-Christian construct through both his affirmation of his identity as a Saracen and his rejection of a Christian identity. In this affirmation of Saracen-ness, the Familiar Saracen validates the Saracen-Christian construct; his actions reflect the fact that as a Saracen, he too subscribes to this construct, that Saracens also regard it as legitimate. In justifying this concept, he reminds the audience that he is a Saracen, and in so doing becomes more Saracen than Familiar, a process that links his fate to those of the countless nameless, faceless Saracen characters who march to their deaths throughout the romances without the fanfare he enjoys.

Saracen Converts

The Familiar Saracen complicates the Saracen-Christian construct through his uncomfortable proximity to Christian characters. But fundamentally, he remains a Saracen, and in the end this is his undoing. However, the romances do present one type of Saracen who, unlike the Familiar Saracen, transcends her/his Saracen-ness, and adopts a new, Christian identity. Within the pages of the romances, the integrity of the Saracen-Christian (European) binary and the concept of Saracen-ness are challenged most dramatically by the Saracen-become-European, the Saracen Convert. In the Saracen Convert, the fundamental ideas of Saracen identity are complicated and brought into question, albeit inadvertently. Within the context of the romances, the very concept of conversion raises a number of questions. If Saracen-ness is primarily, implicitly an ethnic/racial classification, can a character truly "convert," and, as such, cease to be a Saracen? What types of Saracens *can* convert, and in so doing, transcend Saracen-ness? What does conversion entail, and what exactly are these Saracens converting *to*? Most importantly, what do these conversion stories (which are found within larger narratives of Saracen-Christian conflict) tell us about the fundamental nature of Saracen-ness, or for that matter, Christian/European-ness?

One aspect of the Saracen Convert that is particularly important is her/his similarity to the Christian characters, particularly in comparison with the other Saracen characters. In appearance and behavior, the Saracen convert is generally (but not always) the most *European* of the Saracens, and therefore the most likely candidate for conversion. Such characters are also the most desirable candidates for conversion; their credentials (beauty and position for Saracen women; the convert is generally a princess; and skill in battle and nobility for Saracen men) serve to mark them in the texts as potential converts. And although the romances do not present the process of conversion as a conventional "battle," it is nonetheless a type of conquest, and one that differs considerably depending on the gender of the Saracen Convert.

Floripas

Princess Floripas (*The Sowdone of Babylone and Ferumbras His Sone Who Conquered Rome*, derived from the Old French *Fierabras*) stands as an excellent example of the prototypical female Saracen Convert. The daughter of the sultan Laban, she is both a source of pride[22] and a trusted counselor. In her first appearance in the text she is advising her father in regard to Oliver and Roland, who have been recently captured, so as to ensure the safety of Ferumbras, who is a prisoner of the French (1,511–26). She quickly distinguishes herself from the other Saracen characters by her unique qualities, establishing her credentials as a potential convert.

If there is a general rule that is in operation vis-à-vis Saracen conversion, it is that the Saracen Convert represents a material loss for the Saracens and a corresponding gain for the Christians. This is particularly true in the case of the Saracen princess, for whom conversion is a matter of conquest through love; the princess is willing to forsake all, including religion, for the love of a Christian knight.[23] Her conversion is a conquest for the Christian knight as a lover and future wife, and a conquest for Christendom, as a flower of the Saracen world has been plucked from its fold, and all that it has to offer is now at the disposal of the Christian community into which the princess has been assimilated. To underscore this idea, descriptions of such Saracen princesses highlight both their beauty and their wealth.

Beauty for these Saracen princesses means strict adherence to medieval Western European (i.e., French)[24] ideals. The princess must be rendered French if she is to be a suitable match for her Christian (French) lover; the Saracen princess must be white. Of the *chansons de geste* (from which the other vernacular romances are derived) produced between 1150 and 1300, twenty-one Saracen princesses are featured; seventeen of them are explicitly described as white.[25] Without exception, each of these white Saracen princesses converts within the course of their respective story. In describing these princesses, the writers employ the conventional language reserved for French princesses. The initial description of Floripas in the Old French *Fierabras* illustrates this phenomenon at work:

> Her gleaming eyes out-glowed the purest gold that day!
> Her face was fairer far than winter's snow and blazed

> With eyes of deeper black than any falcon's gaze.
> Her cheeks were both as red as roses on the spray,
> Her mouth just made to kiss, so sweetly was it framed
> With lovely lips the hue of peaches' bloom in May.
> Her breasts were small and firm, like apples in their shape,
> And whiter than snow upon a winter's day.
> She was truly more fair than any words could say.[26]

The reader is presented a description of the Saracen Floripas that emphasizes the very European nature of her beauty (her white face and breasts, her rosy cheeks), reinforcing her suitability as a match for the hero, and her sexual desirability.

The binary formulation Christian/white/good and Saracen/black/evil, established early within the narrative of the romances, necessitates the rendering of the Saracen princess (who will choose the Christian knight and Christianity over her family, her people, and her religion) as European in order to ease anxieties over the proposition of an interracial coupling. The Saracen princess as religious Other is addressed within the story through her eventual conversion to Christianity; her status as political Other is addressed through her collusion with the hero to defeat the Saracens (led by her father). Her status as racial Other cannot be addressed so easily; either Christian European (i.e., French) society will have to change to accommodate racial difference, or she will have to "change" to accommodate it. Invariably, the writers choose the latter option, presenting a French princess in a Saracen land, with (racially) Saracen siblings and parents,[27] following the Saracen religion. The white Saracen princess makes the process of assimilation easier for Christian European society; she need only sever her Saracen political and religious ties because her racial difference has already been conveniently erased by the text itself.

The Saracen princess is not only desirable for her great beauty, she is also desirable for both the wealth she possesses, and the wealth she represents. The Saracen princess represents the wealth of the East[28] in her physical attractiveness and in the wealth displayed in her adornment. In *Fierabras*, Floripas' wealth is on display in the description of her clothing. Shortly before recounting her role in freeing the French prisoners from captivity, the writer presents an image of the princess that draws attention to her physical desirability and wealth:

> Good people, let me dwell on the beauty of this maid! . . .
> Her figure was bewitching, both slender and well shaped . . .
> Her hips were low, and lissome and slender was her waist
> That wore Galician velvet with saffron overlaid.
> The fey that made her garment had studded it with swathes
> Of golden stars that shimmered and shed a wondrous ray.
> Its belt was finely threaded with seams of golden chain,

> And fastened by a buckle with gleaming gold ornate . . .
> Her legs were clad in trousers of silk with gold brocade,
> And on her feet were slippers, adorned with chequered lace
> And finished very finely with gold and silver paint.
> Across her pretty shoulders a lovely cloak was draped . . .
> Her cloak was sable crested, and scented so it made
> The smell of mint or lily seem very small and faint.[29]

The description directs the audience's attention to the appeal of the princess in terms of her wealth and her suitability as a sexual partner. However, the Saracen princess does not merely display wealth; as the heiress to her father, she represents the wealth of the Saracen kingdom, which is the goal (stated or unstated) of the Christian hero.

In the Middle English derivative of *Fierabras*, *The Sowdone of Babylone*, it is Floripas' intelligence that is on display, quickly becoming a tool at the disposal of King Charles and the Twelve Peers. Through the course of the text, she becomes a means through which the Christian characters can inflict pain and suffering upon the Saracens in general, and Laban in particular. Long before she is baptized, before she has joined forces with King Charles and the Peers, she is working for their benefit, and to the detriment of her father and his forces. Her desire to meet the imprisoned Oliver and Roland leads her to dispose of first her governess, and then the jailer (ll. 1,563–78; 1,584–1,606). After disposing of the jailer, she works quickly to gain custody of the two prisoners, lying to her father in the process, and promising to protect them from harm (ll. 1,607–46); upon the arrival of the remainder of the Twelve Peers into her custody, she informs Sir Naymes (and the audience) of her long-standing love for Sir Guy and her desire to be baptized for his sake (ll. 1,891–6). Floripas consistently places both her natural gifts and the gifts she has accrued as a consequence of her position at the disposal of the Christian forces.

Having given herself to Sir Guy, and thus to the cause of King Charles and his forces, Floripas not only becomes a willing instrument in the undoing of her father, but appears to derive genuine satisfaction from his discomfiture. When Lukafer, one of Laban's trusted advisors, is burned alive by Naymes, Floripas expresses her approval, and soon after advises the Peers on how to proceed against her father (ll. 2,018–26). Once her allegiance to the Christian forces is revealed, she joins the fray in full, trading insults with Laban (ll. 2,212–30), providing the Peers with alternative sources of sustenance (ll. 2,299–2,306), and later weapons with which to repel Laban's forces during a siege of the castle (ll. 2,475–86) (which they have commandeered), working in tandem with the Christian knights against her father and his forces. It is Floripas who recognizes the banner of the advancing King Charles, and alerts the Peers in a timely fashion, ensuring their participation in the rout of the assembled Saracen forces (ll. 3,083–94). She is instrumental in the Christian victory over her father and his allies.

In her actions on behalf of the Christian forces subsequent to her declaration of love for Sir Guy, Floripas highlights a key concept in the trope of the Saracen Convert in medieval popular fiction: the essential convergence of religious and political affiliation.[30] Having allied herself with the forces of King Charles and assured them of her eventual conversion, it is not sufficient that she merely recognize her fate as being linked to their fate. Rather, she must actively participate in the ongoing conflict against the Saracens, among whom are members of her family (excluding her brother Ferumbras, who has already been baptized, unbeknownst to her), taking part in the conflict in a manner that would be both unexpected and inappropriate for a Christian princess in the context of a romance. However, as a Convert (or prospective Convert), she must demonstrate her allegiance to her new faith, which in practical terms means an allegiance to the Christian sovereign, which can best be accomplished by actively severing all ties to the Saracen political and social system to which she belongs. In the romances, both Saracens and Christians view conversion as an act of betrayal (or realignment), necessitating action on the part of the Saracen Convert to allay any fears on the part of other Christians that they will be the victims of a similar betrayal at some point in the future.

For her part Floripas, like many other Saracen Converts, displays a particular zeal in bringing about the downfall of former companions, as, through their defeat and eventual annihilation, she is born anew within the context of her new community. By itself, the account of a trusted and loved princess who murders her governess, collaborates with an outside force to bring about her father's downfall, and witnesses his execution without protest would be reprehensible; Laban's imprecations against her upon first seeing her subsequent to his capture[31] would be appropriate. However, as the actions of a Saracen Convert, they are both necessary and appropriate; they are part of a rite of passage, as Floripas, like all other Saracen Converts, must completely sever all ties with Saracen society, and thus their Saracen selves, in order to obtain a place in Christian society.

Within the romances, the Saracen princess becomes the literal and figurative embodiment of the Saracen wealth and power the heroes wish to possess. Beautiful (in an acceptable, European manner), wealthy and powerful, her collaboration with the Christian heroes presages their eventual victory. Jacqueline de Weever sees in the white Saracen princess and her presentation of her body and wealth to the Christian European heroes the articulation of latent imperialist desire. She describes it as "a shaping fantasy of Western power to this day – that the conquered East chooses Western culture."[32] More than any other figure in the romances, the Saracen princess as Convert represents both the allure of the East and the aspirations of the European heroes (and the medieval audience). She is perhaps the most complex, problematic character in the romances.

Ottuell

The converted Saracen princess is often noted for her beauty; however, it is martial prowess and nobility that are often the distinguishing characteristics of the converted Saracen knight, qualities that, subsequent to his conversion, are used in the service of the Christian sovereign under whom he now lives, and the Christian community of which he is now a part. A fitting example of the converted Saracen knight (as mentioned earlier in this chapter) is Sir Ottuell of *The Romance of Duke Rowlande and of Sir Ottuell of Spayne* (Otinel in the *chanson de geste Otinel*). In Ottuell one finds the prototypical Saracen Convert both prior and subsequent to his conversion.

From his introduction as a character, Ottuell is clearly presented as both an uncommon knight and a loyal Saracen. He first appears as a messenger, delivering an ultimatum to King Charles on behalf of the Saracen emperor Garcy. In delivering the message, he identifies himself as a loyal servant of his Saracen sovereign and ardent devotee of the Saracen faith, and through his bravado and threats, a knight of similar standing to Roland:

> my lorde þe Emperour Garcy . . .
> In Paynym ne es none so doghety,
> He hathe the flour of cheuallrye . . .
> Charles I ne maye noghte honour the,
> For þou hase greuede Mahoun & me,
> þat alle þis worlde has wroghte.
> And Rowlande, if euer I may the see
> At Batayle or at any Semble,
> thi dedis schall dere be boghte.
>   (ll. 98; 100–1; 103–8)

For further emphasis, Ottuell follows his pronouncements with an account of the Saracen attack of Lombardy, the ensuing massacre of fifty thousand Christian knights, and his role in both the destruction of the city and the massacre (ll. 134–50). It is only after he has slain Sir Estut (who, upon hearing the account, attacks Ottuell) and secured the protection of King Charles against his barons, whose collective wrath he has aroused (ll. 151–83), that the Saracen knight actually delivers the message for which he was sent to Charles's court: the king is to renounce Christianity, adopt the Saracen religion, and recognize Garcy as his emperor; in return, he will be given England and Normandy to govern, and certain members from among the Twelve Peers will also be granted additional lands over which to rule (ll. 203–46).

Ottuell's standing as a knight becomes obvious during his duel with Roland, when King Charles himself prays for Roland's success and the conversion of the "gentill knyghte/ þat es so hardy and so wighte" (ll. 511–12). For his part, Roland offers both the king's daughter Belesant and his friendship, along with Oliver's friendship, as incentive for conversion (ll. 517–28). However, in a response typical of the Saracen knight of the romances, Ottuell rebuffs Roland's offer, returning threats of further violence, and the duel continues (ll. 529–40). Ottuell's manner of declining Roland's offer highlights his qualities as a knight, for although his refusal to convert to Christianity is on the one hand an affront, it would be unseemly for a warrior engaged in a duel to capitulate instead of fighting. In the context of the duel, Sir Ottuell's rejection of Roland's offer is as expected as is Charles' rejection of Garcy's demands that he renounce Christianity in exchange for land; both responses originate from a similar sense of personal and national pride. Indeed, the prayer of the French king and his knight's offer set the stage for Ottuell's moment of conversion and emphasize his formidable nature, as he cannot be brought to the baptismal font through the efforts of men, even men of the stature of King Charles and Roland.

Ottuell's conversion can only be effected through divine intervention; in this case, coming in the form of a dove sent from the heavens that alights on his helmet and inspires him to convert (ll. 577–85). Yet even in these circumstances he remains unconquered; neither his opponent nor any of the spectators are cognizant of his decision to convert prior to his announcement to Roland, and his decision takes place at a time in which the outcome of the duel is in doubt to the degree that the French king feels compelled to offer yet a third prayer for his knight.[33] Ottuell's conversion diminishes the collective strength of the Saracens, but the manner in which it is accomplished actually enhances his position within the text.

Ottuell's first demonstration of loyalty to his new king and community subsequent to his conversion comes immediately after his baptism, when he declares that he will "distruye þe heythyn blode," precluding all things, including marriage to the king's daughter (ll. 648; 658–60). As a Saracen Convert, he is cognizant of his precarious position relative to the Saracen community he has just abandoned, and the Christian community he is attempting to enter, as well as the fact that his entrance into that community is dependent upon his success in completely erasing all vestiges of his Saracen past. King Charles will become his ally only if Garcy becomes his enemy, and such a radical shift can be accomplished only through violence initiated by Ottuell and directed against his former sovereign. Ottuell acknowledges this reality in his pledge to destroy the Saracens, retake Lombardy, and capture Garcy (who, as well as being the emperor, is also his uncle); in effect, he must reverse the damage he helped inflict upon Christendom. Before he can enter Charles' court, he must efface the most powerful symbols of his Saracen past: his works as a Saracen knight, and his personal connections to the Saracen world.

The reality of Ottuell's insecure status as a Saracen Convert is underscored by Christians' and Saracens' reactions to him after his conversion. As a new convert, he has yet to be fully integrated into the brotherhood of the Christian knights, and therefore is not a member in full standing of Charles's

Twelve Peers. Despite Roland's previous assurances to Ottuell that he would be the member of a new trio with Roland and Oliver, upon their arrival in Lombardy, it is Roland, Oliver, and Ogier who set off in search of adventure (ll. 760–8). As one eager to join the Christian community and the fraternity of the Peers, Ottuell lacks the requisite body of work by which King Charles and his knights can judge him, and through which bonds are formed within this closed community of warriors. Consequently, Ottuell remains on the periphery of his new community, awaiting an opportunity to demonstrate his loyalty and his value as a knight.

While the attitude of the Christian knights towards Ottuell is one of acceptance tempered by a degree of ambivalence, the Saracens regard the Saracen Convert with open hostility. Within the context of the romances, conversion represents a shift of temporal allegiance for the characters; the Saracen Convert is regarded as having committed an act of treason. However, until the conversion is confirmed through the Saracen Convert's actions, other Saracens are slow to believe his or her claims of conversion. In the case of Ottuell, it is the aforementioned Familiar Saracen Clarell who first learns of his conversion; his expression of disbelief and anger are typical of Saracen attitudes toward conversion.[34]

Implicit in Clarell's advice is that Ottuell must consider the implications of his actions and repent of them while he can. When Ottuell refuses, the duel between the two knights is a necessary consequence. For Clarell, Ottuell's act constitutes treason, and must be punished as such. For Ottuell, the duel represents an opportunity to sever his ties to the Saracen community and his Saracen past by championing the cause of Christianity against his former religion, to make real his earlier conversion in the eyes of both Saracens and Christians. In this context, the religious overtones of the duel benefit Ottuell's cause, which is used to solidify his new position within the Christian community.

With the death of Clarell during the course of the duel, Ottuell's conversion is firmly established for both Christians and Saracens, and his relationship to each group is fundamentally altered. His position among the Christian knights is strengthened, and each subsequent act serves to further improve his situation, while his links to the Saracen community are irrevocably severed. Ottuell becomes as much an enemy to the Saracens as King Charles and the Peers; Garcy's reaction to the sight of Ottuell on the field of battle expresses his new standing in the eyes of his uncle and former ally: "alas, . . . / . . . Renayede thefe my Cosyn was, / he ledis vs here a wikkede pase, / bothe with traye and tene" (ll. 1,513; 1,516–18). Ottuell's affiliation with both the Saracen community in general, and with his immediate family in particular, is all in the past tense in the eyes of the Saracen emperor.

Ottuell's subsequent actions (capturing Garcy and marrying Belesant) bring the narrative to a close in a predictable manner. But for all practical purposes, the narrative of his conversion ends with the death of Clarell. While the capture of Garcy enables Ottuell to assume the position in

Christian society promised to him by King Charles, it is his victory in a duel in which he champions Christianity that assures a place for him in Charles' kingdom and in Christian society. Prior to the duel, Ottuell's position, like that of other Saracen Converts, is very much in doubt. Like other Saracen Converts, he establishes a place for himself in his new community through his actions against his former allies on behalf of his new allies.

The King of Tars[35]

The King of Tars (also known as *The Soudan of Dammas*) offers one of the most interesting examples of the Saracen Convert. Unlike other converts, whose conversion is read as an act of betrayal toward their sovereigns, the Soudan is himself the sovereign, and thus the betrayal implicit in many of the other tales of Saracen conversion is largely absent in his case. The Soudan as an individual and *The King of Tars* as a work raise interesting questions regarding the nature of Saracen-ness, religious performance, and conversion. By the story's end the Soudan has left all vestiges of his Saracen past behind, and in a manner that fundamentally distinguishes him from other Saracen Converts.

The Soudan is first presented to the reader as a love-struck would-be suitor of the beautiful daughter of the Christian King of Tars. However, even as he declares his desire to marry the Princess of Tars, he adheres to a stock feature of Saracen kings in the romances – the resort to violence in the place of persuasion – declaring that he will win her father's approval for the marriage or, "And ells I swere, withouten fayle,/ I schul hire winnen in pleyn batayle,/ With mony an heih lording" (ll. 31–3). The threat of force is soon realized as the King of Tars, who is repulsed by the idea of his daughter marrying a Saracen (as is his daughter), rejects the Soudan's proposal, which results in war between the King and the Soudan. In the ensuing conflict, the Christians are thoroughly defeated, and the Princess announces that she will marry the Soudan to prevent the continued slaughter of Christians on her behalf: "Fader, ichulle him serve at wille,/ Erli and late, loude and stille,/ And leeven on god almiht; . . ./ Certes, I nul no lengor drye/ That Cristene men schul for me dye,/ Thorw grace of god almiht" (ll. 229–31, 235–7). In so doing, the Princess offers herself as a sacrifice of sorts, a Christ-figure working to save the lives of the Christians of Tars. A medieval European audience would have been familiar with the image of Christ sacrificing himself for the living and then entering Hell to rescue the souls of the righteous dead; here the Princess will sacrifice herself through marriage to the Soudan to save the lives of the Christians of Tars, and then enter the land of the Saracens in order to "rescue" the souls of the unconverted Saracens of Dammas, beginning with the soul of the Soudan himself.

From the beginning of the relationship, religious differences are a source of concern, particularly for the Princess, who enters as the daughter of a defeated king, and as a Christian who will be living in a Saracen land. The text itself articulates the fear that the Princess will be converted, or at the least "Saracenized" (if there is a difference between the two states; the text does not draw a distinction between the two). After their initial meeting, the Princess is led to a chamber to wait for the Soudan. At this point, she is described as being clad "With riche clothes heo was clede,/ Hethene as thaugh heo ware" (ll. 359–60). The passage subtly implies that the line of demarcation between Christian and Saracen is so thin that merely altering one's style of dress can bring one's status as a Christian into question.

The Princess's fears manifest themselves in a dream in which she is approached by one hundred black hounds that bark at her, one of which is particularly menacing, and appear intent on doing her bodily harm; the hounds are accompanied by three devils (ll. 397–408), which is perhaps symbolic of the "Saracen trinity" that Saracens were believed to worship.[36] However, when she remembers Jesus, she realizes that neither the hounds nor the devils can harm her, and that she should have no fear of the Saracen deities, and she awakens reassured (ll. 409–31). This marks a turning point for the Princess, and when the Soudan takes her to a Saracen temple and insists that she renounce Christianity,[37] she readily agrees, asking to be instructed in the rites of his religion (ll. 457–68).

From this point, the Princess operates as a crypto-Christian. Publicly, she openly professes a belief in the Saracen religion; however, the audience is assured that inwardly she remains a devout Christian: "When heo was hire self alone/ To Jhesu Crist heo made hire mone" (ll. 490–1). Her faith and her Christian identity has become portable, which distinguishes her from other Saracen and Christian characters, who are unquestionably one or the other.

After the Soudan and the Princess are married,[38] she soon becomes pregnant. With the birth of their child, the differences between the Soudan and Princess come to the forefront. The child is deformed: "For lymes had hit non;/ But as a roonde of flesche icore/ In chaumbre lay hire bifore,/ Withouten blod or bon . . ./ Hit hedde nouther neose nor eiye,/ But lay stille as a ston" (ll. 543–6, 548–9). The birth of a deformed child recasts the marriage (and sexual union) of the Soudan and the Princess as something unnatural, an inter-species union rather than an interfaith/interracial union. The child's condition stands as proof of the abhorrent nature of the marriage. Both the Soudan and the Princess view the child's affliction as divine punishment; for the Soudan it is due to his wife's lack of faith in the Saracen deities (ll. 551–64), while the Princess states unequivocally that she will believe in them only if they can heal her child (ll. 565–84). However, the text implicitly places the blame for the child's deformity on the Soudan; the child's condition is the physical manifestation of the father's spiritual imperfection as a heathen.[39] The affliction is universally acknowledged as being primarily spiritual in nature, setting the stage for a confrontation between Christianity and the Saracen religion, with the child's health in the balance.

It is the Princess's challenge that leads to the Soudan's eventual conversion. Like many of the other male Saracen Converts of the romances, the Soudan renounces his faith in the Saracen deities as a result of their inability to help him in his hour of need; however, the case of the Soudan is unique in that his request is selfless in nature; he sincerely prays for a cure for his child. For the Soudan it is concern for his child, rather than the quest for self-preservation or for self-aggrandizement, that leads him to reject the Saracen deities. When his prayers go unanswered, he rebukes the deities in a manner reminiscent of other Saracen Converts, declaring "On yow nas never help at need,/ Fy on ow everichon" (ll. 611–12)! In a literal and symbolic severing of ties, he seizes a staff, knocks down the idols, and beats them until they are destroyed (ll. 613–31).

Having lost faith in the Saracen deities, the Soudan is now amenable to the Princess's suggestion that they find a learned Christian man amongst the many Christians he has imprisoned and have their child baptized; he declares that he too will convert if the baptism is successful in curing their child (ll. 663–70). The child is baptized and named John; he immediately becomes the picture of health (ll. 746–57).

At this point the racial difference between the Soudan, his wife, and now also his son, becomes apparent. When the Soudan next meets with his wife and son, he is described as "so blak" (l. 773), highlighting the racial difference between the still Saracen Soudan and his Christian wife and son.[40] Upon his entrance, his son speaks, encouraging him to renounce the Saracen deities (ll. 776–8); his wife is more emphatic, pointing in particular to the ways in which his choice of faith will impact their relationship: "No, sire, i wis, seith heo,/ But thou weore cristene as hit is,/ Thou nast no part therof I wis,/ Nouther of child ne of me" (ll. 787–90). The cure and conversion of their son has tilted the balance of power in the Princess's favor; she is no longer content to practice her religion in private, or even to countenance another faith in her family; everyone to whom she is connected must be Christian.

After the Soudan is baptized, the difference between Saracens and Christians suddenly becomes pronounced in a manner heretofore unseen. The Soudan, whose given name has yet to be disclosed in the text, is baptized as Cleophas.[41] Moreover, the baptism announces not only a religious conversion, but an accompanying *racial* conversion as well: "His colour that lodlich and blak was,/ Hit bi com feir thorw godes gras/ And cler withoute blame" (ll. 854–6).

Saracen-ness is now equally tied to a racial and religious identity. However, this act of racial/religious conflation would appear to complicate the narrative by raising questions that are not answered within the text. Will other Saracens who convert also experience an accompanying racial transformation? Moreover, if one's Saracen-ness is a religious *and* racial condition, how was the Princess (who presumably never underwent a racial transformation) able to dissemble as a Saracen so effectively? The Soudan's dramatic transformation presupposes and then highlights differences that a medieval European, Christian audience (and perhaps to a greater degree, religious authorities) may have wanted to assume existed between Christians and Muslims through a bit of dramatic license, but it inevitably complicates the narrative even as it attempts to tie together a few loose ends.

The conversion of the Soudan is also accompanied by a change in behavior in both the Soudan and Princess, who heretofore had been very accommodating in her interactions with Saracens. Upon the Soudan's conversion, she immediately suggests that he send for her father, the King of Tars, so that he can marshal a force and bring it to the Soudan's kingdom and baptize his subjects. She is unequivocal about the punishment that should be reserved for those who refuse baptism: "And hose nil not cristned be/ Hong hem heighe uppon a tre,/ Withouten eny dwelling" (ll. 894–6). The behavior of the Soudan himself also reflects a similar change; he not only accepts his wife's plan, but also gathers his Saracen knights (who apparently had been uninformed of his radical change in appearance), announcing his conversion, and demanding that they follow suit: "For ichave Mahoun forsake,/ To Jhesu Crist ich have me take,/ And sertes so schul ye;/ And hose wol not so don,/ He schal ben honged swithe son" (ll. 975–9). Having left Saracen-ness both religiously and racially, the Soudan now embarks upon the task of leaving it politically, demanding the conversion of his subjects so as to change the nature of his kingdom from a Saracen to a Christian polity.

The conversion of the Soudan, which has a religious, racial, and now political component, is made whole with the predictable, yet necessary severing of ties with his Saracen past through armed struggle. Five Saracen kings from neighboring territories declare war on the Soudan for abandoning the Saracen deities; in the ensuing battle (in which the King of Tars and his assembled forces are participants as allies of the Soudan) the five kings are killed and their Saracen forces are decimated. Thus *The King of Tars* closes with the Soudan having successfully turned the page on his Saracen past, and opened upon a presumably bright Christian future.

The Soudan as a Saracen Convert stands apart from other Saracen Converts in several important areas. His conversion does not arise out of a desire to better his circumstances or preserve his life, but rather is a product of his sincere wish to see his child's health improve. Moreover, his conversion manifests the conflation of race and religion in the characterization of Saracens and Saracen-ness; he simultaneously becomes Christian *and* "European" upon his baptism. He is also given a Christian name, which further distinguishes him from other Saracen Converts. When the Soudan takes the final step of announcing his conversion through combat – his baptism in Saracen blood – the act is perhaps even more symbolic than it is political. Unlike converts like Ottuell and Floripas, he has actually *ceased* to be Saracen in any tangible way, a fact that in and of itself renders most questions of his Saracen affiliation moot. While many Saracen Converts are able to successfully leave their former Saracen identities, the Soudan stands apart as the only one among them to actually *transcend* his very Saracen-ness.

In the medieval romances the question of conversion is inextricably linked to questions of identity and loyalty, in which the Saracen Convert comes to represent both a benefit and a threat to her/his new Christian companions. While the act of conversion represents a step for the Saracen Convert, it is but an initial step, and will not result in admission into Christian society without the equally important steps represented by the active severing of ties to the character's Saracen past, the annihilation of her/his Saracen identity. The Convert is a welcome addition in terms of the material benefit s/he brings to the Christians in their struggle against the Saracens. However, the Convert represents a threat in that s/he blurs the boundaries between Saracen and Christian identity, suggesting that that identity is a malleable thing. Despite the assertions of theologians such as St. Jerome that "Christians are made, not born,"[42] social, cultural, and religious environment have always played a large part in identity formation. As such, conversions as radical re-formations of portions of the identity of an individual or group represent an implicit threat to the social and structural foundations within which individual and group identities are formed.

Within the context of the romances, the choice of the Saracen Convert is simultaneously an embracing of the Christians and a rejection of the Saracens; in effect, the Saracen Convert is committing an act of treason. The threat posed to her/his former Saracen allies is clear, but there are also disturbing implications for her/his new Christian allies as well. For leaders such as King Charles, the conversion is an implicit reminder of the possibility of Christian conversion. More importantly, it is an indication of the limits of sovereigns' ability to control the actions of their subjects. After all, for the Saracen Convert, Saracen society remains a viable alternative as long as links remain, as Clarell's offer to Ottuell after his conversion demonstrates. It is only by destroying that option that the new Christian can ensure his or her position in Christian society as a *former* Saracen (a title that will be inextricably linked to the character). In order to become fully integrated into the new society, the Saracen Convert must cast his or her lot entirely with Christian society, and kings are often quick to act to cement bonds of loyalty with Saracen Converts (e.g., King Charles' offer of Belesant to the newly converted Ottuell). For the other characters (including knights), all breaches of loyalty are to be viewed with suspicion; a traitor cannot be trusted to be loyal in the future. In most cases (the Soudan of *The King of Tars* being an obvious exception), the Saracen Convert must demonstrate her/his loyalty and value to the Christians, and this can only be accomplished at the expense of former Saracen companions. It is only after the door to the Saracen world and a Saracen past has closed for the Convert that a new door opens to reveal a Christian future within the Christian world in which s/he is now a member.

Conclusion

Within the context of the romances, the Familiar Saracen and the Saracen Convert make powerful statements about the fundamental nature of medieval European identity, about who could and could not be European. The

Familiar Saracen and the Saracen Convert mark the boundaries of European identity, which, for Saracens, operate as inflexible lines of demarcation, permeable only through conversion. But in the context of the romances, what do conversions accomplish vis-à-vis Saracen and European identity? In what ways are Saracen Converts changed via their conversion; how does conversion make these characters *European* in a way that is obvious to all? *Does* conversion make Saracens Europeans, or simply Christian Saracens (and is it possible for a character to be a Christian Saracen, or are the terms mutually exclusive)? Saracen Converts are seldom recognizable *as* converts to Saracen or Christian characters, and particularly in the case of Saracens, who remain incredulous until the conversion is made "real" through acts of violence. It would appear that European identity is as vaguely defined a construct as that of Saracen identity within the romances, and that it is dependent on a number of widely held, mutually reinforcing ideas.

The act of conversion is important as a repudiation of the construct – the idea itself – of Saracen-ness, and all of the associated conflations of ethnicity/race, culture, and religion. The conversion of the Saracen is a crucial step leading to her/his becoming European because it distances her/him from the associated ideas linked to Saracen-ness that are perceived as being in opposition to, threatening to, European-ness. Because the individual Saracen represents the racially, culturally, and geographically distant Saracen Other that is perceived as posing an existential threat to Europe, a formal break with this identity is necessary before the assumption of a European identity is possible. Conversion is a religious act; however, in the romances, it is often the temporal implications of this act that are of primary importance. Floripas' conversion is meaningful in that through it she breaks her bonds of relation with her father, Laban, who embodies the Saracen military threat; in a less direct way she also distances herself from Saracen monsters like Astragoth,[43] who embodies Saracen racial difference. Similarly, Ottuell's conversion is significant in that through it he severs ties with his uncle, Garcy, who poses a military threat to the Christian King Charles. In each instance, the texts do not bear witness to the conversions through baptism, but rather through acts of violence perpetrated against other Saracens, acts of violence that formalize the Converts' entrance into a temporal Christian polity, much as the baptisms mark their spiritual entrance into Christianity.

For the Familiar Saracens, their refusal to abandon a Saracen identity, an identity that carries certain associated aspects that are at odds with European identity (as articulated – albeit implicitly – in the romances), is the flaw that seals their fate. If Saracen-ness is inherently un-European, the Familiar Saracen is the Other, and will remain the Other to the extent that s/he maintains a Saracen identity. Clarell is marked as the enemy through his association with the emperor Garcy, who embodies a military threat to King Charles, and, by extension, to all of Europe. To the extent that he affirms his identity as a Saracen to any degree, he is a Saracen in the same respect as Garcy, who has situated Saracen collective military and political power in opposition to that of the most powerful Christian polity by declaring war on Charles. Despite his undeniable proximity to certain European ideals, as a Saracen, and in particular as a knight, he nevertheless represents the Saracen threat (made real by his emperor), a threat that must be effaced within the text. The fact that he is killed in a duel with Ottuell, which ultimately marks the latter's entrance into the confidence of King Charles and the Twelve Peers, highlights the divide between the Converted Saracen and the Familiar Saracen and their relationships to the idea of European identity. One character joins Christian European society through repudiating his Saracen identity in word and deed; the other affirms his Saracen identity and is ultimately defeated. Through the two character-types, the lines demarcating the boundaries between Saracen and European identity are shown to be almost imperceptible (at times), but always fiercely maintained, when necessary through violent acts of exclusion. Such lines of demarcation, which are omnipresent in the romances, hint at a similar situation in the Medieval Latin West, particularly in the areas in which Muslim and Christian societies were in relatively close, if uneasy, contact.

Notes

1 Siobhain Bly Calkin, *Saracens and the Making of English Identity: The Auchinleck Manuscript* (New York: Routledge, 2005), 183–4.
2 The term "European" itself speaks to a specific set of cultural, political, and historical realities, which are largely associated with the last half of the second millennium. In the medieval period, to the extent that they were united, Western Europeans were united by a common faith (Christianity) and a perceived common cultural/historical heritage (the Roman Empire). The idea of Europe as a cultural and historical entity was preceded in Medieval Western Europe by the idea of Christendom, which largely consisted of the Christian areas of Western Europe that had been Roman colonies, or had been influenced to some degree by Roman culture. Both the Roman cultural and historical ties and the Christian nature of an area were important; without one of the aforementioned attributes, a kingdom's place in Christendom was uncertain. For example, despite their deep historical and cultural ties to Rome, Spain and Portugal existed outside of Christendom for much of the medieval period because of their status as Muslim-ruled nations with large Muslim populations. In a similar manner, many of the Christian Eastern European nations occupied a nebulous position within Christendom because they did not share a Roman past with their Western neighbors. However, because the idea of Europe (Western Europe in particular) embodies much of what the term "Christendom" signified, the terms "Europe" and "Europeans" will be used to refer to the region during the Middle Ages. Western Europe will also be referred to as the "Latin West," as the term encapsulates the region's historical connection to the Roman Empire.
3 See the discussion in Chapter 1.
4 The portrayal of the Saracen was largely a function of his/her role in the romance.
5 The term "Westerner" is itself problematic, in that rather than referring to someone who lives in the Western hemisphere, in its popular usage it often excludes non-white residents of Central and South America and the Caribbean, and yet includes Australians. In fact, in terms of its general application, it can be said to apply almost exclusively to residents of European descent in Western Europe, the United States, Canada, and Australia.

6 Both terms can include definitions that are in fact self-referential; a European or a Muslim can be said to possess European and Muslim/Islamic culture, respectively, without much in the way of elaboration on what makes a culture European or Muslim. Rather, the culture is European or Muslim/Islamic to the extent that it is held by Europeans and Muslims.
7 Notable changes have included the addition of "American" (i.e., United States of America), Canadian, and Australian cultural identities under the umbrella of Western identity. In the case of each addition, it is interesting to note that each of the countries in question has significant indigenous and resident non-white (non-Western[?]) populations within their borders, populations that somehow do not factor into the countries' positions as Western nations and extensions of European culture and history.
8 The end of the Reconquista came in January 2, 1492 when the Amir Muhammad ibn 'Alī, also known as Abu 'Abdallah [Boabdil, in the Christian sources], the leader of the final Muslim kingdom in Spain, Granada, officially surrendered the kingdom to King Ferdinand. A. Hernando del Pulgar, "*Cronicas de los reyes de Castilla 1492*," *Medieval Iberia: Readings from Christian, Muslim, and Jewish Sources*, Trans. Teofilo Ruiz, Ed. Olivia Remie Constable (Philadelphia: U of Pennsylvania P, 1997) 344; for the name of the Amir, cf. "*Nubdhat al-'asr*," *Medieval Iberia: Readings from Christian, Muslim, and Jewish Sources*, Trans. L.P. Harvey, Ed. Olivia Remie Constable (Philadelphia: U of Pennsylvania P, 1997) 350.
9 The next century saw the establishment of Christian rule over the Muslim population of Granada and the surrounding areas, with accompanying attempts to assimilate these populations (including pressure to abandon their pre-conquest customs, beliefs, and language, as well as pushes toward conversion that, among other things, required the registration of children between the ages of three and fifteen in order to instruct them in the Christian faith, all through a succession of official decrees). Rebellions led to greater pressure toward assimilation and conversion, culminating in the proclamation of an edict of expulsion on September 22, 1609, that in the course of five years resulted in the forced immigration of approximately five hundred thousand Muslim Spaniards. After over eight centuries, this marked the end of a large, continuous Muslim presence in Spain. Anwar G. Chejne, *Muslim Spain: Its History and Culture* (Minneapolis: U of Minnesota P, 1974) 104, 132.
10 The term "European," as it is here employed, is meant to signify something akin, phenotypically, to a Western European. However, even the term "Western European" can be problematic, as its meaning has not always been static across time. As such, it is difficult to apply terms that convey a modern understanding of the region to a time antecedent to such an understanding in discussing the various groups of the region. In this context, it is more appropriate to speak of Latin Europe or the Latin West, that part of Europe covering a vast ethnically and linguistically diverse territory in which the various peoples followed the Roman Catholic Church (as opposed to the Greek Orthodox Church or a traditional, non-Christian religion), than to speak of Western Europe, or Europe in general. In a very real sense, the Latin West is the cultural, political, and religious ancestor of Western Europe specifically, and the "West" in general. Robert Bartlett, *The Making of Europe: Conquest, Colonization and Cultural Change 950–1350* (Princeton: Princeton UP, 1993) 1–2.
11 This is evident in the *muwashshah* and *zajal* poetry that emerged in al-Andalus (Muslim Spain) beginning in the tenth century. This is also evident in the discourse over race/ethnicity that was ongoing within al-Andalus during the period, initially between the Arab and the Berbers (who made up the majority of the initial conquering forces, and who appear to have been marginalized in the early

years following the Conquest; one can only speculate on the extent of discrimination against the Berbers, as "Arab" is an even more nebulous racial/cultural marker than European), and later between the indigenous communities and Berber/West African forces of the Almoravid and Almohad dynasties. See Chejne, *Muslim Spain*, 222, 231, 233 ff.; cf. 110–15 for the social/ethno-racial dynamic.
12 Indeed, the re-conquest of Spain either is or becomes an objective of King Charles in romances such as *Fierabras* and the *La Chanson de Roland*.
13 However, the theological position was not always in accord with the popular sentiment or with political exigencies, and sporadic, often brutal eruptions of violence directed against Jewish communities was an unfortunate reality in medieval Western Europe.
14 Moreover, Jews' part in the final days, as a group destined to be converted or destroyed, necessitated their continued existence. Jonathan Boyarin, *The Unconverted Self: Jews, Indians, and the Identity of Christian Europe* (Chicago: U of Chicago P, 2009) 43.
15 Gil Anidjar, *The Jew, the Arab: A History of the Enemy* (Stanford: Stanford UP, 2003) 35.
16 Ibid. See Chapter 1 for a detailed discussion of other aspects of Muslim identity as envisioned by medieval European scholars.
17 Boyarin, *The Unconverted Self*, 43.
18 Ibid.
19 Sidney J. Herrtage (Ed.), *The Romance of Duke Rowland and of Sir Ottuell of Spayne* (London, 1880) ll. 849–55. Subsequent citations will appear parenthetically.
20 See the discussion of the racialized descriptions of Saracen women in medieval romances and their implications as it relates to Saracen Converts in the coming section.
21 Ottuell is one of the primary examples of the Saracen Convert; his role in the present text, and his position as a Saracen Convert is examined in detail in the coming section.
22 The first mention of Floripas comes courtesy of her brother, Ferumbras, who offers her in marriage to Oliver, along with a fiefdom in exchange for renouncing Christianity. Emil Hausknecht (Ed.), *The Romance of the Sowdone of Babylone and of Ferumbras His Sone Who Conquered Rome* (London: N. Trübner, 1881) ll. 1, 220–6.
   The work will henceforward be referred to as *The Sowdone of Babylone*; subsequent citations will appear parenthetically.
23 The exemplar (and most popular) of the Convert Saracen princesses is Orable of the Old French *Guillaume* cycle (in particular *Prise d'Orange*; after converting, she assumes the name Guibourg). An African princess, Orable is the daughter of Desramez, sister of Rainouart, and wife of Tiébaut, all of whom are black. Nevertheless, in keeping with convention, the reader is assured that she is white, and is a veritable French princess in Africa. In the course of the *Prise d'Orange* she frees the French warriors (including Guillaume, her future husband), cuckolds her husband, and is instrumental in the conquest of her father's kingdom. Moreover, within the *Guillaume* cycle as a whole, she is implicated in the deaths of her children, all of whom are murdered by Guillaume, with whom she does not produce an heir. Orable/Guibourg's portrayal as a white Saracen, her betrayal of her family and country, her inappropriate (adulterous) behavior vis-à-vis the French heroes, and the writers' identification of her as a heroine in spite of the overwhelming evidence to the contrary, are staples of the depictions of Convert Saracen princesses in the romances. Jacqueline de Weever, *Sheba's Daughters: Whitening and Demonizing the Saracen Woman in Medieval French Epic* (London: Garland, 1998) 9, 37, 159.

24 The *chansons de geste* (and the derivative vernacular romances) reflect the ideals of the medieval French society in which these works were originally produced.
25 de Weever, *Sheba's Daughters*, 5.
26 *Fierabras and Floripas: A French Epic Allegory*, Trans. Michael A.H. Newth (New York: Italica, 2010) ll. 254–62.
27 Nowhere is the intellectual disconnect involved in the rendering of the Saracen princess as European more evident than in the fact that she is the *only* white Saracen; when presented, the members of her immediate and extended family are generally presented as black/dark, and commonly as grotesque figures. Questions regarding the likelihood of the existence of such a family go unaddressed within the contexts of these works.
28 de Weever, *Sheba's Daughters*, 33.
29 *Fierabras and Floripas*, ll. 3511–12, 3520–5, 3531–4, 3539–40.
30 Siobhain Bly-Calkin provides an in-depth examination of religious identity as political identity in the medieval romances in *Saracens and the Making of English Identity: The Auchinleck Manuscript*. Principal in the conception of religious identity as political affiliation is the reality that "Saracens and Christians resemble each other so closely in their martial comportment and values . . . change of religion amounts to a change of sides in a war." Bly-Calkin, 44. Because the distinction of Saracen or Christian is the only distinguishing feature of the characters of the romances, and one of the principal features of the genre is the constant conflict between Saracens and Christians, loyalty to the Saracen or Christian faith is often understood as loyalty to a Saracen or Christian king within the context of the works, and the conversion of a character thus becomes a military and political gain for one side, and a corresponding loss for the other. As Norman Daniel so aptly states, the lack of difference between the religious practices of Saracens and Christians in the romances lends itself to the conception of religious identification *as* allegiance. This understanding of religious affiliation as being closely connected to a balance of power between two competing factions recasts conversion as a political act, an act of treason. Norman Daniel, *Heroes and Saracens: An Interpretation of Chansons de Geste* (Edinburgh: Edinburgh UP, 1984) 192.
31 "[F]ye on the, stronge hore, / Mahounde confound the!" (*Sowdone of Babylone*, ll. 3,131–2).
32 de Weever, *Sheba's Daughters*, 191.
33 Ottuell differs from other male Saracen converts, such as Ferumbras (Floripas' brother), in that his decision to convert is largely the product of divine intervention and free will, whereas in the case of Ferumbras and others the desire to convert arises out of necessity, and is often accompanied by a disavowal of the Saracen deities that are perceived to have abandoned the Convert in his time of need. Ottuell's status as an undefeated Saracen Convert suggests the existence of a discourse between *Otinel* and works such as *Fierabras*, in which the narrative of conversion as an act of submission on the part of the defeated Saracen is countered by a scene in which the spiritual aspects of conversion are privileged. Marianne Ailes, "*Otinel*: An Epic in Dialogue with the Tradition," *Olifant* 27 (2012): 20–3.
34 Cf. Clarell's response to news of Ottuell's conversion in the section on Familiar Saracens.
35 All citations are from "The Kyng of Tars; and the Soudan of Dammas," *Ancient English Metrical Romances, Vol. II*, Ed. Joseph Ritson (London: W. Bulmer and Company, 1802) 156–203. Subsequent citations will appear parenthetically.
36 The idea of a "Saracen trinity" was commonplace in medieval literature (particularly in medieval romances and drama), with one of the figures being Mahoun/Mahound. This popular myth reinforced on a popular level clerics' charges that Islam was a form of heresy rather than a religion.

37 "Forsake thou most thi false lay" (l. 448).
38 The two are married "In the maner of his lay" (l. 527).
39 Jane Gilbert, "Putting the Pulp into Fiction: The Lump-Child and Its Parents in *The King of Tars*," *Pulp Fictions of Medieval England: Essays in Popular Romance*, Ed. Nicola McDonald (Manchester: Manchester UP, 2004) 105.
40 Early in the story, the Princess is described as being "White so fether of swan" (l. 12).
41 Cleophas, after the name of the priest who performs the ceremony (ll. 851–3); he is the same priest who baptizes and names the Soudan's son.
42 Karl F. Morrison, *Understanding Conversion* (Charlottesville: U of Virginia, 1992), 73.
43 See the discussion regarding Saracen monsters (in which Astragoth is cited as an example) in Chapter 5.

5 Foreign Saracens

Of the three Saracen types, the "Foreign" Saracen occupies a space most distant from medieval Christian Europeans. Within the romances – indeed, within medieval literature as a whole – the Foreign Saracen is the archetypal Other, incomprehensible, hostile, and in its most extreme manifestations marginally human. The Foreign Saracen presents none of the ambiguities or complexities of identity associated with the Familiar Saracen or the Saracen Convert; here is a figure that audiences could despise wholeheartedly, and from whose discomfiture they could derive satisfaction. This figure, in all of her/his manifestations, is a figure that exists far beyond the Saracen/Christian boundary, and is marked by appearance and/or behavior as a representative of the most urgent aspects of the perceived Muslim threat, a threat that is utterly annihilated within the romances.

The most obvious way to mark a character as Other is through physical description which renders that character different, even grotesque. This is as true for the Saracens of medieval European literature as it is for any of the other foreign groups that find their way onto the pages of medieval texts, and is particularly true of the Saracen monsters[1] that appear in some of the romances. The Foreign Saracen represents an extreme type of Saracen-ness, a caricature of the historical medieval Muslim, which in all cases is different in terms of religion and culture. In the case of the Saracen monsters, the characters are also markedly non-Christian/European in form and physical features as well. Such characters are often portrayed as demonic; language connecting them directly to demonic elements can be found in their physical descriptions. In such instances, the characters' physical appearance reinforces their separation from the protagonist and his group (of which the writer is a part), and most importantly, from righteousness.

This physical distance from virtue often situates such characters beyond the pale of salvation; Saracen monsters (and Foreign Saracens in general) are not the targets of conversion efforts. In the few instances in which a Foreign Saracen or Saracen monster does convert, the conversion may or may not be accompanied by a physical change, as is the case with the Soudan in the *King of Tars*, who changes from black to white after his baptism.[2] By his nature the Soudan is evil; in order to join the ranks of the righteous he must literally become something else. In his story of conversion, the Soudan differs from another famous convert from amongst the monsters, the Dog-Headed St. Christopher, who remains a monster after his conversion.[3]

Examples such as the Soudan and St. Christopher notwithstanding, conversion to Christianity is not the lot of most Foreign Saracens or Saracen monsters; for Saracen monsters, their physical appearance serves to highlight the gulf between the world of the writer and his audience and this Saracen Other. The outlandish depictions of these characters serve to strip them of their humanity, and in so doing, to remove them from areas of familiarity in which the audience might relate to them. The defining characteristic of such characters is their appearance; their difference is inscribed in a way that renders them unconvertible, even in comparison with other Saracen characters. The romances themselves often take a hostile stance toward Saracen monsters; such monsters are often depicted as something akin to a frightening natural phenomenon plaguing the Christian armies. Unlike other Saracens, they are understood to be beyond salvation; their appearance is evidence of their status as unregenerate Saracens. This form of Saracen Other is beyond the pale of Christian charity, and all efforts directed toward it focus on its annihilation. Among all Saracens, the Saracen monster is the enemy incarnate, a strange body upon which the protagonist(s), and by extension the writer and his audience, can focus their rage through acts of violence, of which a grotesque description serves as the first volley.[4]

There are numerous examples of the Saracen monster to be found in the pages of the medieval romances. Among them, one of the most striking examples is Astragoth, a Saracen giant in the army of the Soudan in the *Sowdone of Babylone*, who is described as a giant from Ethiopia.[5] Astragoth participates in the Saracen siege of Rome; from the description provided, it is immediately clear that his appearance dramatically differentiates him from his Christian adversaries and from humanity in general: "With bores hede, blakke and donne/ For as a bore an hede hadde . . ./ This Astrogot of Ethiop,/ He was a king of grete strength;/ There was none suche in Europe/ So stronge and longe in length" (ll. 347–8, 353–5). The next step in the description of Astragoth is to infer that he is not human at all, but something akin to a demon: "I trowe, he were a develes sone,/ Of Belsabubbis lyne,/ For ever he was thereto I-wone,/ To do Cristen men grete pyne" (ll. 356–9). This assertion, that the sole purpose behind Astragoth's existence is to inflict pain on Christians, seems to be borne out by Astragoth's actions, the first of which is to kill the heroic Senator Savaris, who had rallied the Romans to the defense of their city.[6] The description of this act of murder conveys a sense of Astragoth's bestial nature, in that he is said to have struck Savaris "as he were madde" (l. 350), as if he were a creature out of control. The description of Astragoth identifies him as physically non-human, and his actions and his Saracen identity identify him as a malevolent force. As a monster, he stands apart from other Saracens, who are associated with the forces of evil, but are not actually manifestations of that evil in the manner of Astragoth. As a character, Astragoth has more in common with figures like Grendel or the Minotaur than the Saracen king he serves. Like these figures, he is presented as an abomination, a monstrous figure that exists to visit disaster upon the protagonists, in this case the Christians of Rome.

Astragoth is situated outside the boundaries of humanity by the author, and as a result, he becomes a thoroughly foreign body upon which the writer and his audience can project their hostility. In the text he operates as an implement of war utilized by the Saracens to great effect rather than a sentient individual. Like the nameless Saracen soldiers who are cut down by the thousands, Astragoth has no real agency or ability to impact his own circumstances; he does not exist outside of his ability to wreak havoc amongst the enemies of the Saracens. He is a bogeyman whose impact on his surroundings is invariably and inevitably negative.

Within the text, the description of his death is the account of something both extraordinary and ignominious, which ironically occurs at perhaps the moment of greatest triumph for the Saracens. As the Saracens are storming the city, a portcullis falls upon Astragoth. Before he dies, he is described as "cryande at the grounde/ Like a deuelle of Helle" (ll. 435–6); in his last moments, he remains a bestial figure. Even in death he is not granted the ability to articulate his pain in a human manner to Saracens, Christians, or the audience. Rather, his cries elicit passive indifference from the other Saracens, and exultation from the Christians, who are heartened by his death.[7]

Astragoth is a dehumanized figure throughout his short appearance in the *Sowdone of Babylone*, and as such, his death does not elicit compassion from the Christian warriors, the author, or the audience. Rather, as an utterly Foreign Saracen, alien even in appearance, he inhabits territory at the farthest remove from European norms, at the very periphery of humanity. Marked by his outward appearance as the Other, his identity as a Saracen serves to reinforce his repulsive appearance, as one whose inward wickedness is writ large on his body. Unlike other Saracens, the audience's revulsion is in equal, if not greater, measure a product of his appearance as it is due to his Saracen identity. Moreover, the fact that he is a *Saracen* monster implies that he is connected to the other, less monstrous Saracens; each one of them is to a varying degree an Astragoth, if not in outward appearance, at least within their innermost selves. It is this basic reality that makes the Saracen threat real in the romances, the fact that at heart *all* but a select few[8] are as alien to their Christian counterparts as Astragoth. He merely exhibits physically what is not as apparent in many of the other characters, but is nonetheless within them.

While Foreign Saracens may or may not be identifiable by their appearance, they are always set apart through their behavior.[9] Whenever they appear, such Saracen characters consistently distinguish themselves from their Christian counterparts through their conduct. Frequently, such characters appear in the form of the Saracen king, over whom the Christians will triumph completely. As a literary figure, the Saracen king fulfills the roles of villain and cautionary figure. As an enemy of Christians – an enemy usually intent on subjugating Christians – he is a despicable, frightening figure, a worthy adversary for heroes like King Charles and Roland. At the same time, the general story of the Saracen kings is instructive of the dangers of overabundant pride. These figures are often undone by their arrogance, which leads them to overestimate their power and underestimate the ability of their opponents. Like Oedipus or King Lear, their pride reveals itself as something akin to a tragic flaw, a flaw that contributes to their eventual defeat, humiliation, and death.

Beyond their place as literary figures, the Saracen monarchs also point to medieval Western European perceptions of the Muslim world. The Saracen king is the personification of the power and wealth of the Muslim societies of the Middle East, North Africa, and parts of Europe during the Middle Ages, particularly relative to much of Western Europe. At a time in which the images of the wealth and sophistication of the Muslim world still endured, the Saracen sultans and emperors of the romances, with their arrogance, their presumptions of Saracen superiority, and their consistently aggressive behavior toward the Christian characters, may reveal as much about European feelings of inadequacy as they do of the ways in which Muslims were lampooned in medieval literature.[10] Indeed, as the Mandeville writer reminds his audience, the material trappings of the Muslim world could be seductive for Christians who were not firm in their faith.[11] In the case of the Saracen kings, their eventual defeat at the hands of Christian heroes, and the accompanying diminution of Saracen power within the texts, serves to minimize this threat to a degree.

The trope of the Saracen monarch (in particular the raving Saracen monarch) was not the exclusive property of the romances. The "Saracen monarch" was employed across genres, and came to represent the archetypical tyrant. Among the various genres outside of the romances, the raving "Saracen" monarch made infrequent appearances in the Mystery Plays of the fifteenth and early sixteenth centuries. In these plays, Saracens are often presented as the persecutors of the righteous Old Testament Israelites or New Testament Christians.[12] In particular, persecuting authority figures are likely to be depicted as Saracens; within the plays, the Saracen ruler becomes synonymous with a type of despot who is not satisfied with the mere oppression of his people, but who is bent upon waging war on the righteous people of God whenever the opportunity presents itself. In this respect, the biblical tyrants of the East did not seem that different from the contemporary figures with whom Christians in Europe were engaged in conflict on various levels. In one example, a "Saracen" Pharaoh (of the Wakefield play of the same name) encourages his legions to "Heyf up youre hertys unto Mahowne" as they prepare to follow the Israelites across the parted Red Sea.[13] In *Passion Play II*, a Saracen Herod proclaims his intent to persecute Christians who will not worship Mahownde, and the satisfaction he derives from the slaughter of Christians.[14] In fact, it is not uncommon to find instances of villains worshiping Saracen "deities" within the Passion plays.[15] In recounting the stories of those who were antagonistic toward or persecuted Jesus Christ and his early followers in the past, the audience's attention was called to those who were perceived as being hostile to Christians in the medieval present.[16] In one notable instance, Jews who deny the miracle of communion (and thus the doctrine of transubstantiation) are depicted as worshipers of the "Saracen deity."[17]

La Chanson de Roland is arguably the most well known of the medieval romances, and in many ways it sets the standard for subsequent works in the genre.[18] It provides the most concise articulation of the romantic ethos relative to Saracen-Christian relations: "The pagans are wrong and the Christians are right."[19] The tale and characters are larger than life; the main characters live and die heroically,[20] and the Saracens appear and are slain in droves. King Charles is old and wise, but he has not lost his vigor, as he demonstrates in the final battle against the Emir, Baligant's forces. The Twelve Peers embody the medieval warrior ethos, preferring death to dishonor.[21] Similarly, the Saracen characters are thoroughly of the genre; they worship idols, are hostile to Christians, and many of the rank-and-file Saracen warriors are monstrous in their appearance.[22]

La Chanson de Roland presents three Saracen leaders of note: King Marsile, his uncle the Caliph, and the Emir Baligant. Among the three, King Marsile best fits the description of the Saracen monarch. He is quickly identified as the nemesis of Charles and the Peers.[23] He is the one with whom Ganelon conspires to betray Charles and the Peers. Moreover, he is also the last of the Saracen monarchs in the text; he outlives his peers, dying at the news of Charles' victory over Baligant (ll. 3644–7), clearing the way for the eventual conversion of his wife, Bramimonde. Marsile's role in *La Chanson de Roland* is unique; he represents the most threatening aspects of the Saracen threat, but also illustrates the impotence of Saracens and the Saracen religion.

Throughout *La Chanson de Roland* Marsile's impotence in the face of Charles and his forces is on display. Charles has been unable to capture Saragossa, but the Saracen king has failed to halt his progress in Spain. His opening speech is a candid admission of his precarious position: "The emperor Charles from the fair land of France/ Has come to this country to destroy us./ I have no army to match his in battle,/ Nor sufficient men to break his army down" (ll. 16–19). His recourse to treachery – feigning a willingness to convert and become Charles' vassal in order to gain a reprieve from the conflict and conspiring with Ganelon to kill Roland – is an indication of both his character and his desperation.

His inability to best the king of the Franks despite outstripping him in wealth and warriors, which has led to subterfuge, is no more evident than in the Saracen ambush of Charles' rear-guard; at the head of two Saracen battalions (each consisting of over one hundred thousand warriors), Marsile is unable to rout the Twelve Peers and the twenty-thousand Franks in the rear-guard. The encounter is a complete disaster for Marsile; both battalions are decimated and put to flight,[24] and he loses his right hand to Roland (l. 1903), which effectively diminishes him as a participant in the drama. He flees the battlefield, unable even to participate in the final defeat of the rear-guard; it is left to the Caliph to oversee the deaths of most of the remaining Peers, including Oliver, whom he fatally wounds, dying in the process. Although Marsile's objective is realized – Roland and the Peers are dead – it is a Pyrrhic victory for him. His forces are annihilated, he is near death himself, and rather than weakening King Charles, the battle has increased the likelihood that all of Spain will fall to the king of the Franks. After the fiasco at Roncevaux, it is left to the Emir Baligant to extend the drama; Marsile is no longer the second most powerful king, merely the second most powerful Saracen king.

Marsile's impotence fuels his frustration, which manifests itself in episodes of rage. These episodes are a common dramatic device in the romances, and can be categorized as part of the trope of the "raving Saracen monarch," who gives vent to his frustration, often in spectacular fashion, after enduring a setback at the hands of the Christian heroes. Marsile, one of the earliest examples of the Saracen monarch – arguably a model for later Saracen monarchs – exemplifies the manner in which Saracen impotence fuels the frustration that leads to unseemly displays. The instances in which Marsile (or his supporters) express their anger in dramatic fashion are all directly or indirectly the product of his relationship to King Charles, a relationship of forced subordination due to military reverses.

In the first such episode, it is Ganelon's delivery of Charles' terms – Marsile must convert and become Charles' vassal (and receive half of Spain as a fiefdom) or else he will be captured, taken to Charles' court in chains and put to death (ll. 430–7) – that provokes the Saracen king's ire.[25] It is only through the intervention of the other Saracens that an altercation between Marsile and Ganelon is prevented (ll. 450–5).[26] Marsile's anger stems from the fact that Charles' message is an explicit reminder of Charles' dominant position. Notwithstanding the fate of the messenger, the message reflects the reality that it is Charles who is in a position to dictate terms. Marsile's anger is rooted in his frustration over the fact that he is powerless to alter the dynamics of his relationship with his nemesis; he may threaten Ganelon, but it is beyond his ability to harm the Frankish king.

The remaining instances are directly attributable to defeats, first to Charles' rear-guard, and then (in absentia) to Charles and his main force. In the first instance, following the defeat at the hands of Roland and the rear-guard (in which Roland cuts off his right hand [ll. 902–3]), it is Marsile's followers who speak for the unconscious king, directing their anger at their gods:

> With her are more than twenty thousand men . . .
> They rush off to Apollo in a crypt,
> Rail against him and hurl abuse at him:

'O, wretched god, why do you cause us such shame?
Why did you permit our king to be destroyed?
Anyone who serves you well receives a poor reward.'
Then they grab his scepter and his crown
And hang him by his hands from a pillar;
They send him flying to the ground at their feet
And beat him and smash him to pieces with huge sticks.
They seize Tervagant's carbuncle
And fling Muhammad into a ditch
Where pigs and dogs bite and trample on him.
(ll. 2578, 2580–91)

The Saracens' actions are indicative of their frustration, this time at the impotence of their gods to accomplish what they themselves cannot. In this episode the idea of Saracen impotence is elevated beyond the level of the two kings; it is now the Saracen gods who are powerless in the face of the Christian God. The Saracens' treatment of their gods – and, in particular, Bramimonde's lament[27] – is telling, as later many of the Saracens of Saragossa, including the queen, will convert.[28]

Marsile's actions in his encounter with Roland and in the aftermath of the battle reveal his lack of character, in sharp contrast to his rival, Charles. After losing both his right hand *and* his only son to Roland, Marsile flees the theatre of war, leaving the fight for his uncle, the Caliph, and his forces (ll. 1904–14). Abandoning the battle before its conclusion, he does not witness the eventual deaths of all of the Peers. Moreover, by eschewing death in combat, or the opportunity to avenge his son's death, he proves himself to be of less worth than the Saracens and Christians who have died in the battle. His comportment in battle is in stark contrast to that of Charles, who when wounded by Baligant, rallies (with the encouragement of the angel Gabriel) and slays his foe (ll. 3602–19). Marsile's behavior after Roncevaux also reveals an unseemly resignation to defeat at the hands of the Frankish king:

King Marsile takes flight to Saragossa;
He dismounts in the shade, beneath an olive tree.
He lays down his sword, his shield and his byrnie;
On the green grass he lies down, a wretched sight.
He has lost his entire right hand;
The blood flowing from it causes him to faint with pain.
(ll. 2570–5)

In removing his battle gear, the Saracen king signifies his unwillingness to continue the fight against Charles, which is confirmed by his relinquishing control of Saragossa to Baligant (ll. 2831–3). And although Marsile swoons due to pain and loss of blood, his actions still appear less heroic than those of Charles, who swoons at the sight of the dead Roland (l. 2880). Unlike

Marsile, Charles will persevere after his lament; bowed but not broken, he will continue the fight. Marsile is content to retreat from the fight, leaving the fight to Baligant, much as he left the fight and the field to the Caliph at Roncevaux. In romances, the battlefield is often the place in which characters prove their mettle. Those who die in combat have met the chivalric ideal by preferring death to dishonor, while those who emerge victorious serve as exemplars of the ideal. By fleeing the field of battle, Marsile consigns himself to ignominy, and the change in status is reflected in his diminished role after Roncevaux and in his eventual fate in the text.

Marsile's final act born of frustration reveals both the depth of his despair and the degree to which he has been defeated. Upon hearing of the victory of Charles' forces and the death of Baligant, he surrenders all hope: "When Marsile hears her, he turns toward the wall;/ He weeps and bows his head low./ He died of grief, oppressed by misfortune;/ He gives up his soul to the living devils" (ll. 3644–7). Marsile has exhausted all avenues to defeat Charles – subterfuge, direct confrontation, abdicating his throne to the more powerful Baligant – all without success. Faced with the prospect of Charles' triumphant entry into Saragossa, his pride and anger will not allow him to witness the total victory of Charles; he dies of grief, perhaps to rob Charles of the pleasure of seeing his adversary in chains. But his death is telling, in that it is indicative of the comprehensive nature of Charles' victory, as life itself offered no prospects for Marsile other than defeat and humiliation before his enemies. His death is not a surprise; throughout the text, Marsile demonstrates that more than the defeat itself, it is often the reminder of the defeat that he finds most vexing. In the end, he is merely true to his character.

Another character that meets the criteria of the Saracen monarch is Laban, the "Soudan" of the *Sowdone of Babylone*. Within the *Sowdone of Babylone*, Laban is first introduced as the archetypal powerful Saracen monarch. He is the ruler of Spain, which is presented as a Saracen land,[29] and a ruler of great power and renown, who has demonstrated his power through his conquests in Asia and of Christian lands, and is acknowledged as such by Christians and Saracens.[30] As the tale unfolds, it is Laban who is the king without rival in arms and dominion, and his enemies who appear to be overmatched. However, through the course of the work, Laban's aura of invincibility diminishes as he comes to be identified as an unregenerate enemy of Christians in general, and of Charles and the Twelve Peers in particular, and a fitting exemplar of the Foreign Saracen.

Laban's credentials as a Saracen monarch are established at the beginning of the *Sowdone of Babylone* through the description of his kingdom, which is reinforced by the idyllic image of him taking a moment to rest during a hunting foray on a spring day (ll. 61–2). However, it is after he learns of the actions of the Romans in plundering one of his vessels that a transition takes place, and he begins to present himself as a Saracen *warrior*-king. Upon hearing the news, he immediately marshals his forces and sets out for Rome at the head of a fleet on a vessel prominently displaying emblems relating to his status as both king and Saracen.[31] But to this point, Laban has yet to distinguish himself as a Saracen villain, let alone as a Saracen who is different from his Christian counterparts in the manner of Astragoth (who is a member of Laban's forces). The possession of a substantial kingdom, his participation in a royal hunting expedition, and his mobilization of forces in response to an act of provocation do not set him apart from Christian monarchs like Charles the Great. Rather, Laban identifies himself as a Foreign Saracen through his prosecution of war against Christians, and in particular the manner in which he carries out this enterprise. It is in the context of this war that he displays the hallmarks of the raving Saracen monarch, and moves from being a somewhat neutral figure to a villain whose demise is necessary for the successful resolution of the story.

The reality of Laban's position as a *Saracen* at war with Christians (regardless of their role in instigating the conflict) situates him securely within the parameters of the Foreign Saracen. Reminders of Laban's Saracen-ness reinforce this idea for the audience, particularly as it figures into the conflict with his Christian enemies. Prior to the actual attack on Rome, Laban affirms his identity as a *Saracen* combatant by pledging to the Saracen gods to destroy first Rome, and then Charles the Great,[32] placing him in opposition to the greatest of the Christian kings (who, at this point, has done nothing to involve himself in the conflict), and thus against much of Christian Europe. Soon after the attack on the surrounding precincts of Rome, in which Christians are slaughtered, and towns, abbeys, and churches are destroyed (ll. 145–6), the Pope appears in the story, heading a council to determine the Christians' course of action (ll. 153–4). It is during this session that Senator Savaris convinces the assembled party of Romans to defend the city without Charles's help, reminding them of the religious aspect of the conflict, promising them that: "Criste is more mighty/ Than here fals goddis alle;/ And he shal geve vs the victorie,/ And foule shal hem this day bifalle" (ll. 196–9). Savaris' proclamation reminds the Romans that Laban is a *Saracen* enemy, a worshipper of false gods. As such, he is already a natural adversary by virtue of his status as a non-Christian. Laban's aggressive behavior makes the preexisting, abstract tension between Saracens and Christians a political and military reality. His subsequent actions and the way in which he is depicted throughout the remainder of the story reflect his new identity as the enemy, or Foreign, Saracen.

The juxtaposition of Saracen and Christian deities is a crucial element in the identification of Laban as a Foreign Saracen. The conflict between Laban and Charles is couched in religious terms throughout the work, even prior to Charles's appearance in the text. When the Romans are successful in repulsing Laban's forces in their next encounter, the Pope thanks God for the victory (ll. 220–3). After the skirmish, when one of the minor Saracen kings (interestingly named Lukafer) produces ten thousand Christian maidens he has captured in raids throughout the countryside, Laban orders that they be slaughtered (ll. 224–9).³³ In ordering the slaughter, Laban states that he does not wish to have his people *polluted* by the maidens (ll. 232–3), articulating a Christian, European concern over the potentially negative consequences resulting from marriages across ethno-religious lines from a Saracen perspective. Laban also often invokes the names of his Saracen deities;³⁴ like the other characters, he works under the assumption that the conflict is a referendum of sorts on the validity of the two religions. Through the course of *The Sowdone of Babylone*, Laban's confidence in and patience with the Saracen deities fluctuates with the news from the front, but his Saracen beliefs continue to shape both his personality and the conflict itself.

Moreover, as a *Saracen* monarch, Laban is aware of his relationship to his Christian counterparts, and is keen to position himself as the preeminent enemy of Christendom (largely the area comprising the Latin West). Early in the story he announces his intention to destroy Christians entirely,³⁵ identifying himself as not just the enemy of the Christians of Rome and/or of Charles's realm, but as the enemy of *all* Christians, and indeed as the enemy of Christianity itself. When given the opportunity, Laban proves himself worthy of his self-proclaimed status as enemy of all Christians. Thus, the capture of Rome by his forces becomes the occasion for widespread slaughter, destruction, and the pillaging of both treasures and of the holy relics by his son Ferumbras.³⁶ The destruction of Rome, which firmly establishes Laban as *the* Saracen enemy, is also the occasion for the appearance of *the* Christian hero, Charles the Great.

The most consistent feature of Laban's personality is his mercurial temperament. Time and again, he is subject to what become predictable fits of anger, in which his reaction exceeds the precipitating event in an exponential sense. Through his behavior, Laban comes to exemplify all of the characteristics associated with the raving Saracen monarch, particularly in his uncontrollable fits of rage, which generally accompany news of a setback at the hands of his Christian adversaries. The first example of this penchant for overreaction comes on the second day of the assault on Rome. When the assembled Saracen forces are unable to penetrate the walls and enter the city, and ten thousand Saracens are killed, Laban makes his displeasure at the news of this reversal plain for all to see.³⁷ In another instance, when the Twelve Peers raid his camp, killing three hundred of his men in the process, he flies into a rage, directing much of his anger at his gods: "O ye goddess, ye faile at nede,/ That I have honoured so longe,/ I shall you bren, so mote I spede,/ In a fayre fyre ful stronge; . . ./ Ye shalle be brente this day ere eve,/ That foule mote you befalle" (ll. 2,431–4; 2,437–8)! On another occasion, in a fit of passion over his forces' failure to recapture his castle, he knocks an idol of Mahound to the ground so that it falls on its face (ll. 2,407–10), and is then compelled by the priests to kneel and ask for forgiveness (ll. 2,511–26). And in yet another instance, on learning of the rescue of Sir Guy, he again threatens to burn his gods, only to be reconciled to them by his priests, who convince him to offer one thousand besants (within the story, a form of Saracen currency) in homage to the gods (ll. 2,761–90). These outbursts and other demonstrations of anger render him comical in his outsized antics, and mark him as irrational, which accords well with the representation of Saracens as an irrational, superstitious people blindly following an irrational, heretical religion.

Throughout the *Sowdone of Babylone*, the impotence of Laban is linked directly to the failure of his gods, often by Laban himself, who does not fail to implicate them in his defeats. In each of the aforementioned examples, news of a defeat is immediately followed by invectives against his gods in which he derides them for failing to reward his loyalty and liberality toward them with success. Laban seems to share the perspective of the writer; he views each loss as an indication of the value of his belief system and the efficacy of his gods. Moreover, as his rage increases in proportion to the magnitude of his defeats, his expressions of discontent toward his gods also become more forceful, expressions that are followed by increasingly outlandish acts of obeisance on his part, and always at the instigation of others. His initial threat to burn his gods is followed by a reconciliation, while his physical attack on Mahound is followed by him kneeling to the fallen idol, and his final threat to burn the gods (at which point he has actually set the fire in which they are to burn) is followed by him offering one thousand besants as a peace offering. Just as he is diminished as a character by each outburst in the *Sowdone of Babylone*, so are his gods and his beliefs diminished by his subsequent actions. While the forces of King Charles ultimately expose his impotence, it is Laban who exposes the impotence of his deities by revealing their inability to help him, or even to punish him when he defies them. His reconciliation with them through the intervention of his priests is fitting, as they are ultimately compatible in their mutual inability to effect change.

In each instance in which Laban flies into a rage, he calls the audience's attention to two realities: his impotence in the face of his Christian adversaries; and the impotence of his deities, and his religion, in the face of Christianity. Despite his best laid plans, his superior numbers, and his natural advantage fighting within the confines of his kingdom, his forces are unable to prevail against the forces of King Charles in combat, whether in a pitched battle, a raid, or a chance encounter. With each subsequent defeat, his rage appears to increase in proportion to the setback, diminishing him in the eyes of the audience, until at story's end he has been reduced from the seemingly invincible destroyer of Rome to a comic foil to King Charles. Laban's rage diminishes him throughout the course of the *Sowdone of Babylone*, particularly as it is contrasted with the calm demeanor of King Charles and the Twelve Peers as they go about the business of defeating him.

Like the Saracen deities, Laban's failure is both consistent and predictable. Each reverse is followed by another opportunity, which inevitably ends in yet another crushing defeat. The bonds of allegiance binding him to his gods replicate those that bind his subjects to him, particularly in that both Laban and his gods signally fail in their primary responsibilities to their devotees/subjects: to protect them and assist them in their hour of need. As such, each reaffirmation of his loyalty to the Saracen gods becomes an implicit reaffirmation of his subjects' allegiance to him as their sovereign. However, despite their connection, Laban cannot help but acknowledge both his impotence and that of the objects of his veneration, even if he is impotent, or unwilling, to change the nature of his relationship to them.

In the end, what marks Laban as a raving *Saracen* monarch is precisely his inability or refusal to abandon his Saracen gods, even in the face of overwhelming evidence of their inability to respond to his pleas. Time and again Laban acknowledges the impotence of his gods; yet despite this recognition, he continues to assume the mantle of champion of the Saracen faith. Unlike his children Ferumbras and Floripas, his recognition of the futility of his worship does not alter his level of commitment to the Saracen faith. It is this aspect of his personality that marks Laban as an unregenerate Saracen. Whereas other Saracen characters either never arrive at this realization, or, as in the case of Ferumbras, convert after coming to this realization, Laban stands as one who perceives that his gods cannot help him, but continues to champion their worship. Despite the evidence of the futility of his cause, Laban continues to fight for it, in a manner reminiscent of a tragic hero blinded by a flaw that impels him toward certain disaster.

This pattern of defeat and impotent rage is brought to an end by Laban's final defeat and subsequent execution at the hands of King Charles and his forces. As the defeated Laban surveys his situation, bereft of his kingdom, his power, and his children,[38] he realizes that he is powerless to act in a meaningful way. His defeat is complete, and it is only at the baptismal font that he is able to regain something of his former aura of invincibility. On the verge of baptism, he lashes out in an attempt to accomplish through words what he knows cannot be achieved through force of arms: the discomfiture of his enemies, and Christians in general: "He smote the bisshope with a bronde/ And gaf him an evel bronte./ He spitted in the water cler/ And cryed oute on hem alle,/ And defied alle þat christen wer./ That foule mote himby-falle" (ll. 3,165–70)! However, he reserves the greater portion of his vitriol for his children, who have not defeated him, as have Charles and the Peers, but rather have betrayed him, and in so doing enabled others to defeat him. In his final address to his children, he speaks not only as a Saracen king to his enemies, but as a Saracen to Saracen Converts:

> Ye and thou, hore serpentine,
> And that fals cursed Ferumbras,
> Mahounde gyfe hem both evel ending,
> And almighty Sathanas![39]
> By you came all my sorowe,
> And al my tresure for-lorne.
> Honged be ye both er tomorowe!
> In cursed tyme were ye born.
> (ll. 3,171–8)

It is here that the true value of the raving Saracen king to a romance is most evident. The raving Saracen king debunks the idea of Saracen might that is based upon historical encounters with Muslims. While Laban's forces serve as bodies upon which the Christian characters can inflict damage, Laban demonstrates his inability to help them and himself, and as each threat and each boast goes unfulfilled, the Saracen menace, the Muslim menace, is diminished. Thus it is Laban and the other raving Saracen kings who complete the mission of their Christian enemies, for while King Charles, the Twelve Peers, and the other Christian heroes of the romances prove that the Saracens can be defeated, Laban and his literary equivalents show that Saracens are not even to be taken seriously.

In their separate ways, Laban, Marsile, and Astragoth are apt examples of the roles and value of the Foreign Saracen in medieval romances. Astragoth is the literary embodiment of the Foreign Saracen and what he represents at a subconscious level, below and beyond the level of articulation: an inchoate specter, repulsive and frightening at a visceral level because of his physical difference. Laban and Marsile are embodiments of medieval Muslim might, threatening with their perceived aggression and arrogance, figures that the romances must reveal to be more contemptible and despicable than frightening. Astragoth is threatening because of *what* he is, a Saracen monster capable of visiting death and destruction on Christians; Laban and Marsile are threatening because of *who* they are, Saracen kings capable of conquering and remaking Christendom through the forces they command, and with the wealth and allies at their disposal. Each character highlights different aspects of Saracen-ness that were repugnant and frightening in a way that identified them as undeniably, unforgivably Saracen, as Foreign Saracens. And in the course of *La Chanson de Roland* and *The Sowdone of Babylone*, as in all romances, each character meets the only fate available to the Foreign Saracen.

Notes

1 The extraordinary descriptions of Saracen monsters found in the romances notwithstanding, the existence of monsters was a widely accepted "fact." Monsters were believed to exist in countries such as Ethiopia and India, beyond the boundaries of the known world. Medieval scholars devoted a great deal of attention to this subject, delineating the supposed myriad races of monsters to be found, their distinguishing features, and their locations. Within the category "monster," scholars identified several different types, including Anthropophagi (cannibals), Cynocephali (monstrous figures possessing a dog's head and a man's body), Blemmyai (headless men), and Cyclopes. While the Saracen monsters of the romances are fictional characters (and literary devices), monsters occupied a real place in the medieval imagination, and were understood to occupy a real place in the physical world. Debra Higgs Strickland, *Saracens, Demons, & Jews: Making Monsters in Medieval Art* (Princeton: Princeton UP, 2003) 44–5.

2 *The King of Tars*, ll. 854–6. See the discussion of the Soudan as a Saracen Convert in Chapter 4.
3 St. Christopher was a giant who was also a cynocephalus. Originally named Reprobus ("Condemned"), he decides to alter his sinful lifestyle after failing to find satisfaction in serving a king, emperor, and the devil, deciding to dedicate himself to Christ. He is initially unsuccessful in his attempts to become a proper Christian; he is converted when he carries Jesus across a river, and is given the name Christopher ("Christ-bearer"). St. Christopher is martyred during the reign of the Roman emperor Decius; after his death, he becomes a saint who looks over travelers. Jeffrey Jerome Cohen, *Of Giants: Sex, Monsters, and the Middle Ages* (Minneapolis: U of Minnesota P, 1999) 120, 135. After his conversion, St. Christopher undergoes a partial transformation; he gains a human face, but remains a giant.
4 The descriptions, which can be (and often are) read as the outward physical manifestation of innate wickedness or perversion, distinguish the Saracen characters from the Christian heroes (as well as the Christian audience). The other outward manifestation of Saracen wickedness is the "worship" of or reference to Saracen deities (as the Saracen religion is understood to be a corruption of Christianity), as well as Saracen behavior in general. Such descriptions, along with accompanying comparisons of Saracen characters to animals, demons, etc. reinforce the idea that these characters are not fully human in the manner of the Christian characters. The inevitable defeat and slaughter of Saracens can then be read as a cleansing or purification of an area of filth, both in the form of the Saracens and their practices.
5 *The Sowdone of Babylone*, l. 352. Ethiopia, India and other distant lands were a favorite address of origin for Saracen monsters. Such places were exotic, on the periphery of the known world for medieval European audiences, and were believed to contain any number of quasi-human and monstrous creatures. In addition, their close proximity to the Middle East and North Africa lent itself well to the idea that such creatures might also be Saracen. Subsequent citations will appear parenthetically.
6 "He smote Sauaryz as he were madde,/ That dede to grounde he felle" (*The Sowdone of Babylone*, ll. 350–1).
7 "Gladde were al the Romaynes,/ That he was take in the trappe" (Ibid, ll. 439–40).
8 The select few are of course the crypto-Christians, the Saracen Converts, who are discussed in detail in Chapter 4.
9 This literary convention is most often found in romances and Mystery Plays in which Saracens appear. Within such works, individual Saracens (most commonly Saracen monarchs) exhibit a type of behavior that marks them as foils for the Christian characters, whose positive attributes are amplified through the contrast provided by their Saracen counterparts. Chief among the characteristics of such Saracen figures are arrogance and bellicosity, arrogance in their presumption of Saracen military superiority, and bellicosity in both their aggressive behavior toward non-Saracens and in their general temperament. In both the romances and Mystery Plays in which they appear, Saracen monarchs become the archetypical despots, and their eventual defeat symbolizes both the triumph of Christianity over Islam and the triumph of just rule (embodied in Christian kings like Charles the Great) over misrule.
10 The David-Goliath aspect of Christian-Saracen encounters in the romances is a consistent feature of the literature. While it likely served to exaggerate the threat posed by the Saracen enemy, so as to magnify the accomplishment of the Christian hero, it may also reflect perceived Muslim power during the Middle Ages,

much as descriptions of the wealth of the Saracen kings reflects similar ideas about Muslim societies at the time.
11 M.C. Seymour (Ed.), *Mandeville's Travels* (Oxford: Clarendon, 1967) 103. Poverty is identified as one of the three reasons for Christian conversion to Islam.
12 A particularly poignant example can be found in the medieval Passion Play "The Scourging." After a crown of thorns has been placed on Jesus' head, one of his torturers says:

> Haill king! Where was thou borne, sich worship for to win?
> We knele all the[e] beforne, and the[e] to grefe will we not blin –
> That be thou bold.
> Now, by *Mahownes* bloode,
> There will no mete do me goode
> To he be hanged on a roode,
> And his bones be cold!
> (ll. 235–41)

David Bevington (Ed.), "The Scourging," *Medieval Drama* (Boston: Houghton Mifflin, 1975) 553–68. ll. 235–41. Emphasis added. "Mahowne" is a reference to Muhammad, who is represented as a Saracen deity. The reference to Mahowne's blood is a direct inversion of a common reference to Jesus' blood/bones/teeth/etc. used by medieval Christians, and drives home the idea that the Saracen religion is a corruption of Christianity.

13 David Bevington (Ed.), "Pharaoh," *Medieval Drama* (Boston: Houghton Mifflin, 1975) 322–36. l. 412.
14   The lawys of Mahownde my powere shal fortefye.
       Reverens to that lord of grace moost excyllent,
       For by his powere, all thinge doth multiplye.
       Yef ony Cristyn be so hardy his feyth to denye,
       Or onys to erre ageyns his lawe,
       On gebettys with cheynes I shal hangyn him heye,
       And with wilde hors tho traitorys shall I drawe!
       To kille a thousand Cristyn, I gif not an hawe.
       To se hem hangyn or brent to me is very plesauns
       (ll. 6–14)

David Bevington (Ed.), "The Passion Play II," *Medieval Drama* (Boston: Houghton Mifflin, 1975) 520–35. ll. 6–14.

15 References to Saracen deities – Mahowne in particular – can be found in the Wakefield plays "Herod the Great" (ll. 1, 10, 54, etc.), "The Scourging" (ll. 3, 39), and in the York play "The Crucifixion of Christ" (l. 61), among others. In the Passion Plays, Mahowne is juxtaposed with Jesus. The role of the Saracen deities within the plays as corruptions of the Christian Trinity underscore the idea that the Saracen religion is a corruption of Christianity.
16 Many of the Mystery Plays provide excellent examples of both raving Saracen monarchs and, in a general sense, of the nebulous nature of the term "Saracen." Within the plays, characters associated with The Old and New Testament such as Pharaoh, Herod, and Pontius Pilate are portrayed as Saracen through invocations to Saracen deities like Mahowne/Mahoun, which serves to situate their anti-Israelite/anti-Christian behavior within the trope of Saracen hostility

to Christians (or in the case of the Israelites in the plays, proto-Christians). In the plays, Mahowne as a deity is associated with the persecutors of pre-Christian Israelites, Jesus Christ, and Christians, regardless of the identity of the villain. This blanket association of Saracens with non-Christians of any stripe, past or (medieval) present, is also borne out in the use of derivations of Mahoun/Mahomet/etc. (Muhammad) in words such as "maumerie/mahumerie" and "maumetrie," which refer specifically to idolatry and/or superstition. The *Middle English Dictionary* defines a "maumerie" or "mahumerie" as "A mosque (in which Mohammedans were thought to worship idols), temple; also, the idols assembled in a temple or shrine" (232). "Maumetrie" is defined in part as "(a) The worship of idols, images, or pagan deities; idolatry; also Mohammedanism" (233–4). The figure Mahoun itself is identified as "1. (a) A pagan god, false god; also *fig*.; (b) in oaths and asseverations; (c) a representation of a pagan god, an idol; (d) the devil; (e) a monster," and finally "2. The prophet Mahomet" (15). While there were specific ethnic/racial and religious connotations to the term, "Saracen" was clearly a term that had a great deal of elasticity, a type of elasticity that extended to words related to the Saracen religion and figures associated with it. Sherman M. Kuhn and John Reidy (Eds.), "Mahoun," "Maumerie," "Maumetrie." *Middle English Dictionary (Lef-Minten)* (Ann Arbor, MI: U of Michigan, 1975) 15, 232–4.

17 This curious conflation of Jew and Saracen occurs in "The Play of the Sacrament." In particular, the character Jonathas, who in the cast of characters is identified as "Judeus primus, Magister" (*Medieval Drama*, 759), gives voice to this curious theological phenomenon:

> Now almighty Machomet, marke in thy magesté,
> Whose laws tendrely I have to fulfill,
> After my dethe bring me to the hyh[e] see
> My sowle for to save, iff it be thy will!
> For min[e] entent is for to fulfill,
> As my glorius god the[e] to honer.
> To do agen thy entent, it shuld gr[e]ve me ill,
> Or agen thin[e] lawe for to reporte.
>   (ll. 149–56)

The association of the worship of a Saracen deity to the Jewish characters, which occurs on more than one occasion, may have been included to further separate them from the Christian characters. As the Jewish characters' sin in the play is unbelief, in this case denial of the miracle of the Eucharist, their denial of one aspect of Christian doctrine is expanded into a wholesale rejection of the (Judeo-) Christian concept of God. Such a conflation may also have served to better mark these characters as enemies of Christians for members of the audience. While the accusation of "Judaeizing" on the part of Muslims was not altogether uncommon, the depiction of Jews worshiping a Saracen deity is unusual. David Bevington (Ed.), "The Play of the Sacrament," *Medieval Drama* (Boston: Houghton Mifflin, 1975) 754–88. ll. 149–56.

18 The term "romance" is used in the medieval sense to signify a text first written in the romance vernacular; in point of fact, the *Chanson de Roland* is a *chanson de geste*.

19 *The Song of Roland*, Trans. Glyn Burgess. (London: Penguin, 1990) l. 1015. Subsequent citations will appear parenthetically.

20 Roland dies, but he is not slain by an opponent; rather, he dies from personal exertion, emotional trauma (particularly over the death of Oliver and the other

Peers), and the accumulation of wounds he has suffered in the course of routing three Saracen battalions.

21 While leading the rear-guard of Charles' forces, Roland and the Peers are ambushed by a Saracen battalion (followed by two more battalions) unbeknownst to their comrades. Their deaths are attributable to Roland's refusal to call for help until it is too late, for fear of besmirching their reputations by requesting assistance in battle.

22 One of Marsile's warriors, Abisme, is described as "black as molten pitch" (l. 1474). In another instance, the Caliph's battalions from Ethiopia ("an accursed land" [l. 1916]) are described in the following terms: "They have large noses and broad ears ... Who are blacker than ink/ And have nothing white save their teeth" (ll. 1918, 1933–4). In yet another instance, Baligant's men – "Milceni" (l. 3221) – are described as being "as bristly as pigs" (l. 3223) along their spines.

23   Charles the king, our great emperor,
    Has been in Spain for seven long years,
    And conquered that proud land as far as the sea.
    There is no castle which can resist him,
    No wall or city left to be destroyed,
    Except for Saragossa, which stands upon a mountain.
    It is held by King Marsile, who does not love God;
    He serves Muhammad calls upon Apollo.
    He cannot prevent disaster from overtaking him.
                                    (ll. 1–9)

24 The third battalion, led by his uncle the Caliph, is also decimated after Marsile flees. It is in the fight with the third battalion that Oliver is mortally wounded; Roland dies soon after.

25 "King Marsile was much perturbed by this;/ He seized a gold-feathered javelin/ And would have struck him, had he not been restrained./ King Marsile changed colour;/ He shook the shaft of his javelin." (ll. 438–42)

26 For his part, Ganelon demonstrates his readiness to engage Marsile in combat (ll. 443–9).

27 In particular, the following lines: "O, Saragossa, how you have been deprived this day/ Of the noble king who held you in his power!/ Our gods committed a grave crime/ In failing him this morning in battle" (ll. 2598–2601)

28 "They take the pagans up to the baptistery;/ If there is anyone who withstands Charles,/ He has him hanged or burned or put to death./ More than a hundred thousand are baptized/ True Christians" (ll. 3668–72)

   Bramimonde later converts, is baptized, and christened Juliana (ll. 3977–87). Interestingly, she alone is converted through reasoning – "through love" (l. 3674) – rather than by force, as are the other Saracens of Saragossa.

29 The characterization of Spain as a Saracen land, and as the power base of the Saracen enemy (as is the case in *La Chanson de Roland*), speaks to its nebulous identity during much of the Middle Ages, as neither a wholly Muslim or Christian land. In fact, by the time of the production of the English version of this work, almost all of Spain was in the hands of Christian monarchs. Only Granada and the surrounding precincts remained under Muslim control, and largely as a result of infighting amongst their Christian neighbors. (Curiously, it was at this moment, when the eventual conquest of Granada by Christian forces appeared inevitable, that construction of the Alhambra Mosque was undertaken and completed.) However, even after the conquest of Granada, the Muslim influence, through first the *mudejars* (Muslims living under Christian rule) and later the *moriscos* (converts to Christianity), would survive well into the seventeenth century. This reality may have been a

contributing factor in the portrayal of Spain as a Saracen land in some of the most famous romances.
30 "Laban, the kinge of hie degree,/ And syr and Sowdon of hie Babilon,/ Conquerede grete parte of Christiante,/ That was born in Askalon." (*Sowdone of Babylone*, ll. 29–32.)
31   Two goddess on hye seten thore
    In the maister toppe, with macis rounde,
    To manace with the Cristen lore.
    The sailes were of red Sendelle,
    Embrowdered with riche araye,
    With beestes and breddes every dele,
    That was right curious and gaye;
    The Armes displaid of Laban
    Of Asure and foure lions of goolde.
                    (ll. 126–34)
32 "He made a vowe to Termagaunte,/ Whan Rome were distroied & hade myschaunce,/ He woolde turn ayen erraunte/ And distroye Charles the kinge of Fraunce." (ll. 137–40)
33 For their part, the maidens are described as resolutely facing their fate: "Martires thai were euerychon,/ And therof were thai all ful fayne" (ll. 230–1).
34 Laban uses the names of Saracen deities in the same manner in which Christian characters use the name of God or Jesus, conferring blessings and invoking curses. Thus, on one occasion, in response to advice from his engineer Mavon, Laban promises "Mahoundis benysone thou shalt have" (l. 289). In another instance, he refers to Mahound's role as a provider, exhorting two of his subjects (Fortibraunce and Mavon) to "Shewe forth here nowe your crafte/ For Mahoundis love, þat gevith man foode" (ll. 424–5). References to Saracen deities, and Mahound in particular, effectively juxtapose the religion of Charles and the Peers with that of Laban and his Saracen hosts.
35 "But I wole distroie ouer all/ The sede over alle Cristiante" (ll. 234–5).
36   The people fled by every waye,
    Thai durst no-where abide.
    The hye wey ful of dede men laye,
    And eke by every lanys side.
    Ferumbras to Seinte Petris wente,
    And alle the Relekes he seased anoon,
    The Crosse, the Crown, the Nailesbente,
    He toke hem with him everychone.
    He dide dispoile al the Cite
    Both of tresoure and of goolde,
    And after that brente he
    Alle þat ever might be tooled.
                    (ll. 659–70)
37 "Whan these tidinges came to Laban,/ His goddess he gan chide./ He waxe both blake, pale and wan,/ He was nyȝe woode þat same tyde." (ll. 308–11)
38 By this time, his children (Floripas and Ferumbras) have both converted, and by their subsequent actions betrayed him. Floripas, in particular, has been outspoken in her rejection of her Saracen past, and of him in particular, at times trading insults with him across battle lines. For his part, Ferumbras also plays a vital role in Laban's eventual defeat. Moreover, it is he who moves for Laban's execution after he refuses baptism, opining "Sir, ye see, it wole not be,/ Lete him take his endynge,/ For he loueth not Cristyante" (ll. 3,180–2).

39 Laban's reference to "almighty Satan" is perhaps the most striking example of the presentation of Islam as a perversion of Christianity in medieval popular literature. The "Saracen Trinity," of which Mahoun is a member, is a common feature of the romances. However, the invocation to Satan marks the Saracen religion as diametrically opposed to Christianity, and drives home the assertion of medieval clerics that it was inspired by demonic forces.

6 Foreign Saracens in accounts of the Crusades

On the final Tuesday in November, 1095, Pope Urban II stood in front of an assembled crowd just outside of Clermont[1] to voice his concerns over the condition of their Christian brethren in the East. His words catalogued the horrors experienced by the Christians of the East at the hands of the Muslims, and enjoined his audience to avenge these atrocities and reclaim the Holy Land for Christianity:

> A race absolutely alien to God has invaded the land of Christians, has reduced the people with sword, rapine and flame. These men have destroyed the altars polluted by their foul practices. They have circumcised the Christians, either spreading the blood from the circumcisions on the altars or pouring it into the baptismal fonts . . . What shall I say of the appalling violation of women, of which it is more evil to speak than to keep silent?[2]

This litany of horrors was followed by a call-to-arms emphasizing the religious imperative and presenting the religious and worldly inducements for those who undertook the task of liberating the Holy Land; it set into motion perhaps the most extraordinary phenomenon of the Medieval Period: the Crusades.

The immediate aftermath of this call-to-arms was the spectacularly successful First Crusade, resulting in the establishment of the Crusader States of Antioch, Edessa, Tripoli, and Jerusalem. However, even as the Latin West basked in the success of this enterprise, the foundations of a Muslim resistance were being laid, a resistance that over the next two centuries would necessitate additional crusades. The Muslim recovery of Edessa in 1144 led to the disastrous Second Crusade of 1148, which ended in an unsuccessful siege of Damascus. Over the subsequent three decades, the relationship between the Christian European Crusader States and the neighboring Muslim states would change drastically, as first Nūr al-Dīn and then Salāh al-Dīn unified the Muslim petty kingdoms under a single sovereign and began the inexorable reabsorption of the Crusader States into the Muslim Eastern Mediterranean, highlighted by the recovery of Jerusalem by Salāh al-Dīn in 1187, which led to the Third Crusade.

The Third Crusade, which featured both the renowned English king Richard I and Salāh al-Dīn, failed to achieve its articulated goal of retaking Jerusalem; however, it was successful in turning back the Muslim advance, ultimately granting the Crusader States a century's reprieve. Moreover, it marked the last time that a Crusade would end to the advantage of the Latin West. The Fourth Crusade was misdirected from the outset, resulting in the Crusader Sack of Constantinople, the capital of the most powerful Christian state in the Eastern Mediterranean, in 1204.[3] Subsequent encounters, particularly the disastrous Fifth Crusade of 1249, highlighted the pronounced Muslim advantage, and under Baybars and the successive rulers of the Mamlūk Sultanate of Egypt, the re-conquest of the Crusader States was resumed with increased vigor. The Muslim recovery of the Levant in its entirety was accomplished with the Fall of Acre in May 28, 1291;[4] by the end of the thirteenth century, the only Crusader stronghold in the region was the island of Cyprus.

The depiction of Muslims as Saracens in medieval popular fiction was in part a reflection of the depiction of Muslims found in historical accounts, particularly the accounts of the Crusades. The understanding of Islam and Muslims discussed in Chapter 1 was largely reserved to the clerics; the public at large appears to have been both unaware of and unaffected by the type of information that was at the disposal of scholars like Albertus Magnus and Roger Bacon. Outside of the romances, the medieval European public's perception of Muslims was largely informed by accounts of encounters between Christian Europeans and Muslims from the Near East and North Africa. Among such accounts, the accounts of the Crusades stand alone due to the importance of the Crusades to medieval Western Europe and for the number and variety of works produced on the subject. The accounts, which differ in their presentation of the facts (both in regard to which of the individual Crusades is recounted, and in terms of partisan loyalties), detail the facts and conditions of the Latin West's most important encounter with the Muslim Other during the Middle Ages. These works provided a medieval European public with an "authoritative" impression of Muslims, and participated in the construction of Muslims *as* Saracens from which the later romances would draw.

Despite the nature of the Crusades as religiously motivated wars between Christians and Muslims for control of the Levant – Jerusalem in particular – the events and figures involved did not lend themselves to being reinterpreted within the framework of the romances. The First Crusade stands as the exception; its history was adapted to the romance form in the earliest accounts, including the partially edited *Estoire d'Antioche*.[5] The facts of the later Crusades – internecine strife within the crusader camps, collusion between Christian and Muslim leaders, Muslim victories, and the tenuous position of the Crusader States (especially after 1187) – belied such attempts. While attractive in theory, the reality of crusading in the Levant – in particular, the military and political situation in the Near East – was a far different matter.

As a result, among medieval accounts of the crusades, one of the staples of the romances, the Foreign Saracen – including the Saracen monarch – is largely confined to stories of the First Crusade. In other accounts it makes sporadic, often gratuitous, appearances,[6] but it is never central to the narrative. But why is the Foreign Saracen at home in accounts of the First Crusade, yet a stranger in the accounts of subsequent crusades? It is tempting to explain its disappearance as the result of a change in perspective relative to the enemy; as Western Europeans became a part of the Levantine landscape, their understanding of Muslims expanded, a fact reflected in the accounts of later crusades. These accounts are more realistic in their depictions of Muslims and Levantine politics. However, there is no indication that medieval Western European audiences insisted upon such attention to detail; the outlandish depictions of Saracens were enormously popular, and continued to appear in romances throughout the Middle Ages.

But perhaps the best explanation for the disappearance of the Foreign Saracen in later accounts of the crusades is that only the First Crusade met the narrative requirements – Christian victory – necessary for the adoption of the conventions of the romances. The First Crusade was the only crusade in which the stated objective was achieved; the later crusades ended in either abject failure or a stalemate.[7] The style of the medieval romances accentuated the narrative of Christian dominance; Foreign Saracens existed to be vanquished; their existence was problematic under any other circumstances. Accounts of other "famous" crusades – such as the Third Crusade or the Crusade of St. Louis – could only employ aspects of the romances sparingly because they were incapable of delivering the type of victory that brought such works to a satisfactory conclusion. The formula for the romances is simple: heroic Christian warriors defeat a seemingly insurmountable Saracen threat – often with divine assistance – to the benefit of Christianity and Christians.

The events of the First Crusade lent themselves to this narrative, to the extent that the memory of the First Crusade became almost indistinguishable from that of the romances. An example of the unique nature of the First Crusade, and the way in which it fit into this narrative, can be found in the *Estoire de la Guerre Sainte*, in which Ambroise, the author, laments the lack of unity within the crusader camp during the Third Crusade:

> When the valiant King Charlemagne, who conquered so many lands and countries, went to campaign in Spain, taking with him the noble band who were sold to Marsile by Ganelon to the dishonor of France, and when he, Charlemagne, had returned to Saxony, where he did so many great deeds and defeated Guiteclin, bringing about the fall of the Saxons by the strength of many valiant men and when he led his army to Rome, when Agoland, through a great undertaking had arrived at Reggio in the rich land of Calabria, when, in another war, Syria was lost and reconquered and Antioch besieged, in the great armies and the

battles against the Turks and the pagan hordes, when many were killed and conquered, there was no bickering and quarreling, at that time and before; then there was neither Norman nor French, Poitevin nor Breton, Mansel nor Burgundian, Flemish nor English; there was no malicious gossip nor insulting of one another; everyone came back with honour and all were called Franks, whether brown or red, swarthy or white ... This is how things should be done and the affairs of today dealt with, that men may follow this example and not attack each other.[8]

Ambroise freely mixes allusions to events and figures from the *chansons de geste* with allusions to events from the First Crusade. In fact, he alludes to a *chanson* based upon the events of the First Crusade, the *Chanson d'Antioche*, demonstrating the legendary status the events of the First Crusade enjoyed during his time. However, unlike the First Crusade, the unsatisfactory outcomes of subsequent crusades required detailed explanations in the accounts, and in these details much of the style and many of the stock characters of the romances were lost.

As the one crusade that did live up to expectations, the First Crusade established a standard by which subsequent crusades would be judged, while serving as motivation for further expeditions into the Near East.[9] Its unprecedented nature and spectacular victories captured the imagination of medieval Western Europe, which is reflected in the accounts of the events and figures of the First Crusade. The nature of the First Crusade – the call to arms by Urban II, the response, the journey to Byzantium and then the Levant, and the battles against Muslim forces, culminating in the conquest of Jerusalem – fit well into the traditional narrative of the romances. Western chroniclers did not fail to capitalize on opportunities to recast events from the First Crusade using the narrative framework and conventions of the romances; their efforts served to generate economic and military support for individual crusaders and the Crusader States as a whole.

The outcome of the First Crusade also allowed for the entrance of familiar stock figures from the romances: Foreign Saracens,[10] in particular, the Foreign Saracen monarch. Subsequent crusades, in which the outcomes were often decisive in favor of their Muslim opponents, did not fit into the narrative framework necessary for the inclusion of the Saracen monarch, who had to be vanquished within the course of the account. But the First Crusade was an ideal fit: the Muslim enemy had every reason to expect victory, the odds were often stacked against the crusaders; most importantly, they prevailed, often in spectacular fashion, resulting in the discomfiture of the Muslim leaders involved. Moreover, the appearance of divine help (which is attested to in accounts of the First Crusade) adds to the epic quality of the First Crusade. Unlike the subsequent crusades, the First Crusade was a success; Jerusalem was captured, and the subsequent decade witnessed the formation of Outremer.[11] The First Crusade ended in the manner of most romances, triumphant Christians faced a future bright with the promise of more conquests to come. Accounts of the First Crusade could adopt the tone and much of the narrative structure of the romances in recounting the story of the accomplishment of spectacular feats in the recent past, while looking forward to the future. And an important factor in the story was the role of the Muslim leaders who were utterly defeated by the Christian heroes.

The preeminent Muslim leader in medieval Western European accounts of the First Crusade was Qiwām al-Dawla Karbughā (Curbaram in the *Gesta Francorum et aliorum Hierosolimitanorum*[12] and Kerbogha in the *Historia Iherosolimitana*), the governor of Mosul.[13] Karbughā emerges as the prototypical Saracen ruler in the accounts because of the central role of the conquest of Antioch and subsequent defeat of the combined Muslim forces outside of Antioch. Although the conquest of Jerusalem was the objective of the First Crusade, the *Gesta*, the earliest and most influential account of the First Crusade, focused more attention on the events related to the capture and defense of Antioch. Because of its standing as the earliest account, later accounts borrowed heavily from its content, and its fixation with Antioch; the battle outside of Antioch became the turning point in the First Crusade, making the eventual conquest of Jerusalem inevitable. Antioch's central position in the narrative of the First Crusade elevated the status of all who were involved in the action, Christian and Muslim. As the preeminent figure among the Muslims, Karbughā became the face of the Muslim response, or rather, the face of the vanquished Saracen.

In the tradition of the romances, Karbughā is introduced to the reader as the ruler of an inestimable Saracen force. After describing Karbughā as the leader of the army of the sultan of Persia,[14] the *Gesta* informs us:

> Now Curbaram had already gathered a large army of Turks, which he had been assembling for a long time, and he had also been given permission to kill Christians by the caliph, their pope. And so he at once began the long march toward Antioch. The emir of Jerusalem came to help him with his army; the king of Damascus came with a great many of his men. And so Curbaram gathered innumerable pagan men, namely Turks, Arabs, Saracens, Paulicians, Azymites, Kurds, Persians, Agulani, and many other innumerable men . . . And all of them came to besiege Antioch and to scatter the gathered Franks.
>
> (p. 71)

The *Historia Iherosolimitana*[15] describes Karbughā in similar terms, as the "general of the Persian king's army,"[16] and includes among his gathered forces "Persians and Medes, Arabs and Turks, Azimitae and Saracens, Kurds and Publicani and many others from various nations."[17] Karbughā is clearly identified within the texts as the greatest threat to the Christians since the beginning of their pilgrimage.[18]

Karbughā's role is reinforced by his arrogance toward the Christian army. When he is presented with weapons that have been taken from poorer members of the Crusader army, his response is typical of the Saracen monarch:

> Such are the ferocious and brilliant weapons that the Christians have brought to conquer us in Asia and with which they confidently think of chasing beyond the farthest reaches of Khorasan, and to erase our name beyond the rivers of the Amazons, they who drove our parents from Romania and from Antioch, the royal city, which is the praiseworthy capital of all Syria.[19]

His ensuing letter to the caliph presents the Saracen monarch in its entire splendor, replete with references to a decadent, warlike Saracen society,[20] Saracen arrogance,[21] and Saracen polytheism;[22] the image of Karbughā, and Muslims in general, is thoroughly imbued with the traditional markers of Saracen-ness that are commonplace in the romances.

Karbughā's arrogance is given fullest expression in his meeting with messengers from the Crusader army.[23] His response to the envoys' message draws upon stock themes from the romances of Saracen arrogance, rejection/hostility toward Christianity, and demands of conversion (with material incentives for conversion):

> We do not want your God or your Christianity. We do not care for them at all. We reject them completely, and at the same time we reject you. We have come here because we are greatly astonished that the leaders and chief lords you mention call their own a land we took away from an effeminate people. Do you want to know what we wish to tell you? Go back quickly and tell your chief lords that if they will become Turks[24] and renounce their God whom you adore on bended knee, as well as your laws, we shall give them this land and still many others besides, along with cities and castles, so that none of you shall remain a foot soldier, but all of you shall be warriors as we are, and we shall always hold them in high friendship. Otherwise, they should know that they shall all suffer the capital sentence, or be led away in chains to Khorasan, and into perpetual captivity, serving us and our children forever and ever.[25]

Karbughā's response, with its threats and its promises of reward for conversion, presages Garcy's message to Charles and his knights in *The Romance of Duke Rowland and Sir Ottuell of Spayne* three centuries later.

However, Karbughā's role in the First Crusade diverges from the traditional narrative of the Saracen monarch in that he largely disappears during the defeat of his forces. When the Turks are defeated[26] (in accordance with his mother's predictions),[27] he is described as fleeing with his men;[28] he is neither killed nor captured. The accounts are deprived of the apogee of the medieval romance: the defeat, discomfiture, and death of the Saracen sovereign.

Karbughā is presented as the classical Saracen monarch within accounts of the First Crusade, but it is the "emir of Babylon"[29] who brings the narrative of Christian-Saracen conflict to a fitting end after the battle of Ascalon. The emir's presence is not primarily as a threat to the Christian heroes; the power of the Saracens is greatly diminished after the crusader victory over Karbughā at Antioch; even the conquest of Jerusalem – central as it was to the First Crusade – receives scant attention in comparison to what is given to Antioch in the accounts. Rather, the emir performs the duty of the defeated Saracen monarch; his speech brings the narrative of triumphant Christianity to an end through the necessary Saracen acknowledgement of defeat:[30]

> O spirit of the gods. Who has seen or heard of such things? Such might, such courage, such an army has never before been defeated by any nation, as has been defeated by these few Christian people . . . I have been defeated by a race of beggars, unarmed and poverty stricken, who have nothing but a sack and a beggar's bag. And they are the ones now pursuing the Egyptian people who used to distribute alms to them when they roamed about, begging all over our homeland . . . I swear by Mohamed and by the splendor of all the gods that never again will I undertake to raise an army because I have been driven off by such a strange people. I brought all kinds of weapons and war machines to besiege them in Jerusalem, and it is they who attacked me two days earlier. Alas! What more can I say? I shall always be dishonored in the land of Babylon.[31]

In defeat, the emir's speech recapitulates the broad themes of the narrative of the First Crusade: the piety and valor of the Christians, the power of Christianity (demonstrated against seemingly insurmountable odds), the arrogance of the Saracens, and the impotence of the Saracens and their religion in the face of the Christians. The emir's comments attest to the comprehensive nature of the Saracens' defeat,[32] confirming the dominant position of the Crusaders, effectively concluding the narrative of the First Crusade.

The First Crusade was unique relative to the subsequent crusades in that its outcome matched the rhetoric at its inception. All of the crusades to the Near East contained the elements of the typical romance: Christian heroes, powerful Muslim enemies, tremendous obstacles, and a compelling objective. However, to this mix the First Crusade added the most important element: a Christian victory, which magnified the other elements in the public imagination. Moreover, the narrative of the First Crusade mirrored that of the romances in that it appeared to be an undertaking that would never be repeated; the enemy would be vanquished and Christian rule would be established in Jerusalem, never to be challenged again. Subsequent crusades proved the illusory nature of this idea; crusading could never fit into the tidy narrative framework of the romances. The Enemy could never be utterly defeated; he would have to be negotiated with; at times, the Enemy ceased

Foreign Saracens in the Crusades 133

to be the enemy. But the First Crusade offered, and appeared to deliver on, the promise of the romances: spectacular, sustainable victory. The First Crusade offered the promise that at least some of the narrative of the romances could be relevant. The reality of maintaining a presence in the Levant asserted itself into later accounts of the crusades. But in the immediate aftermath of the First Crusade, anything seemed possible, and this is conveyed in the events and figures presented within the accounts.

Notes

1 Thomas Asbridge, *The First Crusade: A New History* (Oxford: Oxford UP, 2004) 1–2.
2 Ibid, 1. The preceding excerpt is from an abridged translation of Robert of Rheims' account of the speech found in *Robert the Monk's History of the First Crusade: Historia Iherosolimitana*, Trans. C. Sweetenham (Burlington: Ashgate, 2005) 79–81. All citations of the *Historia Iherosolimitana* in this volume are from this version. (For the speech in its entirety cf. Robert the Monk, *Historia Iherosolimitana*, RHC Occ. III, pp. 727–8.)
3 The Crusaders' misadventure in Constantinople came to a violent end in 1261, when the Byzantines overthrew the Crusader government and drove the Crusaders from the city. The carnage and wholesale slaughter of the Crusaders mirrored the brutality of the Crusaders themselves during the Sack of Constantinople in 1204.
4 Jonathan Riley-Smith, *The Crusades: A History*, 2nd ed. (New Haven: Yale UP, 2005) 244.
5 Jennifer Gabel de Aguirre, *La Chanson de la Première Croisade en Ancien Français d'après Baudri de Bourgueil: Edition et Analyse Lexicale* (Heidelberg: Universitäetsverlag Winter, 2015).
6 For instance, in its account of the Third Crusade, the *Itinerarium Peregrinorum et Gesta Regis Ricardi* includes the following description of two groups of warriors that accompanied the Turkish regulars:

> After these ran a devilish race, very black in colour, who for this reason have a rather appropriate name: because they are black [*nigri*] they are called 'Negroes'. Also there were the Saracens who travel about in the desert, popularly called 'Bedouins': savage and darker than soot, the most redoubtable infantrymen, carrying bows and quivers and round shields. They are a very energetic and agile race.

Here, the Foreign Saracen is not merely a literary device evoked to elicit a desired response from the audience; in a sense, it has more in common with the wonders described in travel literature than the demonic figures and Saracen giants encountered in the romances. Helen J. Nicholson, *Chronicle of the Third Crusade: A Translation of the Itinerarium Peregrinorum et Gesta Regis Ricardi* (Brookfield: Ashgate 1997) 247.
7 The Third Crusade ended in such a manner; it failed to achieve its goal, the recovery of Jerusalem, but was successful in halting the Muslim advance in the Levant, preserving the crusader presence in the region for another century.
8 Ambroise, *The History of the Holy War: Ambroise's Estoire de la Guerre Sainte*, Trans. Marianne Ailes (Woodbridge: Boydell and Brewer, 2003) ll. 8,459–90; 8,495–8. The work will henceforward be referred to as the *Estoire*.
9 The First Crusade was not intended to be the first in a series of military campaigns, but rather as a mission to "free" Jerusalem from Muslim rule and establish Christian

134 *Foreign Saracens in the Crusades*

control over the city. In a manner of speaking, the subsequent crusades were largely attempts to recover territory that had been won during the First Crusade (and in its immediate aftermath) but lost in the ensuing decades, to re-establish the kingdom carved out by the First Crusade.

10 Thus, the *Gesta Francorum et aliorum Hierosolimitanorum* speaks of an encounter with Turkish soldiers in which they "began to let out shrieks and to jabber and shout in high-pitched voices, uttering I do not know what diabolical sounds in their own tongue" (p. 41). *The Deeds of the Franks and Other Jerusalem-Bound Pilgrims (Gesta Francorum et aliorum Hierosolimitanorum): The Earliest Chronicle of the First Crusades*, Ed. and Trans. Nirmal Dass (Lanham: Rowman & Littlefield, 2011).

11 "Outremer" was the name given to the collective Crusader States: Jerusalem, Antioch, Edessa, and Tripoli.

12 The *Gesta Francorum et aliorum Hierosolimitanorum* will henceforth be referred to as the *Gesta*. All references to the *Gesta* in this chapter refer to *The Deeds of the Franks and Other Jerusalem-Bound Pilgrims (Gesta Francorum et aliorum Hierosolimitanorum): The Earliest Chronicle of the First Crusades*, Ed. and Trans. Nirmal Dass (Lanham: Rowman & Littlefield, 2011).

13 Qiwām al-Dawla Karbughā was maligned in both Muslim and Christian sources. In Ibn al-'Athīr's account of the Muslim defeat at Antioch, the thirteenth-century historian places the blame squarely on Karbughā's shoulders:

> When Qiwām al-Dawla Karbughā heard of the Franks doings and their conquest of Antioch, he gathered his forces and marched to Syria. He camped at Marj Dābiq, where the troops of Syria, both Turks and Arabs, rallied to him, apart from those who were in Aleppo. There assembled with him . . . the likes of whom are not to be found. Hearing of this, the Franks' misfortunes increased and they were fearful because of their weakness and their shortage of provisions. The Muslims came and besieged them in Antioch, but Karbughā behaved badly toward the Muslims with him. He angered the emirs and lorded it over them, imagining that they would stay with him despite that. However, infuriated by this, they secretly planned to betray him, if there should be a battle, and they determined to give him up when the armies clashed.

Ibn al-Athīr, 'Izz al-Dīn and Carl Johan Tornberg, *The Chronicle of Ibn al-'Athīr for the Crusading Period from al-Kāmil fī'l-ta'rīkh Part I, the Years 491–541/1097–1146; The Coming of the Franks and the Muslim Response*, Trans. D.S. Richards (Burlington: Ashgate, 2006) 15–16.

It is interesting that in this Muslim account Karbughā is portrayed in a manner that is reminiscent of the Saracen monarchs of the romances, particularly in his arrogance and his treatment of others.

14 *Gesta*, 71.

15 The *Historia Iherosolimitana*'s content is largely derived from the *Gesta*, with a more detailed account of Urban II's famous call to crusade, and a greater focus on the conquest of Jerusalem. It is similar to most other accounts of the First Crusade in its dependence on information found in the *Gesta*. However, the *Historia Iherosolimitana* is distinguished by its popularity; over one hundred manuscripts of the work have survived to the present day. *Robert the Monk's History of the First Crusade (Historia Iherosolimitana)*, Trans. Carol Sweetenham (Burlington: Ashgate, 2005) 11.

16 *Historia Iherosolimitana*, 150.

17 Ibid.

18 The term "crusade" was not used during the time of the crusades, but was coined centuries later. Rather, each crusade was understood as an (armed) pilgrimage to

Jerusalem. Christopher Tyerman, *Fighting for Christendom: Holy War and the Crusades* (Oxford: Oxford UP, 2004) 4.
19 *Gesta*, 73.
20 "Satisfy yourselves joyfully, and with a festive resolve, fill your stomachs. And let commands be given and announcements made in all the region for everyone to give free rein to their passion and their lust and by this pleasure conceive many sons who shall fight bravely against the Christians." *Gesta*, 73.
21 "Let everyone also know that I have all the Franks locked up right inside Antioch, and that I hold the citadel in my power; they are down below in the city. I have them now all in my hands, and they will be either given the capital sentence or led to Khorasan in wretched captivity, because they threatened us and wanted to drive us back with their weapons and chase us out of our borders, as they chased our parents from Romania and from Syria." *Gesta*, 73.
22 "Also, I swear to you by Mohamed and by all our gods that I shall not again present myself before you until I have taken by the strength of my right hand the royal city of Antioch, and all of Syria and Romania, and Bulgaria, right up to Apulia, in honor of the gods, and of you, and of all who are of the race of the Turks." *Gesta*, 73.
23 The account differs slightly in the *Historia Iherosolimitana*; the members of the Crusader embassy refuse to bow before Kerbogha, deliver their message, and trade insults with Kerbogha (pp. 165–6). *Robert the Monk's History of the First Crusade (Historia Iherosolimitana)*, Trans. Carol Sweetenham (Burlington: Ashgate, 2005).
24 Yet another expression of the nebulous boundary between religious and racial affiliation, as the Crusaders are invited to renounce Christianity and "become Turks," reinforcing the idea of conversion as a fundamental change in racial, political, and religious identity.
25 *Gesta*, 84.
26 Both the *Gesta* (p. 84) and the *Historia Iherosolimitana* (p. 168) mention the fact that Karbughā refused to allow his soldiers to pick off the Christian soldiers when they were most vulnerable, as they marched out of Antioch over a narrow bridge; however, credit for the victory is given to the help of celestial forces and the bravery of the soldiers. Ibn al-'Athīr's account offers another perspective; it identifies Karbughā's aforementioned decision, along with his arrogance towards his peers, as the key factors in the Crusader victory:

> On the fifth day they went out of the gate in scattered groups of five or six or so. The Muslims said to Karbughā, 'You ought to stand at the gate and kill all that come out, because now, when they are scattered, it is easy to deal with them.' He replied, 'No, do not do that. Leave them alone until they have all come out and then we can kill them.' He did not allow his men to engage them. However, one group of Muslims did kill several that had come out but he came in person and ordered them to desist.
>
> When the Franks had all come out and not one of them remained within, they drew up a great battle line. At that, the Muslims turned their back in flight, firstly because of the contempt and scorn with which Karbughā had treated them and secondly because he had prevented them from killing the Franks. Their flight was complete. Not one of them struck a blow with a sword, thrust with a spear or shot an arrow. The last to flee were Suqmān ibn Artuq and Janāh al-Dawla because they were stationed in ambush. Karbughā fled with them. When the Franks observed this, they thought it was a trick, since there had been no battle such as to cause a flight and they feared to pursue them. A company of warriors for the faith stood firm and fought zealously, seeking martyrdom. The Franks slew thousands of them and seized as

136 *Foreign Saracens in the Crusades*

booty the provisions, money, furnishings, horses and weapons that were in the camp. Their situation was restored and their strength returned.

(p. 17)

He also presents a different account of the crusader embassy to Karbughā: after having conquered Antioch, the Crusader army languishes there for twelve days without food. Out of desperation, the crusaders attempt to negotiate a surrender of the city, but are rebuffed by Karbughā, who tells them, "My sword alone will eject you" (p. 16). Ibn al-Athīr, 'Izz al-Dīn and Tornberg, *The Chronicle of Ibn al-'Athīr for the Crusading Period from al-Kāmil fī'l-ta'rīkh Part I*, 16, 17.

27 *Gesta*, 74–6; *Historia Iherosolimitana*, 154–7.
28 *Gesta*, 87; *Historia Iherosolimitana*, 170.
29 The Fatimid Caliph of Egypt, al-Musta'li. Prior to the Crusader conquest, Jerusalem had been under the control of Fatimid Egypt; it was during the rule of the Fatimid Caliph al-Hākim that the Church of the Holy Sepulcher was destroyed in 1009. The *Historia Iherosolimitana* names the emir "Clemens," possibly in an effort to draw a connection between the most recent Antipope, Clemens III, and Saracens for potential audiences. *Historia Iherosolimitana*, 204. n. 29.
30 The speech attributed to the emir in the *Historia Iherosolimitana* is far longer than that of the *Gesta*; only Urban II's call-to-arms rivals it in length. Moreover, the *Historia Iherosolimitana* assures its audience that the emir's speech and actions were recounted by a Saracen eyewitness who later converted and took the name of Bohemond, so as to allay the concerns of any skeptics (p. 207).
31 *Gesta*, 107.
32 "[N]ever again will I undertake to raise an army" (*Gesta* 107).

7 Western Europeans in Muslim accounts of the Crusades

The sudden appearance of thousands of soldiers from Western Europe in the Levant in 1097 was both wholly unexpected and militarily and politically devastating for the Muslims of the area. As a region, the Levant was disorganized, fragmented, and militarily vulnerable to outside interference, and had been so for a few years; the result of the Western European invasion was a number of sweeping, stunning European victories, and the establishment of "Crusader States" in relatively short order. The newly established Latin Kingdom of Jerusalem (comprised of Jerusalem, Antioch, Tripoli, and Edessa) was protected militarily by its supply of European soldiers in the Levant and its access to reinforcements on continental Europe, and politically by both the support it received from Europe and by the internecine feuding between the Muslim leaders in the surrounding areas, who appeared to prefer the existence of a kingdom ruled by Christian Europeans to the prospect of a Muslim ruler increasing his sphere of influence through the recovery of the Crusader-controlled areas at the expense of the territorial integrity of his Muslim neighbors.[1] The lack of unity among the Muslims not only ensured the continued existence of the Crusader States, it allowed for their expansion in the early twelfth century, as other parts of the surrounding area were conquered by the Crusaders, thus strengthening the nascent European community in the Levant. The intersection of these circumstances produced a new reality for Levantine Muslims, one in which the Crusaders' place in the Levant was guaranteed in the present and the foreseeable future.

With the success of the European forces, the Muslims of the Levant (and, to a lesser degree, Egypt) were faced with a new reality, a Christian Western European kingdom in their immediate vicinity, one that had been carved out of some of their own territory, including the sacred city of Jerusalem, with which they now had to co-exist. The lack of unity among the Muslims which had facilitated the Crusader successes in the Levant was largely attributable to the recent deaths of a number of capable, powerful Muslim leaders in both the Levant and the Eastern Mediterranean as a whole;[2] it was now left to second-tier rulers to find a way in which to peacefully co-exist with this new military and political force in the area, inasmuch as they did not have the means by which to expel the Crusaders.

This lack of capable leadership was exacerbated by entrenched sectarian and political hostility amongst the competing Muslim groups in the Levant and Egypt that made any united, decisive action unlikely.[3] Realistically, the best each Muslim ruler could hope to accomplish was the protection of the territorial integrity of his realm from outside invasion – Muslim or Christian – at the individual level, and the limitation of the expansion of Crusader power into other Muslim areas in the Levant at the collective level. With these circumstances established as the new reality for the Muslims of the Levant, there were no other options but to adjust to the present situation, allow for the limited assimilation of their new neighbors into the political milieu of the Levant, and await more direct and decisive action from another corner of the Muslim world, help that would not come in a substantial form for many decades.

The establishment of the Latin Kingdom of Jerusalem inaugurated a new period of uncertainty in the Levant, uncertainty for the Muslim rulers, the ordinary inhabitants of the area, and most certainly for the Crusaders themselves. A contributing factor to this uncertainty was the fact that for the inhabitants of the Levant, the First Crusade did not appear to come to a speedy conclusion. While the First Crusade is most commonly associated with the Crusader capture of Jerusalem in 1099, the Western presence in the region was originally felt with the arrival of the Crusaders in Constantinople in 1096,[4] and felt definitively on July 4, 1097, with the Crusader victory over the Seljuq sultan Qilīj Arslān I and his Turkish forces at Dorylaeum.[5] The length of the period of uncertainty is appreciable when one considers the fact that the expansion of Crusader territory in the Levant would continue, largely unchecked, until 1122–3, when Tyre fell to the Western forces (with the Venetians playing a pivotal role in its capture).[6] While Jerusalem, which was revered by Crusaders and Muslims, was given the most attention by chroniclers on both sides of the struggle as the crown jewel of the Levant, its fall to the Crusaders did not signal the end of the Western forces' military action in the area.

The Crusaders' continued activity necessitated decisive action from the Muslims in the Levant and the adjacent areas. When it came, the response of the Muslim leaders tended to fall into one of four categories: active opposition, conciliation, general indifference, or a combination of the three. For the local Seljuq rulers in the Levant, the response was a combination of active opposition and conciliation through negotiated truces with the Crusaders (which generally involved the payment of tribute by the Muslim leaders).[7] As a general rule, the local sovereigns were most concerned with their positions of power, fearing outside interference in the form of either Western Christians bent on conquest or Muslims from the East bent on re-asserting a more centralized Seljuq power from Iraq; they had little regard for abstract concepts of Muslim unity.[8] For the Fatimid rulers in Egypt, the response was initially one of relatively active opposition, followed by a gradual withdrawal from the military situation in the Levant.[9]

For the Muslim rulers of the East (the 'Abbāsid caliphs, who were the nominal rulers of Iraq, Iran, and much of Central Asia, and the Seljuq Turks, who were the *de facto* rulers), the response was initial indifference, followed by unsuccessful attempts at military intervention, and then a return to a more pronounced indifference. The Eastern rulers' initial feelings of indifference toward the plight of the Muslims in the Levant were moderated only by the direct calls to action that were issued by some of the refugees from the affected area.[10] However, in each instance in which a Seljuq sultan responded to the refugees' calls for assistance, his forces were thwarted by the intransigence of the local Seljuq overlords in the Levant, who suspected ulterior motives on the part of the power brokers in the East.[11] The result of the abortive attempts at military intervention, largely due to the refusal of the local rulers to assist the Eastern forces, was a withdrawal of support from the main centers of the Muslim world in the East. The situation could not have been better for the Crusaders; the local rulers in the Levant were not united, and were individually too weak to oppose the Western forces, and the Muslims in the lands further East, who could check their progress, were largely indifferent to the situation. With this set of circumstances, the expansion of Crusader power continued largely unabated, and by the end of 1109 the forces from Western Europe had carved out four Crusader States: Jerusalem, Edessa, Antioch, and Tripoli,[12] and the Muslims in the Levant were faced with a new, entrenched foreign power in the area.

The initial reactions of the Levantine Muslims to the First Crusade were those of shock and anger: shock at such an unexpected and devastating attack coming from an unexpected quarter, and at the Crusaders' astounding rate of success in conquering substantial areas of the Levant; anger at both how the Western forces treated the inhabitants of many of the conquered areas and at the appropriation and "conversion" of sacred Islamic monuments and spaces. Along with these feelings of shock and anger (which would be the enduring emotions associated with the Crusades and the Crusader presence in the Levant), there was also a feeling of confusion for the Muslims who witnessed these events unfold, whether up close or from a distance. The first area of confusion concerned the identity of the Crusaders. Initially, at least some of the Muslims in the area appear to have confused these Western Christians with the more familiar Christians with whom there was a pre-existing history of sporadic conflict, the Byzantines.[13] This apparent confusion was further fueled by the fact that the initial Crusader forces assembled in Constantinople and did in fact have a working relationship of sorts with the Byzantine emperor, Alexius Comnenus. However, during his reign, the Byzantine-Crusader relationship soon became strained.[14] Moreover, while there was a vague awareness of Western Europe and its inhabitants in the collective conscience of the peoples of the Eastern Mediterranean, there was not, initially, a real understanding of the differences between

Western European and Byzantine Christians, though there would be on the part of the Muslim[15] chroniclers in the years to come.[16]

The second area of confusion concerned the motives of the Crusaders for an undertaking of that magnitude. By and large, the historians of the area did not recognize either the destruction of the Church of the Holy Sepulcher under the Fatimid Caliph al-Hākim in 1009–10,[17] or the Byzantine calls for assistance from the West in its efforts against the Turks on its eastern borders as motivating factors.[18] Instead, many of the chroniclers perceived in the First Crusade a broader pattern of conquest, beginning in Muslim Spain, through which Western Europeans looked to conquer large portions of the Muslim world.[19] In his *al Kāmil fī'l-ta'rīkh* ("The Complete Work of History"),[20] the thirteenth-century historian Ibn al-'Athīr refers to the past European conquests of Muslim lands before beginning his account of the Crusades:

> The power of the Franks and their increased importance were first manifested by their invasion of the lands of Islam and their conquest of part of them in the year 478 [1085–6], for [that was when] they took the city of Toledo and other cities of Spain, as we have already mentioned.
>
> Then in the year 484 [1091–2] they attacked and conquered the island of Sicily, as we have also mentioned. They descended on the coasts of Ifrīqiya and seized some part, which was then taken back from them. Later they took other parts, as you shall see.[21]

In this excerpt, Ibn al-'Athīr reflects the opinion of a number of Muslim historians, both before and after his time, who saw in the Crusades a larger geopolitical movement on the part of the Western Europeans. By the time of Ibn al-'Athīr, there was an understanding of the religious dimension of the Crusades, but the idea that the conquest of substantial parts of the Levant was connected to a larger Western European program of expansion in the Eastern Mediterranean and North Africa remained a compelling one for the chroniclers.

The Muslim historians' confusion regarding the Crusaders' motives for invading the Levant was also reflected in the way the initial Crusading forces were depicted in Muslim writing. The Western armies are clearly identified as the enemy and there is no doubt about their religious affiliation, but any indications that the invasion is religiously motivated escape the chroniclers' notice. Consequently, the religious dimension of the conflict goes largely unexplored in many accounts of the initial wave of Western European conquest in the Levant during the First Crusade. There are, perhaps, a few reasons for the absence of religious coloring in the overall portrait of the First Crusade, notwithstanding the initial failure of the Muslim chroniclers to recognize the role of religion in the Crusaders' sudden appearance.

For the Muslim chroniclers, the Crusaders were *al-Ifranj*, ("the Franks"), as opposed to *al-Rum* (the Byzantines),[22] a term that would be used in reference to the Western Europeans consistently throughout the period of the

Crusades. In time, the designation "Frank" would distinguish Western Europeans from Armenian, Byzantine, and Syrian Christians both in regard to religious practice and race. But for the First Crusade, the chroniclers' accounts are almost entirely devoid of any outside information regarding the Crusaders beyond the names of their leaders. Rather, the focus is on the Franks' military actions and related subjects, so much so that at times they almost appear to be a regular part of the military and political landscape of the Levant.

In the Muslim sources that deal with the Crusades, there are four areas in which the chroniclers focus their attention: the military and political aspects of the conflict (military encounters, negotiations, etc.); individual Crusaders of note (famous leaders); religious issues (beliefs and practices); and Crusader culture. While the military and political aspects of the Crusades are the focus of all of the Muslim accounts, questions of Crusader culture and society, and even of religion, are the provenance of the accounts that cover events from the mid-twelfth century forward; such issues go unnoticed in accounts of the First Crusade because of the fluidity of the situation in the Levant at the time, along with the lack of an established Western European presence (which would be a part of the fabric of the area in the twelfth and thirteenth centuries). The historians' focus on the Crusaders outside of the military and political arenas in accounts dealing with this period is a reflection of the new reality on the ground; the Western European presence was firmly established and would be a factor in the Levant for the foreseeable future. This acceptance of a Western presence was unique to the twelfth and mid-thirteenth centuries. Such an outlook was unlikely at the time of the First Crusade, and from the 1250s onward the situation had changed drastically; the re-conquest of the Levant began to appear inevitable, and the embattled "Syrian Franks" who remained no longer cast the shadow, militarily and politically, that their ancestors had in the previous century.

Both the periods of immense Crusader strength and weakness are reflected in the way Muslim sources portray the Muslim leadership of the time. In their coverage of the conquests of the First Crusade and subsequent years, the chroniclers' focus is on the lack of effective leadership and unity among the Muslims of the Levant, Egypt, and the East. From the time of the rise of the Mamlūk dynasty in 1250, the historians' attention shifts to the strength of the Muslim leaders, and the Crusader leadership begins to disappear into the background. It is during the period which included the Second and Third Crusade, when the military and political situation was relatively stable (despite the ongoing conflict), that some of the chroniclers directed their attention toward aspects of Crusader culture.

The Muslim chroniclers' accounts of Crusader culture, religious practices, and leaders of note are not uniform in the manner of the accounts from the other side of the conflict. Unlike many of the Western, Christian chroniclers, who were similar in their approaches toward the enemy (differing mainly in their personal allegiance to individual leaders of the Crusades), the Muslim historians' approaches to the "Franks" and "Frankish" issues can, and do, vary widely. A writer such as Usāmah ibn Munqidh presents himself as an expert on matters of Crusader culture and law, while others are more reliable resources for intra-Crusader politics. However, each of the historians' accounts provide real insight into an aspect of the Muslim experience of the Crusades and the Crusaders; when taken together, the accounts are an accurate reflection of the Muslim perspective of the Crusaders in times of war and peace.

Perhaps the most interesting arena of Crusader-Muslim contact, and one that offers valuable insight into Levantine Muslim perceptions of Western Europeans, was the ordinary interaction between members of the two groups, removed from the military and political drama that is the focus of most Muslim and Christian accounts. Unfortunately, such encounters went largely unreported in favor of accounts of battle and political intrigue. Most of the Muslim and Christian chroniclers were clerics, and such instances of fraternization with the enemy were not viewed favorably; on the Crusaders' side, there are instances in which respected leaders were criticized for being on friendly terms with Muslims.[23]

For accounts of Crusader-Muslim interaction away from the theatre of war, the most valuable resource is Usāmah ibn Munqidh's autobiography, the *Kitāb al I'tibār (Book of Instructions with Illustrations)*. Unlike the majority of the Muslim and Christian chroniclers, Usāmah ibn Munqidh was not a scholar by trade, although he was a voracious reader. Rather, he was a statesman, the Amīr of Shayzar (Caesarea), and one of the few Syrian Arabs whose role in the Crusades was recorded.[24] Moreover, the position of this amīr (who was born in 1095, the year Urban II issued the call to Crusade)[25] enabled him to traverse the broad spectrum of local Crusader and Muslim societies, providing him with valuable insight into both groups, despite his preexisting biases. In his youth, the amīr witnessed the Crusader conquest of significant portions of Syria and the resulting formation of the Crusader States, but he lived to see the Muslim resurgence under 'Imād al-Dīn Zangi and Nūr al-Dīn, and he died during the year that followed the Muslim recovery of Jerusalem under Salāh al-Dīn in 1187.

But what makes Usāmah ibn Munqidh's account so valuable is the fact that he was more than a passive spectator during this turbulent period; he was also a skillful politician. He enjoyed relationships with the Shi'ite Fatimids of Egypt (who were deposed by Salāh al-Dīn at the behest of Nūr al-Dīn) and Nūr al-Dīn, among others;[26] however, in the final years of his life he found himself observing the triumphs of Salāh al-Dīn from a distance, far removed from the intrigues of court to which he had grown so accustomed.[27] Moreover, his experiences among the Crusaders was as rich and varied as those amongst his coreligionists; he rubbed shoulders with Crusaders of all types, from the leaders of the Crusader armies, to the everyday soldiers making a new life for themselves in the Levant,[28] and his autobiography details these encounters. Despite writing of these experiences amongst Muslims and

Crusaders, Usāmah remains the amīr from Shayzar in his outlook; his accounts of both his experiences and those of his friends among the Franks are valuable for the light they shed on Muslims' perspective on their new neighbors from the West.

For Usāmah, despite his close relationships with a few individuals, the Franks are the enemy, and more often than not some type of malediction accompanies references to them. His stories involving the Franks are intended to denigrate Frankish culture, customs, and beliefs. Some of the anecdotes appear far-fetched, and at times lurid, as if crafted to evoke popular stereotypes of Christian Europeans.[29] For example, the following account is intended to illustrate Frankish men's lack of jealousy concerning their spouses:

> Here is an illustration which I myself witnessed: When I used to visit Nāblus, I always took lodging with a man named Muʿizz, whose home was a lodging house for the Moslems. The house had windows which opened to the road, and there stood opposite to it on the other side of the road a house belonging to a Frank who sold wine for the merchants. He would take some wine in a bottle and go around announcing it by shouting, "So and so, the merchant, has just opened a cask full of this wine. He who wants to buy some of it will find it in such and such a place." The Frank's pay for the announcement made would be the wine in that bottle. One day this Frank went home and found a man with his wife in the same bed. He asked him, "What could have made thee enter into my wife's room?" The man replied, "I was tired, so I went in to rest." "But," said he, "my wife was sleeping together with thee!" The other replied, "Well, the bed is hers. How could I therefore have prevented her from using her own bed?" [. . .] "By the truth of my religion," said the husband, "if thou shouldst do it again, thou and I would have a quarrel." Such was for the Frank the entire expression of his disapproval and the limit of his jealousy.
>
> (pp. 164–5)

The preceding story is a caricature of Western Europeans, employing extant stereotypes of Franks' loose morals and husbands' lack of an "appropriate" level of vigilance regarding their wives and their honor, presenting a tale in which both stereotypes are highlighted for the amusement of his audience. Usāmah is careful to present an unsympathetic figure to the audience: a Frank, part of an unwanted presence in the Levant, and a wine-seller, an occupation that places him beyond the boundaries of what is religiously acceptable.[30] This double-screen, established within the context of the narrative, effectively moves the Frankish husband from being potentially pitiable, as one who has been cuckolded, and positions him as a comic figure, one who receives ample recompense both as an enemy of Muslims, and as one who profits from a forbidden practice.

For Usāmah, the Franks' singular positive attributes are their courage and skill in battle, qualities that, according to him, are highly valued in Frankish society. As the following passage illustrates, it is the most important criterion in Frankish society:

> The Franks (may Allah render them helpless!) possess none of the virtues of men except courage, consider no precedence or high rank except that of the knights, and have nobody that counts except the knights. These are the men on whose counsel they rely, and the ones who make legal decisions and judgments. I once brought a case before them, relative to certain flocks of sheep which the lord of Bāniyās[31] had taken from the forest in the course of a period of truce between them and us. At that time I was in Damascus, so I said to King Fulk, son of Fulk,[32] "This man has trespassed upon our rights and taken away our flocks at the lambing time. The sheep gave birth and the lambkins died. Then he returned the sheep, after having lost so many of them." The king said to six, seven knights, "Arise and judge this case for him." The knights went out from his audience chamber, retired by themselves and consulted together until they all agreed upon one thing. Then they returned to the audience of the king and said, "We have passed judgment to the effect that the lord of Bāniyās should be fined the amount of the damage he wrought among their sheep." The king accordingly ordered him to pay that fine. He pleaded with me, urged and implored me until I finally accepted from him four hundred dīnārs. Such a judgment, after having been pronounced by the knights, [. . .] not even the king nor any of the chieftains of the Franks can alter or revoke. Thus the knight is something great in their esteem.
>
> (pp. 93–4)

Having established the knight's central role in Frankish society, he discusses the physical attributes that are esteemed in a Frankish knight.[33] Coming after a discussion of the influence knights wield in Frankish society, it portrays the Franks as shallow in giving so much weight to appearance as a factor in choosing such important figures.

In portraying Frankish society as militaristic, Usāmah ibn Munqidh is quick to acknowledge the Franks' ability to recognize and appreciate martial prowess in allies and enemies alike. In this vein, the amīr reports an encounter with a Frankish knight during the course of a battle in which he took part during his first encounter with the Franks on the battlefield:

> In the rear guard of the Franks was a cavalier on a black horse, large as a camel, wearing a coat of mail and the full armor of war. I was afraid of this horseman, lest he should be drawing me further ahead in order to get an opportunity to turn back and attack me. All of a sudden I saw him spur his horse, and as the horse began to wave its tail, I knew it was

already exhausted. So I rushed on the horseman and smote him with my lance, which pierced him through and projected about a cubit in front of him. The lightness of my body, the force of thrust and the swiftness of my horse made me lose my seat on the saddle. Moving backward a little, I pulled out my lance, fully assuming that I had killed him. I then assembled my comrades and found them all safe and sound . . .

My uncle (may Allah's mercy rest upon his soul!) returned a few days later from his visit to Najm-al-Dīn Īlghāzi (may Allah's mercy rest upon his soul!). A messenger came to summon me to present myself before my uncle at a time in which it was not his custom to call me. So I hurried to him, and, behold, a Frank was in his company. My uncle said to me: "Here is a knight who has come from Afāmiyah in order to see the horseman who struck Philip the knight, for verily the Franks have all been astounded [. . .] on account of that blow which pierced two layers of links in the knight's coat of mail and yet did not kill him."

(pp. 68–9)

The Franks are capable of appreciating martial prowess within any context and in any individual, even if it comes at the expense of one of their own. In this particular instance, Usāmah points to shared values; the warriors on both sides demonstrate an appreciation for individuals who excel in the art of warfare.

However, the amīr's compliments toward the Franks rarely come without a qualification that largely negates the positive attribute in question, and his remarks concerning the Franks' valor is no exception. While Usāmah readily acknowledges that courage and martial prowess are found in great measure among the Franks, he makes it clear that these are the only qualities they possess, portraying the qualities as instinctual rather than being indicative of any type of cognitive process:

Mysterious are the works of the Creator, the author of all things! When one comes to recount cases regarding the Franks, he cannot but glorify Allah (exalted is He!) and sanctify him, for he sees them as animals possessing the virtues of courage and fighting, but nothing else; just as animals have only the virtues of strength and carrying loads.

(p. 161)

Here, Usāmah recasts his earlier comments on the Franks' proficiency in battle, transforming it from a positive attribute into something akin to a distinguishing physical characteristic, such as might be found among animals. For Usāmah, the Franks are not courageous in battle in the manner of his companions; rather, they have the distinguishing characteristic of being war-like, just as other animals possess the characteristics of speed or strength.

The amīr further expounds upon the barbarity of the Franks when he discusses the role of violence in the Crusader courts. Having already explained the status accorded to Frankish knights for their skill in battle (p. 93), Usāmah provides an illustration of some of the negative implications of their overreliance on violence, in this case as it relates to the use of violence as a determiner of justice, through an anecdote of the case of a farmer accused of aiding and abetting a group of thieves from an adjacent Muslim area:

> I attended one day a duel in Nāblus between two Franks. The reason for this was that certain Moslem thieves took by surprise one of the villages of Nāblus. One of the peasants of that village was charged with having acted as guide for the thieves when they fell upon the village. So he fled away. The king[34] sent and arrested his children. The peasant thereupon came back to the king and said, "Let justice be done in my case. I challenge to a duel the man who claimed that I guided the thieves to the village." The king then said to the tenant who held the village in fief, "Bring forth someone to fight the duel with him." The tenant went back to his village, where a blacksmith lived, took hold of him and ordered him to fight the duel. The tenant became thus sure of the safety of his own peasants, none of whom would be killed and his estate ruined.
>
> (p. 167)

To this point in the narrative, Usāmah has painted a picture in which it is unlikely that justice will be served; a legal matter – the question of the peasant's guilt or innocence in rendering assistance to a group of brigands – is to be settled through a duel, which is not likely to establish anything conclusively outside of which of the two combatants is the superior warrior. Moreover, the peasant is denied even the opportunity of facing his accuser in combat, but rather the accuser is able to offer a proxy, in this case a strong yet apparently "expendable" young blacksmith, whose participation in the duel ensures that the lord of the village will not have to risk losing one of his field hands to the vicissitudes of such combat.

As the duel unfolds, the picture becomes more disturbing. The challenger, "an old man . . . strong in spirit," (p. 167) comports himself well against a younger opponent in a scene that abounds with grisly images.[35] When, at the instigation of the viscount (p. 168), the duel comes to an end, with the young blacksmith victorious, Usāmah describes the aftermath, in which the authorities attempt to add a veneer of justice to the proceedings:

> They then fastened a rope around the neck of the dead person, dragged him away and hanged him. The lord who brought the smith now came, gave the smith his own mantle, made him mount the horse behind him and rode off with him. This case illustrates the kind of jurisprudence [. . .] and legal decisions the Franks have.
>
> (p. 168)

In this example, the "barbarity" of the Franks is on full display for the audience, for whom the lesson is that courage and enthusiasm for battle, admirable traits in the context of combat, are inappropriate in circumstances that call for patience and reflection, such as the administration of justice. The preceding anecdote is a clear illustration of the fact that the Franks have not come to this understanding, but rather have allowed their propensity for violence to spill over into other aspects of society. For the amīr, this is but one example of the negative implications of the natural bellicosity of the Franks, and the reason that it is more deserving of censure than praise.

In another example intended to reinforce the violent, capricious nature of Crusader justice, Usāmah recounts the tale of a blind young man, who had been in the habit of killing Frankish pilgrims (p. 168). Over time, the Franks began to suspect him of these crimes, and in accordance with their customs, the man was put on trial:

> They installed a huge cask and filled it with water. Across it they set a board of wood. They then bound the arms of the man charged with the act, tied a rope around his shoulders and dropped him into the cask, their idea being that in case he was innocent, he would sink in the water and they would then lift him up with the rope so that he might not die in the water; and in case he was guilty, he would not sink in the water. This man did his best to sink when they dropped him into the water, but he could not do it. So he had to submit to their sentence against him – may Allah's curse be upon them! They pierced his eyeballs with red-hot awls.
> (pp. 168–9)

Although this "trial" happened, in this particular instance, to arrive at an appropriate verdict, for Usāmah ibn Munqidh it lacked both the appearance and substance of justice. This example, much like the previous one, serves to reinforce stereotypes of Frankish barbarity, stereotypes that the amīr evokes and endorses in his discussions of other aspects of Frankish culture and customs.

If the Franks' innate courage can be both a positive and negative attribute in Usāmah's estimation, there is no such ambiguity in his discussion of his Western neighbors' constancy; the Franks are duplicitous by nature, and are not to be trusted. Even when there is an existing agreement, the Franks will seek to circumvent it to the greatest degree possible. To illustrate this point, Usāmah provides one particularly poignant example, recounting his family's ordeals in traveling through the territory of Baldwin III[36] en route to Damascus. According to Usāmah, the sultan Nūr al-Dīn had obtained safe passage for his family from the Crusader king (p. 60). However, despite this agreement, his loved ones encountered trouble soon after entering Crusader territory:

> Al-Sālih transported my family on one of his private boats to Dimyāt,[37] provided them with all the money and provisions they needed and gave

them the proper recommendation. From Dimyāt they sailed in a Frankish vessel. As they approached 'Akka [Acre] where the king (may Allah's mercy not rest upon his soul!) was, he sent, in a small boat, a few men who broke the vessel with their axes under the very eyes of my people. The king mounted his horse, stood by the coast and pillaged everything that was there.

One of my retainers came swimming to the king, taking the safe-conduct with him, and said, "O my lord the king, is this not thy safe-conduct?" "Sure enough," replied the king. "But this is the usage for the Moslems. Whenever one of their vessels is wrecked near a town, the people of that town pillage it." "Art thou going, then, to take us captive?" inquired my retainer. "No," replied the king. The king (may Allah's curse be upon him!) then put them in a house, had the women searched and took everything they all possessed. In the vessel were jewelry, which had been intrusted to the women, clothes, gems, swords, weapons and gold and silver amounting to about thirty thousand dīnārs. He then sent my people five hundred dīnārs and said, "This will see you home," though they were no less than fifty persons, men and women.

(pp. 60–1)

For the amīr, this is a clear example of Frankish duplicity. Baldwin III puts forth the utmost effort to circumvent his guarantee of safe passage to the Muslim travelers, violating the spirit of the agreement through his extemporaneous, literal interpretation of the covenant. While Usāmah's family and their retinue do arrive safely in Damascus (p. 61), they are greatly imperiled by the very individual who is ostensibly the guarantor of their safety in traveling through his kingdom.

Unlike his discussions of Crusader justice and duplicity, Usāmah assumes a different tone in the area of Frankish marital relations, depicting the men as comic figures rather than villains. One of his examples of Frankish men's overabundant trust in their spouses has already been cited; this particular example is more in keeping with the conventions of the *fabliaux* than that of a chronicle or memoir. However, the tale in question is largely representative of the amīr's characterization of Franks' marital affairs. Perhaps the most serious observations he offers on the subject can be found in his prefatory comments on the topic:

> The Franks are void of all zeal and jealousy. One of them may be walking with his wife. He meets another man who takes the wife by the hand and steps aside to converse with her while the husband is standing on one side waiting for his wife to conclude the conversation. If she lingers too long for him, he leaves her alone with the conversant and goes away.
>
> (p. 164)

In this passage, Usāmah identifies his main concern regarding Frankish conjugal relations: husbands are not jealous of their wives, presumably because they do not appropriately value the importance of marriage and the way in which it reflects on them and their standing within their community. From this point, the discussion takes a turn toward the farcical, as Usāmah relates the aforementioned story of the Frankish wine-seller in Nablus, which is followed by an even more outrageous "anecdote" involving a Frankish knight, his wife, and a Muslim bath house attendant.[38] These two "examples" are then followed by an interesting observation by the amīr concerning Frankish behavior in general, and Frankish courage in particular: "Consider now this great contradiction! They have neither jealousy nor zeal but they have great courage, although courage is nothing but the product of zeal and ambition to be above ill repute" (p. 166). For Usāmah, the courage of the Franks is all the more curious a characteristic because it does not appear to be the outward manifestation of a sense of honor and the accompanying desire to protect that honor. Since the Franks do not attach honor to the appropriate institutions, they must not have a sense of honor. This observation further distances the Franks from other peoples, setting them apart as a race without an identifiable motivating force behind that courage regularly exhibited by them on the battlefield; their works of heroism appear to be instinctual rather than the products of meditated action.

While Usāmah's portrayal of the relationships between Frankish men and women tends toward the comical, one of his contemporaries, 'Imād al-Dīn al-Isfahani, who served as both Nūr al-Dīn's secretary and Salāh al-Dīn's chancellor,[39] exploits another local stereotype regarding Western Europeans' behavior, one which emphasizes Frankish women's loose morals and wantonness. In one passage, he describes the arrival of a group of prostitutes from Europe come to ply their trade:[40]

> There arrived by ship three hundred lovely Frankish women, full of youth and beauty, assembled from beyond the sea and offering themselves for sin. They were expatriates come to help expatriates, ready to cheer the fallen and sustained in turn to give support and assistance, and they glowed with ardour for carnal intercourse. They were all licentious harlots, proud and scornful, who took and gave, foul-fleshed and sinful, singers and coquettes, appearing proudly in public, ardent and inflamed, tinted and painted, desirable and appetizing, exquisite and graceful, who ripped open and patched up, lacerated and mended, erred and ogled, urged and seduced, consoled and solicited, seductive and languid, desired and desiring, amused and amusing, versatile and cunning, like tipsy adolescents, making love and selling themselves for gold, bold and ardent, loving and passionate, pink-faced and unblushing, black-eyed and bullying, callipygian and graceful, with nasal voices and fleshy thighs, blue-eyed and grey-eyed, broken- down little fools. Each one trailed the train of her robe behind her and bewitched the beholder with her effulgence. She swayed like a sapling, walked

proudly with a cross on her breast, sold her graces for gratitude, and longed to lose her robe and her honour.[41]

Here 'Imād al-Dīn, in the ornate style for which he is famous,[42] portrays these Frankish women in a manner different from that of the amīr of Shayzar, as cunning seductresses rather than as mere participants in the cuckolding of their husbands.

For Usāmah ibn Munqidh, the focus is on the perceived indifference of Frankish men regarding their wives; the moral laxity is, in a sense, a by-product of the men's failure to effectively safeguard their marriages, much in the manner of the cuckolded husbands of the *fabliaux*. For 'Imād al-Dīn, who is writing chiefly as a partisan propagandist for Salāh al-Dīn, the concern is the moral laxity that allegedly runs rampant among the Franks. These divergent objectives on the parts of the two writers result in two different portraits of the same enemy's sexual mores. While the amīr's approach to the subject is more personal, that of a married man who is observing other men's interactions with their wives, the chancellor deals with the issue from a distance. This personal approach distinguishes Usāmah ibn Munqidh from 'Imād al-Dīn and the majority of the other Muslim chroniclers. This difference distinguishes his accounts; Usāmah's comments, which are based on his observations, are more likely to reflect what Muslims who actually encountered the Franks thought of them than are those accounts which merely repeat stereotypes.

Another incident that, for the amīr, is representative of Crusader culture in general, takes place on the occasion of a holiday celebration in Tiberias:

> I found myself in Tabarayyah[43] at the time when the Franks were celebrating one of their feasts. The cavaliers went out to exercise with lances. With them went out two decrepit, aged women whom they stationed at one end of the race course. At the other end of the field they left a pig which they had scalded and laid on a rock. They then made the two aged women run a race while each one of them was accompanied by a detachment of horsemen urging her on. At every step they took, the women would fall down and rise again, while the spectators would laugh. Finally one of them got ahead of the other and won that pig for a prize.
>
> (p. 167)

Through his account of this bizarre scene, Usāmah buttresses extant stereotypes of Frankish barbarism and filth. The knights' presence reinforces the idea that violence is part and parcel of Frankish society, while their actions, obstructing the progress of two old women and holding them up for ridicule rather than helping them, points to the barbarizing effects of privileging violence to the extent Usāmah would have the reader understand is the case in Frankish society. The idea of a pig being made the object of the women's endeavors underscores the larger idea of Franks as unclean, polluting the Levant through their presence. The image of the two old women racing (and falling) is simultaneously barbarous and comical, barbarous in its implications for the treatment of individuals who are deserving of better treatment, and comical both for the immediate image it presents,[44] and as representative of Frankish society as a whole as violent, haphazard, and uncivilized.

For Usāmah, the best Franks are those who have been tempered by prolonged contact with Muslims, Franks who have become, by degrees, familiar with Muslim customs, adopting many of them, and losing some of their innate Frankish barbarism (p. 169). To illustrate this point, he relates the story of a friend who, while in Antioch, is invited to the house of a knight who had come as a part of the First Crusade and subsequently taken up residence in the Levant (p. 169). Upon arriving, he finds that a splendid repast is prepared for the knight and his company; however, the narrator refrains from eating due to his concerns over upholding the integrity of his dietary restrictions. Noticing this, his host assures him that he has nothing to fear; the knight has Egyptian cooks who prepare only local cuisine; moreover, he does not eat pork (pp. 169–70). This is sufficient for the narrator, who proceeds to eat, but in a cautious manner (p. 170). Later, this same knight saves the life of Usāmah's friend when a Frankish woman mistakes him for a man who had slain her brother. The narrator, who is unable to communicate with the woman, is surrounded by a group of Franks and fears the worst, but the knight appears and resolves the situation (p. 170). For Usāmah, this knight represents the "evolved" Frank, whose prolonged contact with Levantine Muslims has had a civilizing effect. Such individuals are the exception rather than the rule in his estimation, as they have been altered by their time in the Levant, and consequently have lost much of their "authentic" Frankish barbarism.

Throughout his account, Usāmah ibn Munqidh vacillates between outright hostility and condescension in his appraisal of Franks and Frankish customs. In matters of war he reveals a grudging admiration for their courage and ability, tempered by his partisan interests as a Muslim involved in the Counter-Crusade. In other matters, he finds the Franks by turns barbarous and amusing, uttering invectives and maledictions upon his Western neighbors as he describes their system of justice and their duplicity, while sharing a good-natured laugh with the reader at the expense of Frankish husbands. However, as it relates to the Franks and their customs, the predominant tone of the amīr is one of condescension. He finds humor in their behavior toward their spouses, and relates the story of the race between the two old women in the hippodrome in the manner of an appalled, yet amused spectator. As we shall see, even in matters of faith his expressions of outrage at the beliefs and practices of the Franks reveal an underlying, yet consistent, tone of condescension.

Usāmah ibn Munqidh's accounts of Frankish beliefs and customs serve to emphasize the superiority of his Eastern Mediterranean Arab-Muslim culture. This bias is provincial in nature, and extends even to coreligionists, as he readily admits that not only is he unfamiliar with any of the "Frankish" languages (p. 95), but also Turkish (p. 180), the native language of many of the amīrs and soldiers with whom he works closely, the language of a group that had been a major presence in the area for centuries. It is the Frankish threat to this hierarchy, in particular the military aspects of this threat, which elicits the full measure of Usāmah's anger and vitriol. Off of the battlefield, when the threat to this hierarchy is greatly diminished, and the relative superiority of his Eastern Mediterranean culture, religion, and values appear self-evident, the amīr relaxes, and when writing of the Crusaders, their customs and faith, assumes the tone of outrage, exasperation, and amusement one might expect to find in a parent's description of a recalcitrant child.

Unlike their Western, Christian counterparts, the Muslim chroniclers did not immediately recognize the religious significance of the Crusades. However, once it became a known factor, Muslim writers found the religious dimension of the Crusades both compelling and of enormous propaganda value, and religion and religious difference came to play an important role in the way Muslim writers viewed the Crusades and the Crusaders. Initially, the religious diversity within the Eastern Mediterranean may have obfuscated the religious nature of the Crusades for the Muslim chroniclers. Religion was a defining characteristic of the two groups during the period of the Crusades; but it was also a defining characteristic of the Christian Byzantines and Armenians, with whom the Muslims of the area were in intermittent conflict, as well as of the indigenous Christians of Syria and Lebanon, with whom they lived in relative peace. Sectarian differences were also a relevant factor, and in certain ways more divisive, in relations with the Shi'ite Fatimids of Egypt, and also played a role in the conflict between various Sunni sovereigns and the Isma'īliyya "Assassins."[45] In each of these cases, religion was the publicly articulated justification for the tension, but political considerations often determined whether conflict or peace would be the order of the day.

Inter and intra-religious strife was by no means exclusive to the Muslims of the Eastern Mediterranean; it was also present among the various Christian groups, and the Crusaders themselves would become embroiled in this soon after their arrival,[46] culminating in the disastrous Fourth Crusade and Sack of Constantinople, in which sectarian and political tensions between the Christians of Byzantium and the Latin West, who were brought into closer proximity as a result of the Crusades,[47] played a large part. Political considerations divided Muslims and Christians alike, resulting in inter-religious alliances between the various Muslim groups and Byzantines, Armenians, and Crusaders; as a result, the religious dimension of the Crusades was not felt by the local Muslim sovereigns to the same degree relative to their Western, Christian counterparts, for whom it was the galvanizing force that had brought them to the Levant. For the local Seljuq rulers, the fact that the Crusaders were Christian was not compelling in and of itself; Muslim–Byzantine conflict was not uncommon, and there had been an ongoing contestation of power between the two groups in the Levant for some time.[48] Equally important in the Muslim leaders and chroniclers' assessment of the Crusaders was the fact that it was not immediately apparent that they constituted a coherent and unified political entity, distinct from the other Christian groups in the Levant. Such distinctions would be drawn in the years following the First Crusade, and it would not be long before the religious dimension of the Crusades would become as prominent in the literature of the Muslim historians as it was in that of their Western, Christian counterparts.

When they did begin to distinguish the Crusaders from the indigenous Christians of the Levant (especially the Armenians and the Byzantines) and to identify the religious dimension of the Crusades, the Muslim chroniclers often focused on the cross and its significance, as well as upon the places regarded as holy by the Western soldiers. The cross was a familiar symbol in the religious milieu of the Levant, but it took on an added significance with the coming of the Crusaders because it came to mark Frankish conquest and colonization: when affixed to a structure in the Levant, the cross represented the appropriation of Islamic sites for Christian purposes.[49] The significance of the cross as an emblem of Christian conquest in the Levant, and the enmity it could arouse within the local Muslim population, can be seen in Ibn al-'Athīr's description of the removal of a cross that had been placed upon the Dome of the Rock by the Crusaders, one of the first acts of Salāh al-Dīn's forces upon their conquest of Jerusalem in 1187:

> On top of the Dome of the Rock was a great gilded cross. When the Muslims entered the city on the Friday, several men climbed to the top of the dome to displace the cross. When they did so and it fell, everyone in the city and outside, both Muslims and Franks, cried out as one. The Muslims shouted 'God is great!' in joy, while the Franks cried out in distress and pain. People heard a clamour so great and loud that the earth well-nigh shook under them.[50]

The cross was acknowledged as an important symbol for the Franks, but also as an important holy relic. In particular, Muslim chroniclers recognized the importance of the True Cross to the Franks, and the demoralizing effects that would accompany the loss of this most holy of Christian relics. In recounting the Muslim victory in the Battle of Hattīn (which crippled the Crusader forces in the Levant and led to the fall of Jerusalem to Salāh al-Dīn and, subsequently, to the Third Crusade), both Ibn al-'Athīr and 'Imād al-Dīn focus on the importance of the capture of the True Cross by the

Muslims during the course of the battle, with 'Imād al-Dīn, who was a member of Salāh al-Dīn's retinue at the time, providing a more dramatic account:

> At the same time as the King was taken the "True Cross" was also captured, and the idolaters who were trying to defend it were routed. It was this cross, brought into position and raised on high, to which all Christians prostrated themselves and bowed their heads. Indeed, they maintain that it is made of the wood of the cross on which, they say, he whom they adore was hung, and so they venerate it and prostrate themselves before it. They had housed it in a casing of gold, adorned it with pearls and gems, and kept it ready for the festival of the Passion, for the observance of their yearly ceremony. When the priests exposed it to view and the heads (of the bearers) bore it along all would run and cast themselves down around it, and no one was allowed to lag behind or hang back without forfeiting his liberty. Its capture was for them more important than the loss of the King and was the gravest blow that they sustained in that battle. The cross was a prize without equal, for it was the supreme object of their faith.[51]

The Muslim chroniclers were well aware of the importance of the True Cross to the enemy, and consequently of the propaganda value that it held for the Muslims in the context of the current struggle. Indeed, the Crusaders themselves attested to the value of the True Cross to their morale after their conquest of Acre in 1191, as its return was one of the conditions for the release of the Muslim prisoners taken after the capitulation of the city.[52]

If the True Cross was the most important relic, the Church of the Holy Sepulcher was the most important monument in Medieval Christianity, a fact of which the Muslim chroniclers were well aware. Derisively referred to as the "Church of Refuse" by some Muslims,[53] they were nonetheless aware, as were Muslims in general, of the significance of the Church to Christians as a pilgrimage site. There are two indicators of the writers' recognition of the Church's importance: the description of the Crusaders' attachment to the Church and desire to maintain possession of it during the days leading to the Muslim recovery of Jerusalem in 1187, and the accounts of the discussions among the Muslim leaders regarding the fate of the holy site after their recovery of the city. Once again, the chronicler 'Imād al-Dīn, as an eyewitness to the events on the Muslim side, offers some insight into the thinking of both camps. As for the Crusaders' desire to maintain possession of Jerusalem, and in particular the Church, a speech attributed to the Franks shows the writer's awareness of the sanctity of the Church in their eyes:

> The Franks said: "Here our heads will fall, we will pour forth our souls, spill our blood, give up our lives; we shall endure blows and wounds, we shall be prodigal of our spirits in defense of the place where the Spirit dwells. This is our Church of the Resurrection, here we shall take

up our position and from here make our sorties, here our cry goes up, here our penitence is performed, our banners float, our cloud spreads. We love this place, we are bound to it, our honour lies in honouring it, its salvation is ours, its safety is ours, its survival is ours."[54]

This speech appears to have at least accurately represented the feelings of the Crusaders, and their desperation in the final days before the fall of Jerusalem.[55] Their devotion to the site itself appears to have made an impression on the Muslim leaders, some of whom, in 'Imād al-Dīn's account, articulate the position that the destruction of the Church would deter Christian pilgrims, armed or otherwise, from coming to the city, a position that is quickly refuted:

> Many discussions were held with him [Salāh al-Dīn] about its fate; some advised him to demolish it and remove all trace of it, making it impossible to visit . . . "When its buildings are destroyed," they said, "and its fires spent and extinguished, and its traces rubbed out and removed, and its soil ploughed up, and the Church scattered far and wide, then the people will cease to visit it, and the longings of those destined to damnation will no longer turn to seeing it, whereas if it is left standing the pilgrimage will go on without end." But the majority said: "Demolishing and destroying it would serve no purpose, nor would it prevent the infidels from visiting it or prevent their having access to it. For it is not the building as it appears to the eyes, but the home of the Cross and the Sepulchre that is the object of worship. The various Christian races would still be making pilgrimages here even if the earth had been dug up and thrown into the sky. And when 'Umar, prince of the believers, conquered Jerusalem in the early days of Islām, he confirmed to the Christians the possession of the place, and did not order them to demolish the building on it."[56]

For the Muslim chroniclers, holy symbols, relics, and monuments carried a special significance to the Franks, and could often encourage them to victory in adverse situations. This had been so since the discovery of the "Lance of the Messiah" by Peter Bartholomew in 1098 and the subsequent Crusader victory over superior numbers outside of Antioch.[57] Of course, Crusaders shared much in common with the Muslims of the Levant in their belief in and reliance upon holy symbols, objects, and places. However, the Western writers do not appear to have had a similar level of awareness about the sacred symbols and objects of their Muslim adversaries, and so the Muslim chroniclers stand out for their understanding of this aspect of the religious dimension of the Crusades.

Beyond the symbols and monuments, the Muslim chroniclers understood, and at times exhibited a grudging admiration for, the religious fervor that transcended concrete objects and places and animated the Western soldiers.

The chroniclers may well have perceived in this crusading ethic something akin to the popular concept of jihad[58] that was being evoked in response to the Western presence in the Levant. Whether or not this was the case, the writers were well aware of the role that religious fervor could play in inspiring Crusaders to greater acts of valor in battle. Bahā' al-Dīn's account of the capture of the fortress of Tibrīn (Toron) in July 1187[59] is an excellent example of a chronicler acknowledging the role of religiosity in the struggle. Bahā' al-Dīn, who served as qadi[60] for the army of Salāh al-Dīn, acknowledges the role of faith in the Franks' resistance to the siege:

> The garrison was composed of men of tried valour and very zealous for their faith, therefore they held out with wonderful endurance; but God came to the Sultan's [Salāh al-Dīn] assistance, and he carried the place by storm on the 18th of the month, and led the survivors of the garrison into captivity.[61]

The qadi provides another example of the role of religious fervor in the Crusader cause in his description of the famine that afflicted the Crusader territories in the latter half of 1190, and the Crusaders' persistence in the face of such hardships:

> We were constantly kept informed as to the enemy; they were suffering severely from scarcity of food, for famine prevailed throughout the territories, and had now invaded their camp. The scarcity reached such a height that at Antioch the price of a sack of corn rose to ninety-six Tyrian dinars. But this only strengthened the resolution of the besiegers.[62]

While such resolve was not displayed by all of the Crusaders at Acre,[63] it is clear that for Bahā' al-Dīn the Franks were buoyed by their devotion to the cause.

Perhaps the most compelling example of the recognition and appreciation of the religious fervor of the Franks and its role in the crusading effort is provided by one of the most famous leaders on either side of the conflict. In his famous work *The Book of the Two Gardens* (*Kitāb ar-Raudatain*), the thirteenth-century philologist and anthologist Abu Shama[64] reproduces a letter attributed to Salāh al-Dīn in which he calls for increased support from the surrounding Muslim kingdoms. In the course of this letter, the Sultan reproaches his coreligionists by comparing their efforts to that of the enemy:

> Where is the sense of honour of the Muslims, the pride of the believers, the zeal of the faithful? We shall never cease to be amazed at how the Unbelievers, for their part, have shown trust, and it is the Muslims who have been lacking in zeal. Not one of them has responded to the call, not one intervenes to straighten what is distorted; but observe how far the Franks have gone; what unity they have achieved, what aims they

pursue, what help they have given, what sums of money they have borrowed and spent, what wealth they have collected and distributed and divided among them! There is not a king left in their lands or islands, not a lord or a rich man who has not competed with his neighbours to produce more support, and rivalled his peers in strenuous military effort. In defense of their religion they consider it a small thing to spend life and soul, and they have kept their infidel brothers supplied with arms and champions for the war. And all they have done, and all their generosity, has been done purely out of zeal for Him they Worship, in jealous defence of their Faith. Every Frank feels that once we have reconquered the (Syrian) coast, and the veil of their honour is torn off and destroyed, this country will slip from their grasp, and our hand will reach out toward their own countries.[65]

The letter is remarkable for its appraisal of the Crusader war effort, including the principles guiding it, and for the writer's assessment of the Muslim war effort by comparison as well. It is all the more noteworthy in light of the statements of the "sultan" on the topic of the moral state of Christendom in *Mandeville's Travels*,[66] because in this instance one finds a historical sultan bemoaning the complacence of the Muslims in combating Christian aggression. When viewed in the light of some of the contemporary Western evaluations of the Christian crusade effort,[67] Salāh al-Dīn's appraisal of the Crusaders' devotion appears hyperbolic. Nevertheless, it is perhaps the highest praise of the devotion displayed by the Western European forces in prosecuting this holy war, and of the religious convictions that motivated the enterprise.

The Franks' devotion was admirable in an abstract sense; however, the Franks remained non-Muslims, beyond the boundaries of acceptable beliefs and practices for the Muslim writers. Within the accounts, there are frequent references to the Franks as idolaters, polytheists, heretics, and other such appellations, in a manner reminiscent of the Western sources' descriptions of the Muslims. For example, 'Imād al-Dīn portrays the conflict in loosely religious terms when he describes Salāh al-Dīn's march to Jerusalem in 1187:

> Saladin marched forward to take up the reins of Jerusalem that now hung loose, to silence the Christian clappers and allow the muezzin to be heard again, to remove the heavy hand of unbelief with the right hand of Faith, to purify Jerusalem of the pollution of those races, of the filth of the dregs of humanity, to reduce the minds to silence by silencing the bells.[68]

In its concern with cleansing Jerusalem of both the "filth" of the Frankish race and the "pollution" of their unbelief, the passage echoes the concerns voiced by Pope Urban II over the Muslim occupation of the Levant in his famous call to Crusade.

Nevertheless, the Franks were but one of several groups of Christians in the Eastern Mediterranean, and simply identifying them as Christians was not sufficient to meet the needs of a well-constructed polemic. In characterizing and lampooning Franks as Christians, Muslim writers integrated other stereotypes of Western Europeans, presenting them as aspects of their faith. In particular, Franks were portrayed as unsophisticated in their beliefs, lacking the mature understanding of Christian doctrine and dogma of their Eastern coreligionists. This lack of refinement in the area of belief is an extension of the stereotype of Franks as a crude, barbarous people, and accords well with the pronouncements of al-Mas'ūdī regarding Frankish inconstancy in religious matters. An example of this Frankish "naiveté" can be found in Usāmah ibn Munqidh's account of a conversation between a Templar and the amīr Mu'īn al-Dīn Anar (d. 1149)[69] in the Dome of the Rock:

> I saw one of the Franks come to al-Amīr Mu'īn-al-Dīn (May Allah's mercy rest upon his soul!) when he was in the Dome of the Rock and say to him, "Dost thou want to see God as a child?" Mu'īn-al-Dīn said, "Yes." The Frank walked ahead of us until he showed us the picture of Mary with Christ (may peace be upon him!) as an infant in her lap. He then said, "This is God as a child." But Allah is exalted far above what the infidels say about him![70]

This anecdote reinforces stereotypes of Frankish simplicity; the knight's presentation of the icon reveals his ignorance of the subtleties of Christian doctrine, especially in conversation with a Muslim, for whom the artistic representations of holy figures is forbidden. Usāmah ibn Munqidh leaves the reader to imagine an incredulous yet amused Mu'īn al-Dīn as he stands before the painting in question listening to the Templar's explanation, undoubtedly sharing Usāmah's sense of amusement and indignation.

For the Muslim writers, this naiveté on the part of the Franks in religious matters also resulted in a credulousness on their part, which could be exploited to advantage. For the chroniclers, this was most apparent in the Franks' susceptibility to being manipulated into believing that ordinary occurrences or phenomena were in fact miracles. Ibn al-'Athīr presents an example of this type of credulity in his account of Peter Bartholomew's discovery of the "Lance of the Messiah" (believed to have been the lance that pierced Jesus' side during the Crucifixion) in Antioch during the First Crusade,[71] an event that was followed by a Crusader victory over a better provisioned, numerically superior Muslim army:

> There was a monk there, of influence amongst them, who was a cunning man. He said to them, "The Messiah (blessings be upon Him) had a lance which was buried in the church at Antioch, which was a great building. If you find it, you will prevail, but if you do not find it, then destruction is assured." He had previously buried a lance in a place

there and removed the traces [of his digging]. He commanded them to fast and repent, which they did for three days. On the fourth day he took them all into the place, accompanied by the common people and workmen. They dug everywhere and found it as he had said. "Rejoice in your coming victory," he said to them.[72]

The discovery of the Lance, and the subsequent Crusader victory, apparently aided by a belief that it had been preordained from on High, is here portrayed as the result of an elaborate hoax contrived by a religious leader from among the Crusaders who presumably "knew" that his countrymen were easily duped in matters of faith, and used this knowledge to advance the objectives of the First Crusade.[73]

The Crusaders' perceived naïveté fed into another stereotype concerning Frankish religiosity: their propensity toward ridiculous or unseemly displays of faith. In his account of the siege of Damascus in 1148, the thirteenth-century historian Sibt Ibn al-Jauzi[74] relates the following account of a priest within the Crusader camp:

> The Franks had with them a great Priest with a long beard, whose teachings they obeyed. On the tenth day of their siege of Damascus he mounted his ass, hung a cross round his neck, took two more in his hand and hung another round the ass's neck. He had the Testaments and the crosses and the Holy Scriptures set before him and assembled the army in his presence; the only ones to remain behind were those guarding the tents. Then he said: "The Messiah has promised me that today I shall wipe out this city." At that moment the Muslims opened the city gates and in the name of Islām charged as one man into the face of death. . . . One of the men of the Damascus militia reached the Priest, who was fighting in the front line, struck his head from his body and killed his ass too.[75]

The priest of this account (regardless of its veracity) serves as perhaps the nearest approximation of the Foreign Saracen of the medieval romances. He is a figure who has taken the concept of religious warfare to its most literal, and absurd, extreme, riding into battle on an ass rather than a charger, and equipped with religious symbols and texts rather than weapons. Like his Saracen counterparts in the romances, he is also destined to become a body upon which his enemies can exact a measure of vengeance through violence, and both he and his ass are killed in the ensuing melee. Moreover, like the Foreign Saracen of the romances, he serves to debunk the threat of the Other, in this instance the Christian Other, by taking its most threatening aspects (here, the religious fervor and enthusiasm of the Crusaders), and rendering them ridiculous. Just as ludicrous depictions of Saracens provided some relief to Christian European audiences in the face of previous reverses at the hands of real Muslims, such depictions of Franks may have offered a welcome diversion for a Muslim audience in the Eastern Mediterranean for whom the memories of Crusaders were still fresh.

The Crusaders' faith was a complex issue for the Muslim historians; it united them with the other Christians in the area, yet distinguished them because of the manner of its outward manifestation. For the Muslims, the religious conviction of the Franks was admirable in that it inspired them to heroic feats in battle and to greater sacrifices for the cause of religion. But it was unbelief, and thus abhorrent, perhaps even more so because the Christianity of the Franks appeared to be at greater variance with Islam than the local and regional denominations of Christianity.

The fact that the Christianity of the Crusaders was not indigenous to the area was perhaps its most distinguishing feature, particularly as it did not have a history of co-existence with the other faiths of the area. The soldiers who came on the Crusades were, for the most part, from parts of Western Europe that did not contain the large non-Christian populations found in Spain or Sicily, to say nothing of the situation in the Levant. Whereas the Armenian, Byzantine, and in particular Syrian Christians had come, in time, to co-exist with their Muslim neighbors (or at least, in the case of the Byzantines, to accept the Muslim presence as a religious, political, and social reality), the Crusaders were unaccustomed to such religious diversity, and had ostensibly come to eliminate it. As a result, the Crusaders distinguished themselves from their coreligionists in the East by their militancy, alienating and antagonizing the general Muslim population as a whole, and the Muslim historians in particular.

However, the primary focus of the Muslim chroniclers of the Crusade was not religion, but the military struggle, and over the prolonged periods of conflict, these writers recorded observations about the martial abilities and tendencies of the Franks. On the whole, the chroniclers' portrayal of the Franks at war accords with Usāmah ibn Munqidh's account: the Franks were courageous, formidable warriors, and were respected as such by their Muslim contemporaries. Since the Franks' perceived skill in battle was regarded as a characteristic of their "Frankish-ness," the writers do not tend to go into great detail concerning displays of valor by individual Crusaders or groups; such incidents are often recorded without comment. For example, in Bahā' al-Dīn's account one finds the following passage regarding the Crusaders' defense of a battle standard during an encounter that took place on November 13, 1190, outside of Acre:[76] "The Franks defended it [the battle standard] zealously, even at the cost of their lives. Their foot-soldiers formed an outer ring like a wall to cover their cavalry, and they used their arbalests and bows with such skill that no one could get near, or single out their horsemen."[77] In this instance Bahā' al-Dīn acknowledges the vigorous defense put forward by the Crusaders and its effectiveness, but appears unmoved by the dedication of the enemy in literally rallying around the flag. Beyond details such as those contained in this example, specific information relating to Crusader tactics are generally relayed in a straightforward manner and without comment from the writer. Beyond the pull of their sympathy for the Muslim cause, it is perhaps a reflection of the level of performance by the Crusaders in combat, in conjunction with the pervasive stereotypes regarding Frankish barbarism, that the Muslim historians generally recount feats of heroism performed by Frankish warriors without comment.

However, there are always exceptions, and in certain instances the behavior of the Crusaders in battle does excite the admiration of the chroniclers. At one point in his account, Bahā' al-Dīn describes the discipline of the Frankish foot-soldiers during a march south of Caesarea, during which they came under attack from Muslim archers:

> Their troops continued to advance in the order we have just described, all the while maintaining a steady fight. The Moslems discharged arrows at them from all sides to annoy them, and force them to charge; but in this they were unsuccessful. These men exercised wonderful self-control; they went on their way without any hurry, whilst their ships followed their line of march along the coast, and in this manner they reached their halting place.[78]

Bahā' al-Dīn continues, praising in emphatic terms the foot-soldiers charged with carrying the baggage and tents due to the general lack of pack animals[79] during this march from Acre to Ascalon: "One cannot help admiring the patience displayed by these people, who bore the most wearing fatigue without having any participation in the management of affairs, or deriving any personal advantage."[80] Such a display of patience among the rank-and-file of the enemy, even in the midst of a skirmish, elicits praise even from the qadi of Salāh al-Dīn's army. Plaudits of this sort for displays of valor by the enemy were, although rare, not unknown within the Muslim sources.

Among the Crusaders' rank-and-file, two groups stood out for both the Muslim soldiers and historians: the knights of the military/religious orders of the Hospitallers and the Templars.[81] These orders are not consistently identified by the writers as performing singular acts on the field of battle, but rather are acknowledged implicitly in the Muslim sources for their overall impact within the context of the larger struggle. One such example of this type of recognition within the sources is found in ʻImād al-Dīn's account of Salāh al-Dīn's treatment of the captured Templars and Hospitallers after the victory at the Battle of Hattīn. In this account, Salāh al-Dīn acknowledges the type of threat posed by the knights of these two orders by allotting a singularly harsh fate for them, setting aside his practice of treating prisoners in a humane manner for which he had become famous:

> On the morning of Monday . . . two days after the victory, the Sultan sought out the Templars and Hospitallers who had been captured and said: "I shall purify the land of these two impure races." He assigned fifty *dinar* to every man who had taken one of them prisoner, and

immediately the army brought forth at least a hundred of them. He ordered that they should be beheaded, choosing to have them dead rather than in prison.[82]

Perhaps the greatest tribute bestowed upon the members of either of the two orders comes in an indirect manner, from the thirteenth-century chronicler Ibn Wasil's account of the complete rout of the Crusaders near Damietta in April 1250.[83] In this excerpt, the compliment comes via a reference to a company of Muslim soldiers and their exploits on the field of battle:

> As Wednesday dawned the Muslims had surrounded the Franks and were slaughtering them, dealing out death and captivity. Not one escaped. It is said that the dead numbered 30,000. In the battle the Bahrite mamlūks[84] of al-Malik as-Salih distinguished themselves by their courage and audacity: they caused the Franks terrible losses and played the major part in the victory. They fought furiously: it was they who flung themselves into the pursuit of the enemy: *they were Islām's Templars.*[85]

For Ibn Wasil, the comparison of this group of mamlūk soldiers to the Templars is indicative of the feats of heroism they accomplished on the battlefield; it is perhaps the most poignant illustration of the level of respect accorded the Templars and Hospitallers in the Muslim sources for the courage and skill displayed by the knights of these orders, even among a people renowned for their courage and martial prowess.

Even amongst the accounts of military encounters, political maneuvering, or cultural and religious "oddities," certain instances stand apart for the way in which they bring the human aspect of the Crusades into focus. A particularly noteworthy Muslim account in which the common humanity of both groups becomes manifest occurs under an unlikely set of circumstances. The writer in question is Bahā' al-Dīn, and the occasion occurs during the early stages of the protracted Crusader siege of Acre (which ended with the capitulation of the city on July 12, 1191):[86]

> The soldiers of both sides grew so accustomed to meeting that sometimes a Moslem and a Frank would leave off fighting in order to have a conversation; sometimes the two parties would mingle together, singing and dancing, so intimate had they become, and afterwards they would begin fighting again. One day, wearying of this constant warfare, the soldiers of both sides said to one another: "How long are the men to fight without allowing the boys their share in the pleasure? Let us arrange a fight between two parties of young fellows, the one from your side, the other from ours." Boys were fetched from the city to contend with the Frankish youths ... This is a strange occurrence such as seldom happens.[87]

Given the protracted nature of the siege, and the suffering it caused in both the Muslim and Christian camps, it is remarkable that such an example of mutual recognition of a shared humanity could be found. It is perhaps equally remarkable that the writer in question, who was emotionally invested in the Counter-Crusade, and who had actually composed a treatise on the proper prosecution of Holy War,[88] deemed this set of incidents to be worthy of inclusion in a biography of Salāh al-Dīn, one of the greatest heroes of the Muslim Counter-Crusade.

Accounts of battles and skirmishes comprise the greater part of the Muslim chronicles of the Crusade; however, the individual Crusader and his behavior on the battlefield appear not to have been subjects of interest for the writers. This lack of interest may be traceable in part to the conception of Franks as innately courageous and fierce in battle. More likely, it reflects a bias on the part of the Muslim historians; like their Christian counterparts, they may have sought to minimize the specific accomplishments and successes of the enemy in favor of Muslim achievements on the battlefield. In this case, it would have been sufficient to acknowledge the enemy as being proficient in battle, without exciting any unwanted admiration for them through specific examples. Most likely, the reason for this lack of attention to these areas was a combination of the aforementioned reasons, in conjunction with the desire of the writers to present their audiences with a narrative of Muslim triumph over a formidable opponent. Since this narrative was often inextricably linked to the success of an individual ruler (to whom the writer in question was connected), it was not in the interests of the writer to narrate the exploits of the enemy. Rather, the enemy was to be defeated (to the extent that the historical reality made this possible), and while he may have shared the stage with the Muslim protagonists as a matter of historical fact, he remained the unquestioned villain.

When the Western European forces of the First Crusade arrived in the Levant in 1097, they unwittingly became a part of a wholly new cultural, military, and political landscape. However, the Crusades were not solely a Western European experience. For the peoples of the Levant and the surrounding area, the sudden appearance of armed forces from the Latin West was both an unexpected and devastating turn of events. Levantines, regardless of religious or political affiliation, were faced with the prospect of having to accommodate a new presence on the Syrian coast that differed in terms of culture, language, and to varying degrees, faith. While the adjustment was difficult for the indigenous Christians of the Levant, as well as for the Armenian and Byzantine Christians of the neighboring areas, it was particularly demanding for the Levantine Muslims, who had occupied a position of religious and cultural prominence in the region. Their situation was exacerbated by the fact that as Muslims, they were the primary targets for the Crusaders, and felt the largest measure of the Crusaders' aggression.

As both the indigenous Levantine Muslims and their Turkish sovereigns resisted the Crusaders unsuccessfully during the First Crusade, adapted to the reality of a Western presence in the Levant, and then embarked upon the counter-offensive which would eventually result in the demise of the Crusader States, their experiences were recorded in the annals of Muslim history by some of the greatest historians of the twelfth through the fourteenth centuries. In the course of their accounts, these writers reveal a Muslim perspective of their new Christian European neighbors and adversaries that is reminiscent of the outlook of their Western, Christian counterparts, in that the accounts display religious, racial, and cultural prejudice, appearing to revel in it on occasion. Like their Christian counterparts, the Muslim chroniclers were confident of the sanctity of their endeavor in the eyes of God, and of the depravity of the enemy. Drawing on preexisting stereotypes of Western Europeans, writers presented accounts of Crusader actions both on and off the field of battle that played upon and reinforced popular local preconceptions of Franks and Frankish society in general. Even aspects of Frankish behavior that the writers find praiseworthy, such as courage in battle and religious fervor, are eventually recast to their detriment in the course of the narratives. The martial prowess of the Franks is explained as being instinctual rather than heroic, while the religious fervor of the Crusaders is portrayed in a manner that suggests that the Franks have a crude, simplistic understanding of their religion. In many ways, the Muslim accounts of the Crusades are eerily reminiscent of the Western Christian accounts, as they are similar in focus, language, and tone, differing only to the extent that the respective writers champion opposing sides in the conflict.

What does distinguish the Muslim historians' accounts is the detailed picture they present of the military and political scene in the Levant, and in the Eastern Mediterranean world beyond the Crusader-Muslim conflict. For the Christian writers, the Crusade is the story; for their Muslim counterparts, it is but one aspect of the military and political history of the individual, dynasty, or area to whom or to which each writer is attached. As such, while Muslim unity against the Franks is a necessity for the individual historians, this concept becomes more of an abstraction for the Muslim leaders, who appear to devote more energy toward consolidating power at the expense of their coreligionists than in combating the Franks, whom they are as apt to receive as allies as they are to encounter on the battlefield.

In the end, the message of the Muslim sources is that the initial failure of the Muslims in repulsing the Crusaders and the reason for the continued existence of the Crusader States was the result of the reluctance of Muslim leaders to privilege the collective good of the Levantine Muslims over their individual ambitions. For the Muslim historians, the leaders who are devoted to the expulsion of the Crusaders are few and far between, and are often limited in the undertaking by resistance on the part of their coreligionists and by dynastic concerns, while the majority of the Muslim rulers are not concerned with the Frankish presence in the Levant. This cynicism on the part of many of the Muslim sovereigns would be justified to an extent by the events of the twelfth century, when on several separate occasions the

"Syrian" Franks placed their own local ambitions above the collective interests of their coreligionists from continental Europe during the Second and Third Crusades, frustrating the larger objectives of the Crusades as a whole in the process. However, the internal strife within the Crusader camp was not of particular interest to the Muslim chroniclers, except for the opportunities it presented to reabsorb the individual Crusader states into the Muslim Levant.

In their concern with the prosecution of the Counter-Crusade, their emotional and ideological investment in the conflict, and their disgust with the fragmentation and political maneuvering amongst the Muslims, the Muslim chroniclers echo the concerns of their Christian counterparts. In both the Christian European and Muslim chronicles of the Crusades, the reader is presented with partisan narratives that betray a cultural and religious bias, exaggerating victories and minimizing defeats at every opportunity. However, despite their shortcomings, these accounts present a realistic representation of the Crusades as they were experienced, and perhaps more importantly, as they were perceived by individuals who either participated in the conflict, or were in some way affected by it. And in that, the chronicles of the Crusades, both Christian and Muslim, are invaluable.

Notes

1 Lack of unity was perhaps the key contributing factor to the continued existence of the Crusader States during the twelfth and thirteenth centuries. The provincial Turkish rulers in the surrounding areas of the Levant jealously guarded their individual kingdoms from their more powerful Muslim neighbors in the East, to the great consternation of their subjects. It was not until the emergence of the atabeg 'Imād al-Dīn Zangi in the mid-twelfth century that the Muslims of the Levant would begin to unite (a process that was continued under his son Nūr al-Dīn, and largely completed by Salāh al-Dīn). This unity would mark a decisive and inexorable shift in the fortunes of the Latin Kingdom of Jerusalem, which would be put on the defensive until 1291, when the last European outposts in the Levant were reabsorbed into the Muslim Levant, and the European military presence in the area was brought to an end.
2 The years 1092–4 were tragic for the Muslim world, as it suffered the deaths of some of its most capable rulers and leaders from Egypt to the eastern reaches. In 1092, the vizier, and effective ruler of the Seljuq Turk Empire, Nizam al-Mulk, was murdered; this was followed by the death of the third Seljuq sultan, Malik-Shāh, one month later. 1094 saw the deaths of the Fatimid Caliph al-Mustansir, who had been in power for fifty-eight years, and of his vizier, Badr al-Jamali, who, among his many accomplishments, had designed and overseen the construction of the wall of Cairo. This year also witnessed the death of the 'Abbāsid Caliph al-Muqtadi. P.M. Holt, *The Age of the Crusades* (London: Longman, 1986) 10–15.
3 The Seljuq Turks of the Levant were Sunni Muslims, and ostensibly ruled under the authority of the 'Abbāsid caliph in Baghdad. In fact, the caliph was powerless to exert any real control over his dominions in the Levant; however, the Turkish rulers of the Levant were fearful that their brethren in Baghdad, who were the *de facto* rulers of the 'Abbāsid Empire, would look to take substantive control of

Syria. The Fatimid caliph was based in Cairo, and as a Shi'ite, was opposed to the 'Abbāsid caliph as well as the Seljuq Turks, who were their closest neighbors. These ideological, military, and political fault lines between the Muslim groups in the area made the possibility of unified action against the Crusaders unlikely. Carole Hillenbrand, *The Crusades: Islamic Perspectives* (New York: Routledge, 1999) 33, 36.
4 Peter Lock, *The Routledge Companion to the Crusades* (London: Routledge, 2006) 21.
5 Ibn al-Athīr, 'Izz al-Dīn and Carl Johan Tornberg, *The Chronicle of Ibn al-Athīr for the Crusading Period from al-Kāmil- fī'l ta'rīkh, Part 1, the Years 491–541/1097–1146: The Coming of the Franks and the Muslim Response*, Trans. D.S. Richards (Burlington: Ashgate, 2006) 14.
6 Andrew Jotischky, *Crusading and the Crusader States* (London: Pearson Education Limited, 2004) ix.
7 Hillenbrand, *The Crusades*, 82.
8 Ibid.
9 Muslim historians of the period closest to the First Crusade tended to blame Fatimid Egypt for what was perceived as a lackluster response. In fact, some historians went so far as to suggest that the Fatimids wanted a buffer between themselves and the neighboring Seljuqs, with whom they were locked in a fierce territorial struggle, and that the appearance of the Crusaders met this need. In his account of the First Crusade, Ibn al-'Athīr says of the Fatimid response,

> It has been said that the Alid rulers of Egypt [the Fatimids] became fearful when they saw the strength and power of the Saljuq state, that it had gained control of Syrian lands as far as Gaza, leaving no buffer state between the Saljuqs and Egypt to protect them . . . They therefore sent to the Franks to invite them to invade Syria, to conquer it and separate them and the [other] Muslims, but God knows best.
> (Ibn al-Athīr, 'Izz al-Dīn and Tornberg, *The Chronicle of Ibn al-Athīr for the Crusading Period from al-Kāmil-fī'l ta'rīkh, Part 1*, 13–14)

10 One such direct call to action is recounted by Ibn al-Qalānisī, who writes of the actions of a group of refugees from Aleppo while in Baghdad, and the subsequent actions of the Sultan (Ghiyāth al-Dunyā wa-Dīn Muhammad; son of the renowned Malik-Shāh):

> On the first Friday of Sha'bān (17th February, 1111) a certain Hāshimite sharīf from Aleppo and a company of Sūfīs, merchants and theologians presented themselves at the Sultan's mosque, and appealed for assistance. They drove the preacher from the pulpit and broke it in pieces, clamouring and weeping for the misfortunes that had befallen Islām at the hands of the Franks, the slaughter of men, and the enslavement of women and children. They prevented the people from carrying out the service, while the attendants and leaders, to quieten them, promised them on behalf of the Sultan to dispatch armies and to vindicate Islām against the Franks and the infidels. On the following Friday they assembled again, went to the Caliph's mosque, and repeated their performance with much weeping and clamour and appealing for help, and lamenting. Shortly afterwards the princess, the Sultan's daughter and wife of the Caliph, arrived at Baghdād from Isfahān, in such magnificence and with such quantities of jewellry, moneys, utensils, carriages and riding beasts of all kinds, furniture, varieties of gorgeous raiment, attendants, guards, slave-girls, and followers, as exceeds all reckoning. Her arrival coincided with these appeals for assistance, and the tranquility of

the city and the joy at her coming were marred and disturbed. The Caliph, al-Mustazhir B'illāh, Commander of the Faithful, was indignant at what had happened, and determined to seek out him who had been its instigator and cause, in order to mete out to him condign punishment. The Sultan prevented him from doing so, and excused the action of those people, and directed the amīrs and commanders to return to their governments and make preparations for setting out to the Holy War against the infidels, the enemies of God.

H.A.R. Gibb, *The Damascus Chronicle of the Crusades: Extracted and Translated from the Chronicle of Ibn al-Qalānisī* (London: Luzac & Co., 1932) 110, 111–12.

11 On one occasion, the Seljuq prince of Aleppo, Ridwān, went so far as to shut the gates of the city to the gathered Seljuq forces from the East (Hillenbrand, *The Crusades*, 115). Another reason for the failure of the undertakings was the fact that they were not, in fact, a high priority for the most powerful Seljuq sultan of the period of the First Crusade, Muhammad, who chose not to accompany his forces to Syria on any of the occasions in which they were sent to help their fellow Muslims. Such a display would have demonstrated a real dedication on his part, and might have provided the type of effective leadership needed for a successful military intervention (Ibid, 80–1).

12 Hans Eberhard Mayer, *The Crusades*, 2nd ed., Trans. John Gillingham (Oxford: Oxford UP, 1988) 68.

13 Nadia Maria El-Cheikh, "Byzantium Through the Islamic Prism from the Twelfth to the Thirteenth Century," *The Crusades from the Perspective of Byzantium and the Muslim World*, Eds Angeliki E. Laiou and Roy Parviz Mottahedeh (Washington, DC: Dumbarton Oaks, 2001) 53.

14 Gibb, *The Damascus Chronicle of the Crusades*, 43.

15 The chroniclers are referred to as "Muslim" rather than "Arab" because, like the local Seljuq rulers in the Levant, many of them were not Arab. Francesco Gabrieli, *Arab Historians of the Crusades*, Trans. E.J. Costello (Berkeley: U of California P, 1969) xiv.

16 El-Cheikh, *The Crusades from the Perspective*, 56.

17 Hillenbrand, *The Crusades*, 50, 286–8.

18 Jonathan Riley-Smith, *The Crusades: A History*, 2nd ed. (New Haven: Yale UP, 2005) 2.

19 Hillenbrand, *The Crusades*, 51–4.

20 Ibn al-Athīr, 'Izz al-Dīn and Carl Johan Tornberg, *al-Kāmil fī al-tārīkh* (Báyrūt: Dar Sáder, 1965). See also *The Chronicle of Ibn al-Athīr for the Crusading Period from al-Kāmil- fī'l ta'rīkh, Part 1*, vii.

21 Ibn al-Athīr, 'Izz al-Dīn and Tornberg, *The Chronicle of Ibn al-Athīr, Part 1*, 13. "Ifrīqiya" refers to the eastern portion of Morocco (n. 3).

22 El-Cheikh, *The Crusades from the Perspective*, 56.

23 One of the most famous examples is that of Richard I, who, according to Ambroise, was criticized for being on too familiar of terms with members of Salāh al-Dīn's court. Ambroise, *Estoire*, ll. 7,429–43.

24 Gabrieli, *Arab Historians of the Crusades*, xxviii. While the citizenry and the lower levels of local leadership were largely composed of Syrian Arabs, the leadership of the Muslim Counter-Crusade was Turkish, with the exception of Salāh al-Dīn and the Ayyubid dynasty he founded, which was Kurdish.

25 Usāmah ibn Munqidh, *An Arab-Syrian Gentleman and Warrior in The Period of The Crusades: Memoirs of Usāmah ibn Munqidh (Kitāb al-i'tibār)*, Trans. Phillip K. Hitti (New York: Columbia UP, 1929) 3. This work will henceforward be referred to as the *Memoirs of Usāmah ibn Munqidh*.

168 Western Europeans in the Crusades

26 ibn Munqidh, *Memoirs of Usāmah ibn Munqidh*, 12.
27 Gabrieli, *Arab Historians of the Crusades*, xxviii.
28 ibn Munqidh, *Memoirs of Usāmah ibn Munqidh*, 16. Further references to this account will appear parenthetically in the text.
29 Hillenbrand, *The Crusades*, 348.
30 Ibid.
31 Paneas.
32 Fulk V, the count of Anjou. ibn Munqidh, *Memoirs of Usāmah ibn Munqidh*, 93.
33 "If the knight is thin and tall the Franks admire him more." ibn Munqidh, *Memoirs of Usāmah ibn Munqidh*, 94.
34 Fulk of Anjou, who by this time had been installed as king of Jerusalem. He ruled from 1131–42. Ibid, 167.
35 The physical contest is described in these terms: "They went on exchanging blows until they looked like pillars smeared with blood." Ibid, 168.
36 The ruler of Jerusalem (1142–1162). Ibid, 60.
37 Damietta.
38 Usāmah relates the following story, courtesy of a bath-keeper named Sālim:

> I once opened a bath in al-Ma'rrah [al-Nu'mān, between Aleppo and Hamāh] in order to earn a living. To this bath there came a Frankish knight. The Franks disapprove of girdeing a cover around one's waist while in the bath. So this Frank stretched out his arm and pulled off my cover from my waist and threw it away. He looked and saw that I had recently shaved off my pubes. So he shouted, "Sālim!" As I drew near him he stretched his hand over my pubes and said, "Sālim, good! By the truth of my religion, do the same for me." Saying this, he lay on his back and I found that in that place the hair was like his beard. So I shaved it off. Then he passed his hand over the place and, finding it smooth, he said, "Sālim, by the truth of my religion, do the same to madame" . . . referring to his wife. He then said to a servant of his, "Tell madame to come here." Accordingly the servant went and brought her and made her enter the bath. She also lay on her back. The knight repeated, "Do what thou hast done to me." So I shaved all that hair while her husband was sitting looking at me. At last he thanked me and handed me the pay for my service.
>
> (Ibid, 165–6)

39 Gabrieli, *Arab Historians of the Crusades*, xxix.
40 There is also a description of Frankish women who participated in some of the battles, disguising themselves as men, in a later portion of the passage. While 'Imād al-Dīn seems surprised by this, the phenomenon of women's occasional participation in military encounters was not exclusive to the Crusaders, as Usāmah ibn Munqidh himself relates several instances of Muslim women participating in battles. ibn Munqidh, *Memoirs of Usāmah ibn Munqidh*, 153–9. Moreover, there is a tradition in the Arabian epics, or *sīra*, of heroic women who distinguished themselves in battle.
41 Gabrieli, *Arab Historians of the Crusades*, 204–5.
42 Ibid, xxx.
43 Tiberias.
44 Hillenbrand, *The Crusades*, 350.
45 However, in the case of the "Assassins," politics, and the politically motivated assassinations for which they were famous, played a more important role.
46 Consider Ibn al-'Athīr's account of the Byzantine emperor's demands upon the soldiers of the First Crusade upon their arrival in Constantinople, and the motives ascribed to them:

After they had decided to march to Syria, they went to Constantinople to cross the straits into Muslim lands, to travel by land, for that would be easier for them. When they arrived, the Byzantine emperor refused them passage through his territory. He said, 'I will not allow you to cross into the lands of Islam until you swear to me that you will surrender Antioch to me.' His aim was to urge them to move into Islamic lands, assuming that Turks would not spare a single one of them, because he had seen how fierce they were and their control of the lands.

(Ibn al-Athīr, 'Izz al-Dīn and Tornberg, *The Chronicle of Ibn al-Athīr for the Crusading Period from al-Kāmil-fī'l-ta'rīkh, Part 1*, 14)

47 There were other instances of Western European and Byzantine Christians living in close proximity prior to and during the period of the Crusades (particularly in southern Italy and Sicily); however, this was the first time that such a large contingent of armed forces from Western Europe was stationed close to the heart of the Byzantine Empire for an extended period of time.

48 A generation before the arrival of the Crusaders (1071), Alp Arslān had led the Seljuq Turks to victory over the Byzantines in the battle of Manzikert, which initiated the gradual process by which Turks from the eastern portion of the Seljuq empire began settling on Byzantine and Armenian territory. However, the Byzantines were not resigned to this eventuality, and continued to be a military presence in the Levant, with the objective of reclaiming the lost territory. Johnathan Riley-Smith, *The Crusades: A History*, 2nd ed. (New Haven: Yale UP, 2005) 2.

49 Hillenbrand, *The Crusades*, 304–5.

50 Ibn al-Athīr, *The Chronicle of Ibn al-Athīr for the Crusading Period from al-Kāmil- fī'l ta'rīkh, Part 2, The Years 541–589/1146–1193: The Age of Nur al-Din and Saladin*, Trans. D.S. Richards (Burlington: Ashgate, 2007) 334.

51 Gabrieli, *Arab Historians of the Crusades*, 136–7.

52 These hostages were later executed at the command of Richard I, and would become both a blemish on the record of the English king's actions in the Levant, and a pretext for the Mamlūk Sultan al-Ashraf's execution of his Christian hostages after the fall of Acre in 1291.

53 In Arabic, the word *qiyāma* signifies "resurrection" and the word *kanīsa* signifies "church"; the Church of the Resurrection/ Holy Sepulcher was referred to as *Kanīsat al-Qiyāma* by the indigenous Christians of the area. In Arabic the word *qumāma*, which is very similar in form, signifies "garbage" or "refuse." Hence, a way in which to belittle Christians for some Muslims was to refer to the Church of the Holy Sepulcher (*Kanīsat al-Qiyāma*) as the "Church of Refuse" (*Kanīsat al-Qumāma*). Cf. Gabrieli, *Arab Historians of the Crusades*, 148, n.1; and also *The Hans Wehr Dictionary of Modern Written Arabic*, s.v. *qumāma, qiyāma, kanīsa* (pp. 923, 936, and 987).

54 Gabrieli, *Arab Historians of the Crusades*, 148.

55 Both Ibn al-'Athīr and 'Imād al-Dīn provide examples of this desperation on the part of the Crusaders in their accounts of the negotiations between the Crusaders and Muslims leading up to the surrender of the city. In one instance, Ibn al-'Athīr records that at one point during the negotiations for the surrender of Jerusalem to Salāh al-Dīn, Balian II of Ibelin became convinced that the Muslim forces would show no mercy to the Franks after the fall of the city. He gives voice to this concern in a speech attributed to him in Ibn al-'Athīr's account:

> O sultan, understand that in this city we are a great host that God alone can comprehend. They are tempering their fighting merely in the hope of terms, thinking that you will grant terms to them as you have to others. They shun

death and desire life. However, if they see that death is inevitable, by God we will slay our sons and women, burn our property and goods and not leave you to benefit from it by a single dinar or dirham, nor take captive a single man or woman. When we have finished that, we shall destroy the Dome of the Rock, the Aqsa Mosque and other sites and then kill the Muslim prisoners we have, 5,000 in number. We shall not leave for you any mount or animal without killing it. Then we shall come forth, all of us, against you and fight you like desperate men fighting for their lives. Not one of us will be killed at that time until he kills many more of you. We shall die nobly or win victory gloriously.

(Ibn al-Athīr, *The Chronicle of Ibn al-Athīr for the Crusading Period from al-Kāmil-fī'l ta'rīkh*, Part 2, 332)

See also Gabrieli, *Arab Historians of the Crusades*, 141–2; 156–7.
56 Gabrieli, *Arab Historians of the Crusades*, 174–5.
57 Ibn al-Athīr, 'Izz al-Dīn and Tornberg, *The Chronicle of Ibn al-Athīr for the Crusading Period from al Kāmil fī'l-ta'rīkh*, Part 1, 16–17, n. 24. Of course, Muslim chroniclers were as likely to attribute a defeat to ineptitude on the part of the Muslim leaders.
58 The popular concept of *jihad* was (and remains) that of armed struggle, primarily, but not exclusively, against a non-Muslim enemy. The other form of *jihad* – what is termed the Greater *Jihad* – is waged against one's baser desires.
59 Bahā' al-Dīn, *al-Nawādir al-sultānīyah wa-al-mahāsin al-yūsufīyah, aw Sīrat Salāh al-Dīn* (al-Qāhirah: al-Mu'assasah al-Misrīyah al-'Ammah, 1964). Translation provided in *Saladin or What Befell Sultan Yūsuf* (Lahore: Islamic Book Service, 1988) 116.
60 The term "qadi" is generally translated as "judge;" however, during this time, religious questions and/or disputes would also have fallen under the jurisdiction of the qadi as well. *The Hans Wehr Dictionary of Modern Written Arabic*, qadi, 904. For Bahā' al-Dīn's service to Salāh al-Dīn, see Gabrieli, *Arab Historians of the Crusades*, xxix.
61 Bahā' al-Dīn, *What Befell Sultan Yūsuf*, 116.
62 Ibid, 223. The "besiegers" in question are the Crusaders who were engaged in a siege of Acre.
63 Both Bahā' al-Dīn and Ambroise mention defections from the Crusader camp due to hunger. Ambroise writes:

Those who remained with the army endured much hardship. No-one can tell you how their sufferings grew, how they endured and suffered during the siege from the time of their arrival. Hear how great is the loss and waste, how great the harm and shame, when a man, whom God made in his own image, denies God because of his misery. In the army the shortage of all kinds of food was so great that many of our people went to the Turks and turned renegade. They denied that God did or could deign to be born of woman; they denied the Cross and baptism – everything.

(*Estoire*, ll. 4,309–26)

Bahā' al-Dīn writes that although the crusaders' resolve was initially strong in the face of the famine, eventually the lack of food began to take its toll: "Nevertheless, the uncertainty of their position and their sufferings from want of food, which grew worse from day to day, caused a great many to desert to us, so as to escape the pangs of hunger." Bahā' al-Dīn, *What Befell Sultan Yūsuf*, 223.

64 Gabrieli, *Arab Historians of the Crusades*, xxx.
65 Ibid, 214–15.
66 M.C. Seymour (Ed.), *Mandeville's Travels* (Oxford: Clarendon, 1967) 100–1.
67 In particular, Ambroise is scathing in his criticism of the Crusaders' lack of unity during the Third Crusade, calling to mind the state of affairs during many of the most notable alliances amongst great leaders during times of war in bygone days of glory, real and fictitious. Cf. Ambroise's critique in Chapter 6.
68 Gabrieli, *Arab Historians of the Crusades*, 147.
69 Ousāma ibn Mounkidh, *The Autobiography of Ousāma*, Trans. George Richard Potter (New York: Harcourt, Brace and Company, 1929) 294.
70 ibn Munqidh, *Memoirs of Usāmah ibn Munqidh*, 164.
71 Jonathan Phillips, *Holy Warriors: A Modern History of the Crusades* (London: Bodley Head, 2009) 19. 17, n. 24.
72 Ibn al-Athīr, 'Izz al-Dīn and Tornberg, *The Chronicle of Ibn al-Athīr for the Crusading Period from al Kāmil fī'l-ta'rīkh, Part 1*, 16–17.
73 Ibn al-'Athīr was not alone in his skepticism, nor was this skepticism exclusive to the Muslim historians. While Peter Bartholomew enjoyed great popularity amongst the rank-and-file of the crusader contingent as a result of the discovery of the Lance and the subsequent crusader victory, his popularity began to wane as his behavior became more erratic. When he began to question the integrity of the soldiers, his fate was sealed. Arnulf of Choques, the chaplain for Robert of Normandy, gave voice to the doubts that many had privately harbored, challenging Peter's visions, including that of the Lance. Peter volunteered to undergo an ordeal by fire. While his supporters and detractors offered different accounts of the nature and origins of the injuries he suffered (his supporters asserted they were the result of the riotous behavior of a jubilant crowd; his detractors maintained that he failed the ordeal), Peter Bartholomew died as a result of the injuries within two weeks of the ordeal. His death dealt a serious blow to belief in the miracle of the Lance among crusaders. Thomas Asbridge, *The First Crusade: A New History* (Oxford: Oxford UP, 2004) 289–92.
74 Gabrieli, *Arab Historians of the Crusades*, xxxii.
75 Ibid, 62–3.
76 Bahā' al-Dīn, *What Befell Sultan Yūsuf*, 226.
77 Ibid, 227.
78 Ibid, 283.
79 Ibid.
80 Ibid.
81 Hillenbrand, *The Crusades*, 334.
82 Gabrieli, *Arab Historians of the Crusades*, 138.
83 Gabrieli, *Arab Historians of the Crusades*, 293. For Ibn Wasil, Ibid, xxxi.
84 Mamlūks were non-African slave-soldiers, generally from Central Asia or Europe, employed by the various rulers of the Eastern Mediterranean. In this instance, the designation "Bahrite" refers to a specific corps of mamlūks. See also *The Hans Wehr Dictionary of Modern Written Arabic*, mamlūk, 1083.
85 Gabrieli, *Arab Historians of the Crusades*, 294. Emphasis added.
86 Ibid, 222.
87 Bahā' al-Dīn, *What Befell Sultan Yūsuf*, 161–2.
88 Ibid, 24.

8 A familiar enemy
Salāh al-Dīn and Richard I in enemy sources

In analyses of medieval Near Eastern Muslim and Western European Christian representations of one another, it is often the grotesque and farcical – the caricatures – that attract the most attention. The inherent appeal of "shock value" in depictions of the Other was an idea that resonated with medieval audiences (as it does for audiences today); the Saracen monsters of the romances and the bizarre creatures that populated Near Eastern *ajā'ib* literature speak powerfully to this fact.[1] These generic characters and storylines are particularly effective in filling in the gaps where real information about an event or individual is lacking; in Western accounts of the crusades many of the speeches attributed to Muslim leaders mirror those of the Saracen kings of the romances in belligerence and bombast. This is indicative of the ways in which both genres, the romances and the accounts, informed one another; equally, it speaks to the fact that chroniclers recognized the need to entertain their audiences, and were not content with merely presenting the facts.[2] However, whereas such characters roam freely through the landscape of the romances and *ajā'ib* literature, their appearance in Western European and Near Eastern accounts is constrained by the exigencies of the texts, providing a face with which audiences are familiar in the absence of information, or simply to embellish an otherwise uninspiring sequence of events within the narrative.

The nebulous boundaries between fictional and historical accounts, between caricature and analysis, change with the emergence of historical figures of note from among the enemy.[3] This is particularly true of Western European chroniclers writing of subsequent crusades; as the fervor that accompanied the First Crusade and its spectacular successes waned, writers assumed a more dispassionate, objective stance toward the events and participants.[4] One of the unexpected results of this stance is that in that many of the Western accounts, the Muslims recede into the background as villains. They remain the principal villains due to the nature and objectives of the crusades; however, Christian "villains" also emerge, and are often the targets of the writers' most pointed criticism.[5] As the *de jure* enemy, Muslims and Muslim leaders are the targets of semi-formulaic expressions of opprobrium related to their status as hostile non-Christians; but as the *de facto* enemies of individual crusaders through political and military rivalries in Europe and the Levant, it is other Christian crusaders of note who are often the victims of faint praise and scathing criticism at the hands of the Western chroniclers, who remain vigilant regarding their patron's reputation as a crusader.

In analyzing medieval Christian and Muslim accounts of the crusades, one is left with the impression that the crusades were more noteworthy for the Latin West than for the Muslim Near East. This apparent lack of interest on the part of medieval Muslim historians has been variously interpreted as either indicative of a more cosmopolitan perspective, in which the activities of a new group in the Levant is deemed unworthy of undue attention, or of the myopic perspective of a stagnant civilization lacking curiosity about the outside world. Both interpretations fail to acknowledge crucial aspects of the political situation in the Levant, and the Muslim Near East as a whole, that contributed to the apparent disinterest of Muslim chroniclers, particularly in the first years of the crusades.

The very nature of the First Crusade – a religiously inspired conflict – was not immediately apparent to Muslim historians. This singular aspect, acknowledged from the outset by Western, Christian historians, which connected four years of political and military activity in the Latin West and the Levant (including preaching of the crusade, recruitment, organizing, travel, and military engagement), was unknown to Muslim contemporaries of the First Crusade, who lacked the information necessary to distinguish it from other past and present Muslim–Christian conflicts in Sicily, Spain, North Africa, and the Near East. This difference in perspective explains the fact that the first Western Christian crusade account, the *Gesta Francorum*, emerged within a few years of the conclusion of the First Crusade,[6] whereas the first Muslim references to the crusades as a phenomenon did not appear for several decades. For Muslim contemporaries of the crusades, the story of a crusade often began with the arrival of Western European forces in the Levant (or, after the Third Crusade, in Egypt).

Muslim historians were also distracted by the local political situation in the decades in and around the First Crusade, which was marked by instability. The type of cohesion that enabled such a disparate coalition of nobles, soldiers, clerics, and ordinary men and women to travel from Western Europe to the Levant was not to be found in the Muslim Near East, which had recently lost its most capable leaders,[7] and was now saddled with individuals unequal to the task of working in concert to preserve its territorial integrity. Like their Christian counterparts, Muslim historians were aligned with powerful individuals and dynasties, but until the emergence of 'Imād al-Dīn Zangi in the mid-twelfth century, the Levant lacked a powerful Muslim leader worthy of their attention as a hero (and patron).

When Muslim chroniclers recognized the crusades as a unique phenomenon, and the crusaders as a distinct entity in the region, they approached the historical and political reality of the crusaders in earnest. For the masses of

Western European men and women, the chroniclers employed a formula not unlike that of their Christian counterparts: a mixture of caricature and demonization. Individual crusaders of note, particularly leaders, were evaluated based on their military and political successes. In Muslim accounts, the amount of attention paid to an individual crusader is a reflection of the degree to which he was able to distinguish himself in a political landscape that included Sunni and Shi'ite Muslims, and Byzantine, Armenian, and indigenous Levantine Christians, a landscape in which internal strife was common, and religious or ethnic affiliation was not a reliable predictor of military or political alliances.

Among the many noteworthy individuals, Crusader and Muslim, no two figures captured the imagination of medieval audiences to a greater extent than did Salāh al-Dīn (Saladin in Western sources) and Richard I. While many heroes emerged – Bohemond of Apulia and Louis IX (Saint Louis) among the crusaders; Nūr al-Dīn and Baibars among the Muslims, to name but a few – Salāh al-Dīn and Richard I are distinguished by their status amongst writers hostile to their cause. Both were acknowledged as the undisputed leaders of the crusade and counter-crusade by Muslim and Christian chroniclers.[8] Richard I emerged as a historically formidable opponent of the Muslims, and Salāh al-Dīn, whose role in the Muslim recovery of Jerusalem in 1187 led to the establishment of the "Saladin Tithe" in France and England for the financing of the Third Crusade,[9] became an exemplar of chivalry for Christian writers; in later ages he would be transformed into something of a quasi-European.[10]

If Richard and Salāh al-Dīn were brought together by the circumstances of the Third Crusade – the last crusade in which the Levant was the staging ground, and the last crusade in which crusader forces achieved a tangible victory[11] – they were also united by their unique individual circumstances. Salāh al-Dīn, an exemplar of the Muslim *mujahid*[12] and the classical Arab warrior ethos, was not Arab like his Levantine Muslim subjects, nor was he Turkish; he was a Kurd. Richard I, who emerged as the *English* hero of the crusades, and who presented himself as the quintessential *milite Christi*,[13] was not English; during his ten-year reign as king of England perhaps an aggregate year was spent in England.[14]

In a similar manner, the Third Crusade, with which they are inextricably linked, was but a small part of the military and political agenda of both figures. For Salāh al-Dīn, the Third Crusade was an endnote to a stellar career that included the reintegration of Egypt into the Abbāsid Empire and the conquest of much of the Levant, which culminated in the recovery of Jerusalem in 1187, a feat that enshrined him among the preeminent Muslim heroes of the medieval world. Richard, whose later fame as a *roi-chevalier* ("warrior-king") was almost entirely derived from his exploits while on crusade, devoted the majority of his efforts as king to solidifying his holdings in France, ultimately dying on April 6, 1199, from a minor wound incurred during the siege of a renegade castle in Chalus-Chabrol in the area of

Limoges in Aquitane.[15] In life, his greatest enemy was not Salāh al-Dīn, but rather King Philip Augustus of France. Both worked assiduously to cultivate their image as warriors for the Faith. In so doing, they proved prescient beyond their wildest imagination, as this is the image of the two men that has endured, eclipsing the other military and political achievements to which they dedicated so much of their lives.

The image of Richard I that emerges from medieval Muslim accounts of the Third Crusade is that of a redoubtable strategist and warrior, who nevertheless engages in morally reprehensible behavior. In a sense, the Muslim historians' depiction of Richard I is in keeping with the assessment of their Western Christian counterparts who were contemporaries of the English king, and who presented him as an indomitable warrior, but a flawed – at times cruel and duplicitous – man.[16] This tension between Richard I's unparalleled ability as a warrior and his questionable character as a man adds to his status as a threat to the Muslims.

As a leader and warrior, the English king is unmatched in the Muslim accounts. Writing of his arrival in Acre, Bahā' al-Dīn compares Richard I with Philip Augustus in the following terms:

> The king of England was very powerful, very brave, and full of resolution. He had distinguished himself in many a battle, and displayed the greater boldness in all his campaigns. As regards his kingdom and rank, he was inferior to the king of France, but he outstripped him in wealth, in valour, and in fame as a soldier.[17]

In explaining the position of Richard I relative to Philip Augustus (the king of France), Bahā' al-Dīn draws a crucial distinction between the two monarchs, between one who possesses the trappings of power and privilege, and one who has the experience necessary to lead ably and the respect of his peers. Later, the qadi describes the atmosphere of the Crusader camp as one of euphoria subsequent to the arrival of the English king:

> The Franks were filled with so great joy at his arrival that they lit huge and terrible fires that night in their camp – a sure sign of the important support he had brought them. Their leaders had oftentimes boasted to us that he would come, and held his arrival as a menace over our heads; and now, according to the people who frequented their camp, they expected, the very moment he landed, to see him fulfil their dearest wish of pushing forward with the siege of the city.
>
> (p. 249)[18]

What is perhaps most remarkable about this description of the Crusaders' estimation of Richard I is not the degree of confidence they are alleged to have in him, but rather that Bahā' al-Dīn appears to validate their feelings with his characterization of the English king: "This prince indeed was justly distinguished for his good judgment and wide experience, for his extreme daring and insatiable ambition" (p. 249).

Equally surprising is the qadi's description of the Muslims' reaction to the English king's arrival; Bahā' al-Dīn is frank in his admission of the fear Richard's reputation inspired among the rank-and-file of the Muslim forces, revealing that prior to his arrival, both his general standing as a leader and his exploits in Cyprus (which he had conquered en route to Acre) generated a great deal of anxiety in the Muslim camp (p. 248). Upon his arrival, and the subsequent reaction within the Crusader camp, the qadi paints a somber picture of an apprehensive Muslim camp, in which only Salāh al-Dīn remains calm, facing the new challenge with the characteristic aplomb that one comes to expect in reading the Muslim accounts of the Sultan: "when the Moslems heard of his arrival, they were filled with terror and alarm. The Sultan, nevertheless, received the news undisturbed, for he counted upon God's favour and protection, and manifested the purity of his motives in warring against the Franks" (p. 249). From the outset, Richard I is identified as an unprecedented, dangerous new threat to the Muslims, a worthy opponent for Salāh al-Dīn.

Richard's standing as a threat is supported by his military successes, at the expense of Salāh al-Dīn, which the Muslim chroniclers readily acknowledge. The writers' candor about Richard's accomplishments in the Levant, and their impact on Muslim morale, further reinforce his position relative to other crusaders of note. In what is perhaps the most revealing admission of the extent of the English king's dominance over the Muslim forces, Bahā' al-Dīn paints a scene of true desperation as Salāh al-Dīn and his forces await an expected attack on Jerusalem,[19] reminiscent of Western accounts of the Crusaders in Antioch during the First Crusade; both describe leaders and soldiers on the brink of collapse, despairing of their mission, and who readily attribute the subsequent dramatic, positive resolution of the situation to divine intervention. However, unlike Karbughā, Richard's reputation as a warrior emerges unscathed; it is his coreligionists, not the Muslims, who are his ultimate undoing.[20]

In addition to his ability to wage war against the Muslims with great success, Bahā' al-Dīn also portrays Richard I as a shrewd and pragmatic politician, capable of using dissension within the ranks of the Muslims to his advantage. On one occasion, the English king is accused of impeding the negotiations for peace in the spring of 1192 in order to capitalize on the political dispute that had surfaced within Salāh al-Dīn's family, hoping that it would lead to his accepting terms more favorable for the Crusaders (p. 331). On another occasion, the qadi complains of Richard's cunning in attempting to use his projected return to England – an event eagerly anticipated by the Muslims – as leverage in negotiating for a more favorable distribution of land for the Crusaders. In this instance, his emissary is quoted as delivering a cleverly couched ultimatum to the Sultan, which elicits a pointed response from Bahā' al-Dīn:

> "The king begs you to allow him to keep those three places [i.e. Ascalon, Dārūn, and Gaza] as they are, and not to demolish them; of what

importance can they be in the eyes of so powerful a prince? The king is forced to persist in his request by the obstinacy of the Franks, who refuse to consent to their being given up ... Therefore, if you will give him the cities in question, peace can be made on every point ... in this way everything can be settled, and the king will be able to depart. If peace is not concluded, the Franks will not suffer him to go, and he could not withstand them." See the cunning of this accursed man! To obtain his own ends, he would employ first force, and then smooth-speaking; and, although he knew he was obliged to depart, he maintained the same line of conduct. God alone could protect the Moslems against his wiles.

(pp. 358–9)

The qadi is perturbed but impressed by Richard's ability to use his presence in the Levant as a negotiating tool at a time in which his allies and adversaries knew that he was under tremendous pressure to return to England (p. 357). For Bahā' al-Dīn this tactic is detestable for the problems it presents to the Sultan and his agenda, but also the mark of a shrewd negotiator.

The English king also exhibits a remarkable pragmatism in his negotiations for peace; in part, this pragmatism manifests itself in the King's ability to differentiate between things that are valuable to the strategic interests of the crusaders and those which are less important, and is apparent in his stance on a potential assault on Jerusalem, which gradually diminishes in importance during the course of the negotiations (pp. 308; 322–3), until the only crucial item is the question of the Church of the Holy Sepulcher (p. 358). On the other hand, items of strategic value remain the key points of contention throughout the negotiations.[21] Through the course of this account, Richard I distinguishes himself for his ability to privilege practical considerations when negotiating for the distribution of territories, which the qadi grudgingly acknowledges.

This pragmatism is also on display in the qadi's account of the English king's candor in representing his personal interests. At various points in the narrative, Bahā' al-Dīn portrays Richard as being frank about his desire to return to England (due to his concerns over his holdings in England and continental Europe).[22] Shortly after his arrival in Jaffa, Bahā' al-Dīn recalls the King's interest in expediting the peace, which he conveys to the Sultan's envoy in no uncertain terms:

"Greet the Sultan from me, and tell him that I beseech him, in God's name, to grant me the peace I ask at his hands; this state of things must be put a stop to; my own country beyond the sea is being ruined. There is no advantage either to you or me in suffering the present condition of things to continue."

(p. 372)

Later, after having successfully repulsed the Muslim forces from Jaffa, an annoyed Richard I refuses the Sultan's chamberlain entry into the city, expressing both his irritation with Salāh al-Dīn's perceived intransigence and his disappointment over his own frustrated ambitions of returning to England: "How long am I to go on making advances to the Sultan that he will not accept? I was anxious above all things to be able to return to my own country, but now the winter is here, and the rain has begun" (p. 377). Later, in a private conversation with the Sultan's chamberlain in which he proposes what will be the eventual framework for the settlement between the two forces, he reveals both the extent of his personal ambitions in the continuing negotiations, and his personal skepticism about the crusading enterprise, with surprising honesty:

> "Beg *my brother*[23] el-Melek el-'Ādel to consider what means can be used to induce the Sultan to make peace, and ask him to request that the city of Ascalon may be given to me. I will take my departure, leaving him here, and with a very small force he will get the remainder of their territory out of the hands of the Franks. My only object is to retain the position I hold amongst the Franks. If the Sultan will not forgo his pretensions to Ascalon, then let (el-'Ādel) procure me an indemnity for the sums I have laid out in repairing its fortifications."
>
> (p. 380)

The Richard I of Bahā' al-Dīn's account is, in matters of war and peace, as pragmatic as his adversary Salāh al-Dīn (p. 380),[24] whose life is the very subject of the text.

Richard I's greatness as a warrior and negotiator is offset by his cruelty and duplicity, a charge also leveled against him by Western, Christian chroniclers. For the Muslim chroniclers, the greatest proof of his cruelty is the mass execution of Muslim prisoners at his behest on August 20, 1191, shortly after the crusader capture of Acre. While the Western sources are consistent in blaming Salāh al-Dīn for the massacre, through his failure to meet the terms of the negotiated surrender of the city in the specified time,[25] Bahā' al-Dīn presents a far different scenario, in which the Sultan attempts to work within the framework of the agreed-upon treaty but encounters an obstinate enemy. According to the qadi, the payments stipulated by the treaty, along with certain Frankish prisoners, were to be delivered in three installments (p. 271). However, the Muslims' inability to locate certain individuals from among the group of requested Frankish captives led the two parties to an impasse at the end of the first period, at which point both parties demanded assurances of good faith from one another that were unfeasible (pp. 271–2). Although Bahā' al-Dīn does acknowledge the fact that Salāh al-Dīn was tardy in fulfilling the terms of the treaty (p. 272), for him the actions of Richard I are a clear breach of the terms of the treaty, and indicative of the bad faith in which the Franks had negotiated the treaty:

> He [Richard I] had promised to spare their lives if they surrendered the city, adding that if the Sultan sent him what had been agreed upon, he would give them their liberty, with permission to take their wives and children with them and to carry away all their movable property; if the Sultan did not fulfil the conditions, they were to become slaves. The king broke the solemn promises he had made them, and openly showed the intentions he had hitherto concealed, and carried out what he had purposed to do as soon as he had received the money and the Frank prisoners.
> (pp. 272–3)

For Bahā' al-Dīn, Richard's actions violated the terms of the treaty, which specified the penalty for noncompliance on the part of the Sultan, which was proof of his true attitude regarding the treaty. The qadi also speculates about the King's reasons for carrying out the massacre, listing two possible motives:

> Various motives have been assigned for this massacre. According to some, the prisoners were killed to avenge the deaths of those slain previously by the Moslems; others say that the king of England, having made up his mind to try and take Ascalon, did not think it prudent to leave so many prisoners behind in Acre. God only knows what his reason really was.
> (pp. 273–4)

For 'Imād al-Dīn, this episode is not only proof of his cruelty, but also of his duplicity:

> every time he made and agreement, he violated and broke it; every time he settled an affair, he twisted things and confused the issue; every time he gave his word, he went back on it; every time he was entrusted with a secret, he did not keep it; every time we said: 'he will be true,' he betrayed us; when we thought he would improve, he got worse; and he only revealed villainy.[26]

It is the lack of the chivalric virtues of mercy and honesty that makes Richard I, the "*roi-chevalier*" the object of 'Imād al-Dīn's opprobrium.

The Richard I of the Muslim accounts of the Third Crusade is a complex figure, admirable for his martial prowess, execrable for his cruelty and treachery. Despite his role in the discomfiture of Muslims, he is a worthy adversary who possesses many of the most prized attributes for a knight and king. Notwithstanding their aversion to some of his actions and tactics, the chroniclers are unflagging in their respect for the English king and his contribution to the cause he champions. Richard I is more than an enemy, he is an unparalleled threat; in the words of Bahā' al-Dīn, "we never had among

180 *A familiar enemy*

our enemies a man more crafty or bolder than he" (p. 350). High praise indeed from the biographer of Salāh al-Dīn.

Within the Muslim accounts of the crusades several heroes emerge: 'Imād al-Dīn Zangi, Nūr al-Dīn, Salāh al-Dīn, Baibars, and al-Ashraf Khalil (under whom the Muslim re-conquest of the Levant was completed in 1291). Amongst these figures, only one captured the imagination of historians and audiences in medieval Western Europe: Salāh al-Dīn (Saladin), whose legend grew to such proportions that at one time he was rumored to have won the affection of Eleanor of Aquitane (Richard I's mother) during her time in Antioch with her then-husband Louis VI.[27] For Muslim chroniclers, Salāh al-Dīn's efforts and achievements against the crusaders were assessed within the broader context of his career as a warrior and statesman in the Levant and Egypt; their evaluations were based on the entirety of his career. The recovery of Jerusalem was a monumental feat;[28] it obscured, but did not efface other less spectacular moments, such as the later reverses at Acre, Arsuf, and Jaffa.

For Christian contemporaries in Western Europe, for whom the crusade effort was the prism through which events in the Levant were viewed, Salāh al-Dīn's conquest of Jerusalem – perhaps the greatest defeat of the crusades (especially for its emotional and symbolic impact) – distinguished him from his Muslim peers. The fall of Jerusalem in 1187 marked a turning point in the crusades; the crusaders were put on the defensive, and with the exception of the reprieve offered by Richard I's exploits, there would never be a return to the heady days of the First Crusade. In fact, after the Third Crusade, Western European forces would never return to the Levant on crusade, as first Byzantium and then Egypt became the staging grounds for subsequent crusades. The triumph of 1187 cemented Salāh al-Dīn's place amongst the preeminent figures of the crusades for medieval Christian historians, and despite their negative impact on the Western crusade effort, his accomplishments added to his legend, enabling him to transcend his identity as a Muslim and become an exemplar of chivalry in the medieval West.

One of the first indications of Salāh al-Dīn's status within the Western accounts is the chroniclers' presentation of him as an enemy. In the *Itinerarium Peregrinorum et Gesta Regis Ricardi*, Salāh al-Dīn's empire is described as stretching from North Africa to India;[29] his army is described in this manner:

> His army contained such a number of people, such dissimilar races with such diverse religious observances that if we were to describe them as fully as the law of history demands the length of the description would defeat our intention of brevity. However, although it was an innumerable multitude its size can be estimated to some extent if we name only the commanders.[30]

The exaggeration of Muslim opponents' wealth and power is a common feature of medieval works (particularly in the romances), as it magnifies the perceived threat; however, the chroniclers' descriptions of Salāh al-Dīn are grounded in fact; they attempt to present Salāh al-Dīn in a manner that is more or less consonant with the historical record. The wholesale mythologizing of Salāh al-Dīn would take place in the years and centuries following the Third Crusade. The *Itinerarium* devotes a section to the origin of Salāh al-Dīn, followed by a fairly extensive account of his conquest of Jerusalem and many of the other major cities of the Levant. It offers this explanation of his name:

> He was from the nation of *Mirmuaenus*. His parents were not descended from the nobility, but neither were they common people of obscure birth. His father's given name was Job [Ayyūb], and his was Joseph [Yūsuf]. Giving Hebrew names of circumcision when their sons are circumcised is a rite which thrives among many of the Gentiles and follows Muslim tradition.
>
> The princes take their names from the title of the law of Muhammad, so that their names may remind them to be studious defenders of that law. Now, in the Gentile language the law is called the *Hadin*. From this he was called *Salahadin*, which translates as "reformer of the law", or "peacemaker". And just as our princes are called emperors or kings, so among them those who are preeminent are named *Soldans*, as if to mean "sole dominion".³¹

Through its explanation of the origins of his personal and family name, the *Itinerarium* distinguishes Salāh al-Dīn, identifying him as the leader of the Muslims, and a worthy adversary.³²

The portrayal of Salāh al-Dīn can be described as generally positive, but it is not entirely positive; Western writers find fault with his actions on several occasions. They are unanimous in blaming Salāh al-Dīn for the massacre of the Muslim hostages after the Crusader conquest of Acre; he is viewed as having dealt in bad faith with the Crusaders, particularly in his failure to deliver on his promise to return the True Cross, and for allowing his loyal soldiers to be slaughtered after they had served him in such exemplary fashion. Both the *Itinerarium* and *Estoire* maintain that Salāh al-Dīn was held blameworthy by many of his own soldiers for his failure to ensure their companions' safe return after the loss of Acre. Salāh al-Dīn is also reproached for negotiating in bad faith with Richard through his brother Sayf al-Dīn.³³ And on occasion, Salāh al-Dīn's valor is brought into question as a result of his reluctance to engage Richard's forces in open combat; this is particularly true of many of the writers' interpretations of his haste in moving his camp after the defeat at Jaffa.³⁴

Instances in which his character is called into question notwithstanding, the writers' overall tone toward Salāh al-Dīn is positive. He is universally acknowledged as a wise leader by the writers and leaders of the Third Crusade; indeed, it is Richard I's respect for Salāh al-Dīn as a tactician that prompts the King and his forces to abandon their march on Jerusalem.[35] This instance is illustrative of both the extent to which the two leaders were aware of one another's capacity to lead, and the objective manner in which they approached the task of prosecuting the Third Crusade. Their mutual admiration for one another is also reflected by an almost friendly competition that manifests itself at certain points in the narratives.[36] The apparent mutual admiration between the two leaders is suggested by both the *Itinerarium* and the *Estoire*, which is at times a source of tension for others. Indeed, both texts mention one occasion in which important members of the Crusader camp were perturbed by what they perceived as an inappropriate level of cordiality between Richard and Salāh al-Dīn.[37]

The level of familiarity between Salāh al-Dīn and Richard was problematic for some of the English king's allies; however, their interconnectedness is a theme in many of the accounts. For Richard I, the Third Crusade itself is in part an opportunity in which to test his abilities against a worthy adversary. Long before their arrival at Acre, the English king conjures up the image of Salāh al-Dīn and his forces to spur his men to action against the inhabitants of Messina, at whose hands they have received abuse and injury. In *The Chronicle of Richard of Devizes of the Time of King Richard the First*, he is quoted as saying:

> O my soldiers, the strength and crown of my realm! You who have endured a thousand perils with me, you who by your bravery have conquered so many kings and cities for me, do you not see that the cowardly mob is now insulting us? Will we overcome Turks and Arabs, will we be the terror of the most invincible nations, will our right arms make a way for us to the ends of the earth after the Cross of Christ, will we restore the kingdom of Israel, if we show our backs to these vile and effeminate Griffons? If we are defeated here in the confines of our own country, will we go any farther? Shall the laziness of Englishmen be made a joke to the ends of the world? My men, is not this new cause of grief to me a very just one? It may be, I think, that you are deliberately sparing your strength now, so that perhaps later on you may fight more boldly against Saladin . . . If I go away from here alive, Saladin will not see me unless I am victorious.[38]

The insults and hostility alone are not sufficient to draw the full measure of Richard's ire; rather, it is the combination of this perceived insolence and the specter of the coming combat with Salāh al-Dīn that oblige him to seek satisfaction for the slights suffered in Messina. For the English king, Messina serves as a location in which to stage a dress rehearsal for the impending conflict in the Levant.

This perceived connection between the two leaders informs the observations of the Western European chroniclers as they relate both individuals' actions and decisions during The Third Crusade, to the extent that both

Richard I and Salāh al-Dīn appear to be cognizant of the way in which their actions will affect their legacies.[39] The massacre of captured Muslim soldiers mentioned in connection with Muslim historians' appraisal of Richard I also serves as an apt example of an instance in which Western European writers pass judgment on him. In this instance, the Christian sources are as unanimous in blaming Salāh al-Dīn for the massacre as the Muslim sources are in blaming Richard. Both the *Estoire* and *Itinerarium* place the responsibility squarely on Salāh al-Dīn's shoulders; he is excoriated for failing to uphold his part of the agreement in the negotiated surrender of Acre, for allowing his soldiers to be slaughtered, and it is assumed that he is the object of the opprobrium of Christian and Muslim soldiers.[40] Another example in which Salāh al-Dīn appears mindful of his image in the Western accounts occurs when some of his soldiers suggest that they exact vengeance on the Christian pilgrims at the gates of Jerusalem for the aforementioned massacre at Acre; Salāh al-Dīn's counselors advise against it because of the harm it will do to their collective name as a result of their violating the negotiated terms of the recent truce that grants the pilgrims access to the city.[41] This idea is also reflected in the actions of those closest to the principal figures, and in particular Salāh al-Dīn's brother, Sayf al-Dīn, indicating the value both individuals ascribed to their reputations.

The relationship between the two men as peers and rivals is articulated in the response of Hubert Walter, the bishop of Salisbury, during his conversation with Salāh al-Dīn, in regard to the question of his opinion of the Sultan:

> "My lord, I can tell you of my lord for he is the best knight in the world and the best warrior, and he is generous and talented. I say nothing of our sins but if one were to take your qualities and his together then we will say that nowhere in all the world would ever two such princes be found, so valiant and so experienced."[42]

The bishop speaks eloquently for the chroniclers and their medieval audiences in opining that Salāh al-Dīn's only deficiency is his Sarcen-ness.

However, the Familiar Saracen is never the *equal* of his Christian opponents, and in Salāh al-Dīn's case there is evidence of the writers' hostility toward him as a Saracen. In the *Itinerarium*, Salāh al-Dīn's widespread popularity is attributed to a tax he imposed on the prostitutes of Damascus and their clients, using these funds to support the arts, essentially winning the affection of his subjects through a corrupt practice.[43] Similarly, Salāh al-Dīn's rise to power in Egypt is ascribed to an act of treachery.[44] The *Itinerarium* is scathing in its description of Salāh al-Dīn during the years leading up to his invasion of Palestine:

> That pimp, who had a kingdom of brothels, an army in taverns, who studied dice and rice, is suddenly raised up on high. He sits among princes, no he is greater than princes! "Holding the throne of glory" [1 Samuel ch.

> 2 v. 8] he rules the Egyptians, he subdues Damascus, he seizes the land of Roasia [al-Ruhā, or Edessa; now Urfa] and Gesira [al-Jazīra] and he penetrates and governs the most remote parts of India . . .
>
> Storming and seizing, now by trick, now by arms, Saladin brings all these kingdoms under his control. Then he makes a single monarchy out of all these sceptres. He alone claims the governments of so many kings! The more he has, the more he wants, and he strives with all his strength to seize the Lord's Inheritance.
>
> Then the opportunity arises for him to obtain his desire. Now he hopes to gain what he had never even dared to wish for.
>
> (pp. 28–9)

The intent of the passage is to shape the audience's opinion of Salāh al-Dīn at an early stage, establishing him as a villain, so that as they progress through the text, they do not form an overly sympathetic opinion of him when he is cast in a positive light through his accomplishments. The passage reinforces the fact that a Familiar Saracen remains Saracen, even in the case of the renowned Salāh al-Dīn.

Salāh al-Dīn is also cast in conventionally Saracen roles in Western accounts of the Third Crusade, generally as a Foreign Saracen in reaction to Crusader victories. As Western chroniclers could only speculate on Muslim leaders' responses,[45] they tended to draw upon the traditional stereotypical images of the raving Saracen monarch found in the romances. In one instance, after Richard's forces sink a Saracen vessel in their first encounter with the enemy, Salāh al-Dīn is described as plucking the hair from his beard in rage.[46] Similarly, after their defeat in the Battle of Arsur, Salāh al-Dīn's censure of his amīrs bears all the markings of the defeated Saracen monarch of popular fiction:

> "So! What magnificent exploits and extraordinary achievements by my most trusted warriors! They used to be so full of boasting and unbearable arrogance; I had bestowed such great gifts on them so often; and now, look! the Christians travel through the land of Syria just as they like without meeting any opposition or resistance. Where are my soldiers great boasts and brilliant exploits now? . . . See! the battle which they sought is now here, but where is the victory they boasted of? How the people of today have degenerated from our noble ancestors who gained so many brilliant and justly memorable victories against the Christians, victories which are retold to us daily and whose memory will endure forever! . . . What a disgrace when our people have become the scum of the earth in warfare! We are nothing in comparison to our ancestors. We are not even worth an egg."[47]

Later, in an interesting contrast to the above excerpt, Salāh al-Dīn is presented as listening in amusement to his soldiers' description of a botched attempt to capture King Richard, finding humor in their ineptitude.[48]

In accounts of Salāh al-Dīn in defeat, the writers revisit (and contribute to) a familiar trope – the raving Saracen monarch – to fill in the "blank spaces," adding a veneer of legitimacy to the images of the Saracen found in the romances in the process. As each genre presents a similar image, the image is reinforced, along with the presumption that it reflects a fundamental truth about the nature of Saracens. The result is an image that is not accurate in an historical context, but is accurate within the construct of perceived Saracen behavior, a construct which ultimately triumphs over other more accurate notions of Muslims and Muslim behavior.[49]

For Christian chroniclers, Salāh al-Dīn was an equally compelling, problematic figure, compelling for his spectacular achievements as a warrior-king, but problematic in that many of them came at the expense of the cause of the crusades. In Salāh al-Dīn the threat of the Familiar Saracen is made plain: the Familiar Saracen confronts his audience with the disturbing fact that Saracens are in fact human, capable of the displays of valor and chivalry associated with Christians. The Familiar Saracen threatens the construct of the Saracen outlined explicitly in the Foreign Saracen and reinforced implicitly in the Saracen Convert. However, unlike the Familiar Saracens of the *chansons de geste*, Salāh al-Dīn remains alive and relevant throughout the course of the Third Crusade; the chroniclers cannot silence his voice through death or defeat. Instead, it is the chroniclers themselves who are constrained by history to recount a narrative in which it is the Saracen ruler who emerges intact, and the Christian ruler who must reconcile himself to fighting another day.

Richard I and Salāh al-Dīn's accomplishments as leaders placed them in exclusive company; this much was acknowledged by even their most inveterate critics. However, for both the English king and the Sultan, the most pointed criticism often came from coreligionists, partisan historians who chafed at the prospects of their patrons being eclipsed by these successful but opportunistic figures. In the eyes of chroniclers hostile to the cause with which Richard or Salāh al-Dīn was associated, their successes stood on their own merits. Salāh al-Dīn was a reprehensible figure for Western Christian chroniclers, as was Richard I for Near Eastern Muslim chroniclers, by virtue of their status as Muslim and Christian leaders involved in the conflict. What distinguished Richard for Muslim chroniclers and Salāh al-Dīn for Christian chroniclers was their effectiveness in advancing their causes, particularly on the battlefield. For chroniclers from the other side of the conflict, their successes engendered grudging admiration for the ways in which each embodied the warrior ethos – the *milite Christi* or the *mujahid* – so esteemed in the Medieval West and Near East, respectively. Both Richard I and Salāh al-Dīn were enemies of the Faith for either Muslim or Christian chroniclers, deserving of the opprobrium reserved for all individuals of their ilk. But they were warriors – warriors who were successful on a grand scale – at a time and for people for whom the idea of the warrior resonated in a profound manner. What was foreign in religion or culture did not obfuscate what was familiar

186 *A familiar enemy*

in the knight or king. In the end, this simple truth, that both exemplified an ideal that was both familiar and respected, is acknowledged by chroniclers on both sides of the crusades.

Notes

1 The most famous Western European Christian accounts of the First Crusade all exhibit a tendency to imitate the *chansons de geste* both in the portrayal of Muslims and in the use of certain literary tropes. For their part, Near Eastern Muslim accounts of the crusades employ popular stereotypes to caricature (and demonize) Western European Christians.
2 Despite some of the chroniclers' protestations to the contrary, their references to classical works; events, figures, and ideas from the Bible; and use of literary tropes from the *chansons de geste* are all indicative of the pride they took in producing works of literature. Indeed, in the prefatory comments of arguably the most popular medieval account of the First Crusade, the *Historia Iherosolimitana*, Robert the Monk informs his audience that he was commissioned to write an account of the First Crusade in part to address the deficiencies of the first account, the *Gesta Francorum*, which some felt was "unsophisticated in its style and expression." *Historia Iherosolimitana*, 75.
3 Western European accounts of the First Crusade are notable exceptions to this rule. The *Gesta Francorum et aliorum Hierosolimitanorum* was heavily influenced by the tradition of the *chansons de geste* (it also served as propaganda for Bohemond of Apulia); many of the later works drew from it, embellishing its "plain" style, but maintaining its *chanson*-esque depiction of the Muslims.
4 Western chroniclers remained wedded to the concept of crusading; however, they were more objective in their analysis of the planning and execution of particular crusades, as well as of the performance and value of individual crusaders. Of course, their objectivity was tempered by their allegiances to powerful individuals, and by extension families and factions, involved with the crusades.
5 This phenomenon is traceable to the portrayals of Emperor Alexius I Comnenus of Byzantium in the accounts of the First Crusade. The chroniclers, who were attached to individual crusaders, reflected those individuals' interests and partisan prejudices within their accounts.
6 *Historia Iherosolimitana*, 4.
7 See the summary of the political situation in the Near East in the years leading up to the First Crusade in Chapter 7.
8 Ironically, both Richard and Salāh al-Dīn enjoyed greater acclaim amongst the historians of the opposition than from their coreligionists. At the hands of their coreligionists, the two suffered the vicissitudes of the partisanship that led each writer to elevate the individual to whom he was aligned by virtue of politics and regional bias, usually at the expense of perceived rivals, whether that patron was King Philip Augustus of France, or Nūr al-Dīn (who, for his partisans, had been the victim of Salāh al-Dīn's political machinations).
9 Jean Flori, *Richard the Lionheart: Knight and King*, Trans. Jean Birrell (Edinburgh: Edinburgh UP, 1999) 64.
10 For example, in *Histoire des croisades*, the twentieth-century historian René Grousset attributes Salāh al-Dīn's chivalric behavior to the fact that as a Kurd he was an Indo-European. René Grousset, *Histoire des croisades, Vol. 1* (Paris: Plon, 1934–6) 535–6. In an example of a similar phenomenon at work in a medieval text, the *Gesta Francorum* goes one step further; in order to account for displays of chivalry amongst Turkish soldiers, it posits that the Turks and Franks have a common ancestor: "Indeed they [Turks] claim to be of the same blood as

the Franks, and claim that no one, apart from the Franks and themselves, have a right to the name of knight." *The First Crusade: The Deeds of the Franks and Other Jerusalemites (Gesta Francorum et Aliorum Hierosolimitanorum)*, Trans. Somerset De Chair (London: Golden Cockerel Press, 1945) 26.

11 Although Jerusalem was ceded to Frederick II Hohenstaufen through a negotiated treaty in 1229, it was not an exclusively crusader territory in the way it had been from 1099–1187.
12 *Mujahid*: One who strives; popularly understood as a holy warrior.
13 *Milite Christi*: Soldier of Christ.
14 Jean Flori, *Richard the Lionheart*, 2.
15 Ibid, 198–200.
16 Ralph of Coggeshall, Gerald of Wales and Matthew Paris all delivered harsh assessments of the king's life and legacy after his death, interpreting the inglorious nature of his death (from a minor wound from a crossbow that turned septic) as a form of divine punishment. However, these writers, all clerics, appear to have been most disturbed by the king's refusal to maintain the traditional privileges of the clergy, in particular, his willingness to tax the Church and appropriate Church funds and property to serve his military and political ends. Ibid, 222–5.
17 Bahā' al-Dīn, *What Befell Sultan Yūsuf*, 242. Subsequent citations will appear parenthetically.
18 For his part, Ibn al-'Athīr describes Philip Augustus as "the noblest of their kings in lineage, although his kingdom was not a great one." Like Bahā' al-Dīn, his appraisal of Richard I reflects the difference between the two kings, a perspective shared by most Muslim historians: "The king was an outstanding man of his time for bravery, cunning, steadfastness and endurance. In him the Muslims were tried by an unparalleled disaster." *The Chronicle of Ibn al-Athīr, Part 2*. 386, 7.
19 Bahā' al-Dīn, *What Befell Sultan Yūsuf*, 347–52.
20 While traveling through the suburbs of Vienna in December 1192, Richard was captured by officers loyal to Duke Leopold of Austria (whom he had insulted in an open, gratuitous manner after the capture of Acre in 1191). Richard's capture was a result of his rivalry with the German Emperor Henry VI, and the activity of Philip Augustus in fomenting rebellion in Aquitaine (in direct contravention of his oath to respect the English king's holdings while he was on crusade); his imprisonment lasted until February 1194. It was prolonged by an excessively burdensome ransom (which put England in financial duress) and interference by Philip Augustus, who sought to keep Richard imprisoned. Flori, *Richard the Lionheart*, 156–62.
21 In particular, the fortress of Ascalon lay at the center of a heated debate between the two parties. Ascalon had been destroyed at Salāh al-Dīn's behest (to prevent it's falling into Crusader hands), only to see Richard I rebuild the fortress at great personal expense. As a result, the Muslims demanded the demolition of the fortress, while the Crusaders sought to preserve it. However, as the time for Richard I's departure drew near, the Crusaders, anticipating a Muslim resurgence in the wake of the king's absence, began to worry that in Muslim hands, the rebuilt fortress would serve as an instrument of their discomfiture. Thus, by the conclusion of the negotiations, both sides were eager to see the demolition of the fortress. Bahā' al-Dīn, *What Befell Sultan Yūsuf*, 358, 372, 380, 386–7.
22 This desire to return to England was primarily motivated by his brother John's attempts to usurp the throne in his absence.
23 Bahā' al-Dīn is drawing attention to the friendship that had developed between al-Malik al-'Ādil (Sayf al-Dīn) and Richard I through the course of the negotiations. Ibid, 320.

188 *A familiar enemy*

24 In an earlier message to the Sultan, he is quoted as saying: "It is my wish that you should divide (the land) in a way that your brother shall be aquitted of all blame by the Moslems, and that I shall incur no reproach from the Franks" (p. 323).
25 For Western versions of the massacre, cf. Ambroise, *Estoire*, ll. 5,160–5,535; see also Canonicus Sanctae Trinitatis Londoniensis Ricardus, *Chronicle of the Third Crusade: A Translation of the Itinerarium Peregrinorum et Gesta Regis Ricardi*, Trans. Helen J. Nicholson and William Stubbs (Brookfield: Ashgate, 1997), 227–9, 231, in which Salāh al-Dīn is accused of negotiating in bad faith. The *Itinerarium Peregrinorum et Gesta Regis Ricardi* will henceforward be referred to as the *Itinerarium*.
26 'Imād al-Dīn, *Conquête de la Syrie*, Trans. Henri Massé (Paris: Librairie Orientaliste Paul Geuthner, 1972) 353–4.
27 Louis VI, the king of France, and Eleanor were in Antioch as a result of his involvement with the Second Crusade. The rumor in question was propagated by the Minstrel of Reims. Flori, *Richard the Lionheart*, 4.
28 Salāh al-Dīn appears to have taken full advantage of the opportunity to maximize the public relations value of this accomplishment; he entered the city on Friday Rajab 27, 583/ October 2, 1187, which was also the anniversary of the Prophet Muhammad's Night Journey into Heaven. Hillenbrand, *The Crusades*, 189.
29 *Itinerarium*, 28.
30 *Itinerarium*, 30.
31 Ibid, 26–7.
32 However, it is the accounts of his acts of magnanimity and justice (along with the demonstrations of mutual respect between he and Richard I) that identify Salāh al-Dīn as a Familiar Saracen, rather than the descriptions of his political power, as such descriptions are often found in reference to Foreign Saracens.
33 Ambroise, *L'estoire de la guerre sainte, histoire en vers de la troisième croisade (1190–1192) par Ambroise*. Collection de documents inédits sur l'histoire de France, 1–2., Ed. Gaston Paris (Paris: Imprimerie nationale, 1897). See also Ambroise, *Estoire*, Vol. II, 131–2. A similar account can be found in the *Itinerarium* (pp. 272–4).
34 Ambroise describes Salāh al-Dīn's retreat in the *Estoire* in the following terms:

> Then was the news brought to Saladin and the account given of the assault on his people. He, the defeated man, more angry than a wolf, was feverish with fear. He did not dare wait there any longer but had his pavilions struck and his tents moved back into the plains.
>
> (Eth vos la novele aportee/ A Salehadins e contee/ Que sa gent [i] ert assaillie/ E il, la persone faillie,/ Qui estoit plus irez que leus,/ Deust ester de peur fevereus./ Si n'osa illoc plus atendre,/ Ainz fist ses paveillons destendre/ [E] ses tries sus es plains ariere . . .)
>
> (*Estoire*, ll. 11, 188–96)

The retreat is described in these terms in the *Itinerarium*:

> Saladin heard that the king had arrived and of his fine combat with his Turks and how he had cut to pieces all he met without distinction. Sudden fears rushed on him, for he was a very timid creature, like a frightened hare. Hurriedly tearing up his tents from their pitches he put spur to horse and fled before King Richard, not wishing to be seen by him.
>
> (p. 357)

35 Had the king carried out the march, it would likely have been a success; Bahā' al-Dīn's account of the time in question informs us that the city was vulnerable, and the Muslim leaders themselves believed that they were not capable of defending the city from the crusaders. Bahā' al-Dīn, *What Befell Sultan Yūsuf*, 347–52.
36 A noteworthy example of this type of one-upmanship between the two leaders takes place during the events following the battle for Jaffa (July 26 – August 1, 1192). After the Crusader victory, Richard pitches his tents in the very place Salāh al-Dīn had recently vacated. For his part, Salāh al-Dīn responds by sending a message to Richard announcing his intentions of capturing him, if he dares await his approach. Of course, the English king affirms through his messenger that he eagerly awaits his approach. *Itinerarium*, 369.
37 This takes place during the course of the ultimately fruitless negotiations (c. November 6, 1191) between the two leaders over the division of the lands of the Levant between the two forces, in particular, the fates of Ascalon and Fort Erach of Mount Royal. The *Itinerarium* (pp. 272–4) provides the details of the substance of the negotiations. Both the *Itinerarium* (pp. 273–4) and *Estoire* (ll. 7,398–7,400; 7,416–33) reveal that King Richard was admonished by some of his peers for his perceived friendliness toward Salāh al-Dīn. Moreover, both remark on the zeal with which Richard renewed his battle with the enemy after the breakdown of the negotiations, spurred on in part by feelings that he had been deceived, and in part by the desire to demonstrate that his desire to wage war against the enemy had not waned.
38 Richard of Devizes, *The Chronicle of Richard of Devizes of the Time of King Richard the First (Cronicon Richardi Divisensis De Tempore Regis Richardi Primi)*, Trans. John T. Appleby (London: Thomas Nelson and Sons, 1963) 20–1.
39 The Western, Christian sources and the Eastern, Muslim sources are of one accord in their portrayal of both leaders' awareness of their legacies, and the role the Third Crusade could play in shaping them.
40 Ambroise, *Estoire*, ll. 7,933–51; *Itinerarium*, 287.
41 *Itinerarium*, 375–6; Ambroise, *Estoire*, ll. 11, 941–78.
42 *Itinerarium*, 378. There is also an account of the conversation in Ambroise, *Estoire*, ll. 12,099–12,110.
43 *Itinerarium*, 27.
44 At that time [1169] a certain Gentile, Shawar by name [Abu Shujā' ibn Mujir Shāwar], had obtained the whole of Egypt [as vizier], under the authority of the Molan [the Caliph:
Abū Muhammad 'Abd Allāh al-'Adid] which means 'Lord' in the language of that country. Amalric the victorious king of Jerusalem had forced him to pay an annual tribute . . .
At that time Saladin was fighting for the Egyptians with his uncle Saracun [Asad al-Dīn ibn Shādhī Shīrkūh]. He treacherously killed these unsuspecting men, and so won the lordship of all Egypt. Later, in fact not long afterwards, Nuradin came to the end of his life. Saladin married his widow, put Nuradin's heirs to flight, and seized the government of the kingdom of Damascus.

(*Itinerarium*, 28)
45 Unless they chose to invent an eyewitness, as in the case of the "convert" who witnessed the speeches of the Saracen leader Clemens in Robert the Monk's *Historia Iherosolimitana* (p. 207).
46 *Itinerarium*, 199.
47 *Itinerarium*, 260.

48 "Saladin is said to have taunted the cowardice of those who had been making boastful promises by asking: 'So where are those who are bringing *Melech* Richard as a prisoner? Who got him first? Where is he, I say? Aren't you going to produce him?'" *Itinerarium*, 368.
49 Edward Said offers an example of such a system in his description of Orientalism as a closed, self-reinforcing system in which each "fact" within the Orientalist system reinforces, and is at the same time informed by, previously held "facts," verifiable only within the context of the system itself. Edward W. Said, *Orientalism* (New York: Vintage, 1978) 69–71.

Conclusion

In the end, the tension, or rather conversation, between desires to understand the outside world and tendencies toward ethnocentrism revolves around responses to difference, the extent to which an ethnic/racial or religious group became the Other. The "Saracens" and the "*iFranji*" are equally concepts formulated in response to questions of identity; they are indicative of the role difference can play in the shaping of group identity. Long before the Crusades, difference had already played a decisive role in the formation of Near Eastern/North African (and Spanish) Muslim and Western European Christian identity. For the Muslims in question, this difference included a religious dimension, among area Muslims, Christians (Armenian, Byzantine, and indigenous Near Eastern groups), and Jews; a racial/ethnic dimension between Arabs, Turks, Persians, and Africans; and a linguistic dimension between speakers of Arabic and speakers of *ajānib* ("foreign") languages. Difference for Western European Christians also consisted of religious, racial/ethnic, and linguistic dimensions: among Christians, Jews, and "pagan" groups; among the various ethnic/racial groups in Western Europe; and among the speakers of the various languages of Western Europe. For both the Muslims and Christians there were languages and cultures that occupied positions of prestige, Arabic as a language and "culture" for the Muslims, and Latin and a Roman ideal that hearkened back to the ancient Empire for the Christians. Yet despite the presence of universally acknowledged dominant languages and cultures, both regions were beset by intra-group tensions stemming from political instability, intra-religious sectarian conflict, and ethnic/racial hostility. Without the presence of "Frank" or "Saracen" interlopers, both groups were already struggling with the "Others" who were integral parts of the fabric of the Eastern Mediterranean and Western European landscape.

For the Latin West, the answer to the question of identity that emerged was to categorize the various groups that fell outside the pale of the Christian, Roman/Latin religious and cultural norms and deal with each group based on its distance from the established norms. Through this categorization of difference, a hierarchy of sorts emerged regarding the status afforded to each group by medieval Western European authorities, religious and secular. Where Christian authorities governed, members of the groups in question were excluded from citizenship on an equal standing with their Christian neighbors; however, the authorities' approach varied according to the group in question. Jews were disenfranchised, segregated, and subject to state-sanctioned persecution, pressure to convert, and outbreaks of violence. However, as adherents of a faith recognized as legitimate by the Church, their existence was necessary to the identity of the Christian state and its role in ultimate salvation as envisioned by the Church. They were permitted to exist, but in a state of economic and social degradation perpetuated by religious and secular authorities, and enshrined in law.

However, "heretical" Christian groups and "pagans" were denied the right to exist in Christian society; their extermination was a prerequisite for the establishment and maintenance of a Christian society. The very existence of heretics and pagans was antithetical to the conception of society for medieval authorities in Western Europe. While the Crusades to the Eastern Mediterranean are a widely known historical phenomenon, during the medieval period there were also crusades against the Albigensians a in the south of France (1209),[1] and a program of crusading against the pagans of Prussia and the Baltic that led to the establishment of crusading orders, most notably the Teutonic Knights.[2]

Medieval Muslims occupied a unique space as an Other for medieval European Christians. Unlike Jews, who were a "Religious Other," an internal threat, Muslims were also a "Political Other," an external threat. Neither Jews nor Muslims could be European without surrendering their identity as Other,[3] but there was a place, degraded as it was, for Jews in medieval Western European society. As an external threat, there could be no room for Muslims in Christian Western Europe. On a variety of levels, a Muslim presence was antithetical to the very idea of the Latin West. The existence of Muslims in an area threatened its identity as a Christian space in a manner that was different from the threat posed by "pagans," Jews or "heretical" Christian groups. Unlike Jews and "heretical" Christian groups, Muslims were a political and military power; there were Muslim-majority polities ruled by Muslim sovereigns, ostensibly in accordance with Muslim religious law. Unlike pagans, Muslims adhered to a faith that was perceived to be a threat on doctrinal grounds in much the same manner as Judaism and the various Christian "heresies." The Muslim threat was a combination of the most disturbing aspects of the threats posed by Jews, heretics, and pagans. The individual Muslim represented the external military and political threat posed by the Muslim world, and the internal religious threat posed by Islam.

For Muslims in the Near East/North Africa, the Muslim world lay at the center of the civilized world, at the crossroads of the earlier Egyptian, Greek, Roman, and Persian empires, having inherited much of the grandeur and intellectual legacies of these empires. The region was also home to multiple racial/ethnic identities, languages, and religions. Above these types of difference, one identity occupied a privileged position within the region, and served as the standard for racial/ethnic, cultural, and linguistic normativity: the Arab. This identity was frequently invoked to legitimize claims to power, particularly in regard to non-Arab figures of note.

However, the reality of the Muslim Near East contradicted the Arabocentric ideal; by the tenth century, the Muslim Eastern Mediterranean was under the *de facto* control of Turkish petty kings. It is worth noting that none of the most renowned Muslim heroes of the Crusades were Arab. Their "Arab" identity, which eventually became an integral part of our understanding of each figure, was provided by the historians who recorded their exploits. Although many of the Muslim chroniclers were not themselves Arab, they understood the necessity of representing the Muslim heroes through the language of the classical Arab warrior, and that evoking these images would enshrine them in the popular consciousness as Muslim heroes in a manner that was not achievable through constant references to these individuals' Turkish or Kurdish identities. To be a full participant in the Muslim Eastern Mediterranean was to recognize the primacy of Arabic language and culture in the region, in much the same way that one had to acknowledge the privileged position of Latin language and culture in medieval Western Europe.

Outside of the Muslim world of the Eastern Mediterranean, the lands and peoples in the immediate vicinity (India, China, Central Asia, and East Africa) were of interest. The medieval Muslim perception of the "Franks" – of Western Europe in general – was informed in part by the lack of information about the area and its inhabitants. The "land of the Franks" was located in the distant North, an area that was generally regarded as being incompatible with civilization. For Muslims in the region, their rivals in Byzantium were the Christian Other; prior to the advent of the Crusades, the Franks were not perceived as being actors of consequence on the world stage.

For Western European and Eastern Mediterranean scholars and audiences alike, studies about the outside world and the peoples found therein often reflected popular prejudices regarding the different areas of the world beyond their borders. The Saracen and the Frank were abstractions, ideas conceived of and delineated by others, manifestations of Western European and Eastern Mediterranean cultural, racial, and religious prejudices, and the fears that such prejudices often engendered. The Saracen was in part a reflection of the Western European understanding of Muslims, but more so of Western European fears of difference within the Latin West, differences of race, culture, and religious orthodoxy. Similarly, the Frank was an expression of Eastern Mediterranean perceptions of Western Europeans, but also of ideas of culture, civility, and barbarism. As designations, Saracen and Frank became synonymous with idolatry and moral depravity (Saracens) and barbarism and lack of intelligence (Franks). Moreover, these terms came to signify a worldview that was wholly self-referential, and that demanded conformity relative to the production of information regarding the outside world, particularly in regard to the specific group(s) denoted by the terms.

For both Eastern Mediterranean Muslims and Western European Christians, the Crusades were instrumental in transforming the Eastern Muslim and Western Christian Other into powerful symbols within the popular consciousness. Saracens and Franks existed as parts of the landscape of the European Christian and Mediterranean Muslim worldview, but it was the Crusades that brought these figures to the forefront. The length of the conflict, the level of participation on both sides, the differences along ethnic/racial and cultural lines, and the intensity of the conflict due to its religious dimension brought about a level of enmity between the two regions that enabled such vaguely defined constructions of the Self and the Other to survive, even to thrive, in the popular consciousness, in subtle and blatant ways, and in symbols that are still salient in the discourse between "East" and "West."

However, the Crusades were part of a larger discourse; the Muslim and Christian accounts of the Crusades informed other works of literature, but were also informed by the romances, travel narratives, and works within the learned tradition. Each genre contributed to the conversation, helping to shape public perception and public expectations relative to the Muslim or Christian Other. The romances and other works (now regarded as fiction) provided both a general narrative framework (the triumph of the true religion and its warriors) to which the Crusade accounts were expected to adhere, as well as tropes (the Saracen monster and Saracen idolatry; Frankish barbarity and simplicity) that appear in both Crusade accounts and travel narratives. In turn, the travel narratives and Crusade accounts reinforce extant stereotypes, while disseminating information derived from personal experience and research in a manner that is more accessible to a wider audience than what is to be found in many of the scholarly works. Finally, the scholarly works serve as the intellectual foundation upon which the discourse on the Other is built. Many of the stereotypes that populate the most popular medieval works have their roots in the erroneous theories/distortions of fact in the works of medieval scholars. Each genre contributes to the image of the Muslim or Christian Other; the resulting images dominated popular conceptions of the Saracen and Frank in Western Europe and the Near East/ North Africa for centuries, and still exist on the fringes of the conversation between "East" and "West."

The peoples of the medieval Muslim Eastern Mediterranean and Christian Western Europe were separated by culture, history, and religion, but inextricably linked by common threads in their worldviews, and by their reactions to perceived threats to their concepts of the world and their places in it. Both held an ethnocentric conception of the world which privileged their civilization, culture, race, and religion. These perspectives were the products of each society's unique cultural, historical, and religious context, the products of an internal dialogue which resulted in a discourse of "otherness" in which the symbols and points of reference were self-contained, informed by considerations and conditions within rather than outside the society in question.

Similarly, each society's discourse on cultural, racial, and religious difference reflected a continuous, evolving internal conversation on the subject, in which the reaction to difference and the articulation and depiction of otherness functioned primarily as a means of engaging and understanding the outside world. The tension between the desire to approach racial, cultural, and religious difference in a responsible, scientific manner and the desire to marginalize it is a function of their constant intersection in the medieval works that have been the focus of this book. These competing desires can be found in scholarly works in which the Other makes sporadic appearances in the form of monsters or monstrous practices, but they can also be found in the romances, in which Familiar Saracens serve as tacit recognition of perceived fundamental similarities between Muslim and Christian society, and Saracen Converts stand as explicit reminders that the borders between the two worlds are not as imposing as the Saracen monsters would have one believe. In both the medieval Muslim and Christian worlds of the Near East/North Africa and Western Europe, works within the learned and popular traditions were in constant conversation, sharing symbols, points of reference, and a framework in which to understand the Other.

The tension between the two goals is most evident in crusade accounts and travel narratives, in their embracing of aspects of both the scientific texts and popular works. Attempting to educate (about the events of the crusades or exotic places and peoples) and to entertain, the works in these genres walk a fine line, seasoning the factual with the questionable, evoking popular stereotypes to maintain their audience's interest. The medieval romances and other works now recognized as popular fiction provided audiences with a set of symbols and frames of reference that were intrinsically connected with the concepts of the Saracen and the Frank, and discussion of either group often involved the adoption of these symbols and frames of reference. Similarly, works from the learned tradition provided the theoretical perspective through which travelers and historians approached the Muslim or Christian Other, especially in the areas of racial, cultural, and religious difference. Crusade accounts and travel narratives were distinct genres; however, they both drew from the learned and medieval romantic/epic tradition. In so doing, travel narratives and crusade accounts embodied the tension between the urge to understand culturally, racially, and/or religiously foreign groups and the desire to assert one's superiority over them, divergent motivations that often emerged within the same text.

The Other was a construct employed by both medieval Muslims and Christians to define and delineate the parameters of difference, as it has been and continues to be used by societies across the globe. In this exercise, the normative community is both the author and audience, imagining, describing, and ultimately giving voice to the "Othered," drawing this Other nearer in order to categorize and characterize it, even while simultaneously rejecting it and confining it to the periphery of humanity for its difference. For both medieval Near Eastern/North African Muslims and Western European

Christians, the concept of Otherness was neither exclusively an attempt to engage difference in a constructive manner nor a reaction born out of fear due to the existence of a racially, culturally, and religiously distinct group with whom they were in economic, military, and political competition. On the contrary, it was the expression of their attempts to articulate a thoroughly ethnocentric worldview, in which the dominant feature was the assertion of the centrality of their position within the world. However, occupying a central, dominant position on the world's stage does not negate the desire to understand the ostensibly subordinate peoples in nearby and distant foreign lands, and this desire often unearthed information that complicated the facile formulation of Self (superior) and Other (inferior). The close inspection of difference often reveals similarity, which is a troubling development when the difference in question has become shorthand for inferiority. But what is perhaps the most troubling result in the study of difference is the discovery that difference itself is dependent upon perspective; the Other has its own Other. The story of the discourse about difference in the medieval Muslim Near East and North Africa and Christian Western Europe was not about whether scholars and lay writers ever arrived at this conclusion, but rather the journey they embarked upon in developing a discourse in the first place, and the fundamental contradictions that are part and parcel of it.

Notes

1 Robert Bartlett, *The Making of Europe: Conquest, Colonization and Cultural Change 950–1350* (Princeton: Princeton UP, 1993) 26.
2 Ibid, 17–18.
3 As the Spanish Inquisition revealed, even after such a forfeiture, life in Western European Christian society was still fraught with peril for such individuals.

Bibliography

Primary sources

Al-Bakrī, Abū 'Ubayd. *Geografia de España: Kitāb al-Masālik wa-l-Mamālik.* Trans. Eliseo Vidal Beltran. Zaragoza: Anubar Ediciones, 1982. Print.

Al-Bakrī, Abū 'Ubayd 'Abd Allah Ibn 'Abd al-'Azīz and 'Abd al-Rahmān 'Alī Hajjī. *Jughrāfīyat Al-Andalus Wa-Ūrūbbā: Min Kitāb Al-masālik Wa Al-Mamālik.* Bayrūt: Dār Al-Irshād Lil-tibā'ah Wa-al-nashr Waal-tawzī', 1968. Internet resource.

Albertus Magnus. *Alberti Magni Liber De Natura Locorum, De Causis Propietatum Elementorum, De Spiritu Et Respiratione, De Longitudine Et Brevitate Vitae, De Nutrimento Et Nutribili – BSB Clm 956a.* S.I., 1494. Print.

———. *An Appraisal of the Geographical Works of Albertus Magnus and His Contributions to Geographical Thought.* Trans. Sr. Jean Paul Tilman Ann Arbor: U of Michigan P, 1971. Print.

———. *The Book of Secrets of Albertus Magnus of the Virtues of Herbs, Stones and Certain Beasts, Also a Book of the Marvels of the World.* Trans. Michael R. Best and Frank H. Brightman. Oxford: Oxford UP, 1973. Print.

———. *Liber de natura Locorum.* München: Bayerische StaatsBibiothek, 1515. Internet resource.

———. *Man and the Beasts (De Animalibus, Books 22–26).* Trans. James J. Scanlan. Binghamton: Medieval & Renaissance Texts & Studies, 1987. Print.

Al-Idrīsī. *Kitab Nuzhat al-Mushtaq fi Ikhtiraq al-Afaaq, Vol. 2.* Cairo: Al-Thaqafa Al-Denia Bookshop, 1990. Print.

Al-Mas'ūdī. *Murūj al-Dhahab wa Ma'ādin al-Jawhar, Vol. 2.* Beirut: Dār al-Kutub al-'Ilmiyyah, 1990. Print.

———. *Kitāb al-Tanbīh wa 'l-Ishrāf.* Trans. S.M. Ziauddin Alavi in "Al-Mas'ūdī's Conception of the Relationship between Man and Environment." *Al-Mas'ūdī Millenary Commemoration Volume.* Eds. S. Maqbul Ahmad and A. Rahman. Calcutta: Little Flower, 1960. 93–7. Print.

Al-Muqaddasi. *The Best Divisions for Knowledge of the Regions: A Translation of Ahsan al-Taqasim fi Ma'rifat al-Aqalim.* Trans. Basil Anthony Collins. Reading: Garnet, 1994. Print.

Al-Muqaddasī, Muhammad A. and Shākir Lu'aybī. *Rihlat Al-Muqaddasī: Ahsan Al-taqāsīm Fī Ma'rifat Al-aqālīm, 985–990.* Bayrūt: Al-Mu'assasah Al-'Arabīyah Lil-Dirāsāt Wa-al-Nashr, 2003. Print.

Ambroise. *The Crusade of Richard Lion-Heart.* Trans. Merton Jerome Hubert. New York: Columbia UP, 1941. Print.

198 Bibliography

———. *The History of the Holy War: Ambroise's 'Estoire de la Guerre Sainte'*, in 2 vols: vol. I 'The Text', eds. Marianne Ailes and Malcolm Barber; vol. II 'The Translation', trans. Marianne Ailes, notes by Marianne Ailes and Malcolm Barber. Woodbridge: Boydell and Brewer, 2003. Print.

———. *L'estoire de la guerre sainte, histoire en vers de la troisième croisade (1190–1192) par Ambroise*. Ed. Gaston Bruno Paulin Paris. Paris, 1897. Print.

Archer, T.A., ed. *English History by Contemporary Writers: The Crusade of Richard I, 1189–92*. New York: AMS, 1978. Print.

Bacon, Roger. *Fratris Rogeri Bacon, Ordinis Minorum, Opus Majus: Ad Clementem Quartem, Pontificem Romanum. ExcCodice Dubliniensi, Cum Aliis Quibusdam Collato, Nunc Primum Edidit S. Jebb, M.D.* Londini: Typis Gulielmi Bowyer, 1733. Internet resource.

———. *The Opus Major of Roger Bacon, Vol. 1*. Trans. Robert Belle Burke. New York: Russell & Russell, 1962. Print.

———. *The "Opus Majus" of Roger Bacon, Supplementary Volume: Containing – Revised Text of First Three Parts; Corrections; Emendations; and Additional Notes*. Ed. John Henry Bridges. London: Williams & Norgate, 1900. 121. Print.

———. *Roger Bacon's Philosophy of Nature: A Critical Edition, with English Translation, Introduction, and Notes, of De Multiplicatione specierum and De speculis comburentibus*. Trans. David C. Lindberg. Oxford: Oxford UP, 1983. Print.

Bevington, David, ed. "The Passion Play II." *Medieval Drama*. Boston: Houghton Mifflin, 1975. 520–35. Print.

———. "Pharaoh." *Medieval Drama*. Boston: Houghton Mifflin, 1975. 322–36. Print.

———. "The Play of the Sacrament." *Medieval Drama*. Boston: Houghton Mifflin, 1975. 754–88. Print.

———. "The Scourging." *Medieval Drama*. Boston: Houghton Mifflin, 1975. 553–68. Print.

Caxton, William. *Caxton's Mirrour of the World*. Ed. Oliver H. Prior. London: Paul, Trench, Trübner & Co., 1913. Print.

de Aguirre, Jennifer Gabel, ed. *La Chanson de la Première Croisade en Ancien Français d'après Baudri de Bourgueil: Edition et Analyse Lexicale*. Heidelberg: Universitäetsverlag Winter, 2015. Print.

The Deeds of the Franks and Other Jerusalem-Bound Pilgrims (Gesta Francorum et aliorum Hierosolimitanorum): The Earliest Chronicle of the First Crusade. Trans. Nirmal Dass. Lanham: Rowman & Littlefield, 2011. Print.

The English Charlemagne Romances, Part VII: The Boke of Duke Huon of Burdeux. Trans. John Bourchier. London: Pub. for the Early English Text Society by Trübner, 1882. Print.

The First Crusade: The Deeds of the Franks and Other Jerusalemites (Gesta Francorum et Aliorum Hierosolimitanorum). Trans. Somerset De Chair. London: Golden Cockerel, 1945. Print.

Frantzius, Johannes Joachimus, Johann Heinrich Boecler and Einhard. *Historia Caroli Magni Imperatoris Romani: Ex Praecipuis Scriptoribus Eorum Temporum Concinnata*. Argentinae: Typis Joannis Philippi Mûlbii, 1644. Print.

Fulcher of Chartres. *The First Crusade: The Chronicle of Fulcher of Chartres and Other Source Materials*. 2nd ed. Ed. and Trans. Edward Peters. Philadelphia: U of Pennsylvania P, 1998. Print.

———. *Fulcheri Carnotensis Historia Hierosolymitana (1095–1127)*. Heidelberg: Winter, 1913. Print.

Gabrieli, Francesco. *Arab Historians of the Crusades: Selected and Translated from the Arabic Sources.* Trans. E.J. Costello. Berkeley and Los Angeles: U of California P, 1969. Print.
Giles, J.A., ed. *Chronicles of the Crusades: Being Contemporary Narratives of the Crusade of Richard Coeur de Lion.* London: Bohn, 1848. Print.
Hausknecht, Emil, ed. *The Romaunce of the Sowdone of Babylone and of Ferumbras His Sone Who Conquered Rome.* London: Pub. for the Early English Text Society by Trübner, 1881. Print.
Herrtage, Sidney J., ed. *The Charlemagne Romances, Part II: "The Sege of Melany" and "The Romance of Duke Rowland and Sir Ottuell of Spayne," Together with a Fragment of "The Song of Roland."* London: Pub. for the Early English Text Society by N. Trübner & Co., 1880. Print.
———. *The Lyf of the Noble and Crysten Prynce Charles the Grete, Translated from the French by William Caxton, and Printed by Him 1485.* London: Pub. for the Early English Text Society by N. Trübner & Co., 1880. Print.
Hill, Rosalind, ed. *Gesta Francorum Et Aliorum Hierosolimitanorum.* London: Nelson & Sons, 1962. Print.
Hugh of St. Victor. *Didascalicon De Studio Legendi.* Turnhout: Brepols, n.d. Internet resource.
———. *The Didascalion of Hugh of St. Victor: A Medieval Guide to the Arts.* Trans. Jerome Taylor. New York: Columbia UP, 1961. Print.
Ibn al-Athīr, 'Izz al-Dīn and Carl Johan Tornberg. *Al-Kāmil fī al-tārīkh.* Báyrūt: Dār Sáder, 1965. Print.
———. *The Chronicle of Ibn al-Athīr for the Crusading Period from al-Kāmil fī'l-ta'rīkh, Part 1, the Years 491–541/1097–1146: The Coming of the Franks and the Muslim Response.* Trans. D.S. Richards. Burlington: Ashgate, 2006. Print.
———. *The Chronicle of Ibn al-Athīr for the Crusading Period from al-Kāmil- fī'l ta'rīkh, Part 2, the Years 541–589/1146–1193: The Age of Nur al-Din and Saladin.* Trans. D.S. Richards. Burlington: Ashgate, 2007. Print.
Ibn Al-Qalānisī. *The Damascus Chronicle of the Crusades: Extracted and Translated from the Chronicle of Ibn al-Qalānisī.* Trans. H.A.R. Gibb. London: Luzac, 1967. Print.
Ibn Al-Qalānisī, Abū Ya'lá Hamzah Ibn Asad, Ahmad Ibn Yūsuf Ibn 'Alī Ibn Al-Azraq Al-Fāriqī, Yūsuf Ibn Qizughlī Sibt Ibn Al-Jawzī and Muhammad Ibn Ahmad Dhahabī. *Tārīkh Abī Ya'lá Hamzah Ibn Al-Qalānisī: Al-ma'ruf Bi-Dhayl Tārīkh Dimashq.* Bayrūt: Matba'at Al-Ābā' Al-Yasū'īayn, 1908. Print.
Ibn Fadlan. *Ibn Fadlan's Journey to Russia: A Tenth-Century Traveler from Baghdad to the Volga River.* Trans. Richard N. Frye. Princeton: Wiener, 2005. Print.
Ibn Fadlān, Ahmad and Sāmī Al-Dahhān. *Risālat Ibn Fadlān (Ahmad Ibn Fadlān Ibn Al-'Abbās Ibn Rāshid Ibn Hammād).* Dimashq: Matbū'āt Al-Majma Al-'Ilmī Al-'Arabī Bi-Dimashq, 1959. Print.
———. *The 13th Warrior (formerly titled Eaters of the Dead): The Manuscript of Ibn Fadlan Relating to His Experiences with the Northmen in A.D. 922.* Trans. Michael Crichton. New York: Ballantine, 1992. Print.
Ibn Hazm. *The Ring of the Dove: A Treatise on the Art of Love and Practice of Arab Love.* Trans. A.J. Arberry. London: Luzac & Company, 1953. Print.
Ibn Jubayr, Muhammad ibn Ahmad. *Rihlat ibn Jubayr.* Beirut: Dār Bayrūt lil-Tabā'ah wa-al-Nashr, 1984. Print.
———. *The Travels of Ibn Jubayr: Being the Chronicle of a Mediaeval Spanish Moor Concerning His Journey to the Egypt of Saladin, the Holy Cities of Arabia,*

200 Bibliography

Baghdad the City of the Caliphs, the Latin Kingdom of Jerusalem, and the Norman Kingdom of Sicily. Trans. R.J.C. Broadhurst. London: Camelot, 1958. Print.

Ibn Khaldūn and Abdesselam Cheddadi. *Al-Muqaddimah.* Al-Dār al-Baydā': Khizānat Ibn Khaldūn, Bayt al-Funūn wa-al-'Ulūm wa-al-Ādāb, 2005. Print.

———. *An Arab Philosophy of History: Selections from the Prolegomena of Ibn Khaldun of Tunis (1332–1406).* Trans. Charles Issawi. Princeton: Darwin, 1987. Print.

———. *The Muqaddimah: An Introduction to History,* Vols. 1–3. Trans. Franz Rosenthal. New York: Pantheon, 1958. Print.

Ibn Mounkidh, Ousāma. *The Autobiography of Ousāma.* Trans. George Richard Potter. New York: Harcourt, 1929. Print.

Ibn Munqidh, Usāmah. *An Arab-Syrian Gentleman and Warrior in the Period of the Crusades: Memoirs of Usamah ibn-Munquidh (Kitab al-'Itibar).* Trans. Phillip K. Hitti. New York: Columbia UP, 1929. Print.

———. *The Book of Contemplation: Islam and the Crusades.* Trans. Paul M. Cobb. London: Penguin, 2008. Print.

———. *Kitāb al-i'tibār.* Ed. Philip Khuri Hitti. Al-Wilāyāt al-Muttahidah: Matba'at Jāmi'at Prinstūn, 1930. Print.

Ibn Rushd. *Averroes on Plato's "Republic."* Trans. Ralph Lerner. Ithaca: Cornell UP, 1974. Print.

Ibn Shaddād, Bahā' al-Dīn Yūsuf ibn Rāfi'. *Al-nawādir Al-Sultānīyah Wa-Al-Mahāsin Al-Yūsufīyah, Aw Sīrat Salāh Al-Dīn.* Al-Qāhirah: Al-Mu'assasah al-Misrīyah al-'Ammah, 1964. Print.

———. *The Rare and Excellent History of Saladin or al-Nawādir al-Sultāniyya wa'l-Mahāsin al-Yūsufiyya.* Trans. D.S. Richards. Aldershot: Ashgate, 2001. Print.

———. *Saladin or What Befell Sultan Yūsuf (Salah ed-Din, 1137–1193 A.D.).* Lahore: Islamic Book Service, 1988. Print.

'Imād al-Dīn. *Conquête de la Syrie et de la Palestine.* Trans. Henri Massé. Paris: Librairie Orientaliste Paul Geuthner, 1972. Print.

Isidore of Seville. *The Etymologies of Isidore of Seville.* Ed. and Trans. Stephen A. Barney. Cambridge: Cambridge UP, 2006. Print.

Isidori Hispalensis Episcopi. *Etymologiarum Sive Originum Libri XX.* Ed. W.M. Lindsay. Oxford: Oxford UP, 1911. Print.

Jeanroy, Alfred, ed. *La Geste De Guilluame Fièrebrace Et De Rainouart Au Tinel, D'après Les Poèmes Des 12e Et 13e Siècles, Par A. Jeanroy.* Paris: Boccard, 1924. Print.

John of Salisbury. *Ioannis Saresberiensis Metalogicon/Enumeratio Formarum, Concordantia Formarum, Index Formarum a Tergo Ordinatum.* Turnholti: Brepols, 1991. Print.

———. *The Metalogicon of John of Salisbury: A Twelfth-Century Defense of the Verbal and Logical Arts of the Trivium.* Trans. Daniel D. McGarry. Gloucester: Smith, 1971. Print.

———. *Policraticus.* Turnhout: Brepols, n.d. Internet resource.

———. *Policraticus: The Statesman's Book.* Ed. Murray F. Markland. New York: Ungar, 1979. Print.

Kölbing, Eugen, ed. *The Romance of Sir Beues of Hamtoun.* London: Pub. for the Early English Text Society by Paul, Trench, Trübner, 1885. Print.

Kritzeck, James. *Peter the Venerable and Islam.* Princeton: Princeton UP, 1964. Print.

Lull, Ramón. *Doctor Illuminatus: A Ramon Lull Reader.* Trans. Anthony Bonner and Eve Bonner. Princeton: Princeton UP, 1985. Print.

McKnight, George H., ed. *King Horn, Floriz and Blauncheflur, the Assumption of Our Lady*. London: Pub. for the Early English Text Society by Paul, Trench, Trübner & Co., 1866. Print.

Orosius, Paulus. *Pavli Orosii Presbyteri Hispani Adversvs Paganos Historiarvm Libri Septem*. Thorunii: Sumptibus Ernesti Lambeccii, 1857. Internet resource.

———. *Seven Books of History against the Pagans: The Apology of Paulus Orosius*. Trans. Irving Woodworth Raymond. New York: Columbia UP, 1936. Print.

Paris, Matthew. *The Illustrated Chronicles of Matthew Paris: Observations of Thirteenth-Century Life*. Trans. Richard Vaughan. Cambridge: Corpus Christi College, 1993. Print.

———. *Matthaei Parisiensis Monachi Sancti Albani Chronica Majora*. Ed. Henry Richards Luard. Nendeln: Kraus, 1964. Print.

Petrus Venerabilis. *Schriften Zum Islam*. Ed. Reinhold Glei. Altenberge: CIS-Verl, 1985. Print.

Ralph of Coggeshall. *Radulphi De Coggeshall Chronicon Anglicanum, De Expugnatione Terræ Sanctæ Libellus, Thomas Agnellus De Morte Et Sepultura Henrici Regis Angliæ Junioris*. Nendeln: Kraus, 1965. Print.

Ralph of Coggeshall, Gervasius of Tilbury, Thomas Agnellus and Fulk Fitz-Warine. *Radulphi De Coggeshall Chronicon Anglicanum, De Expugnatione Terræ Sanctæ Libellus, Thomas Agnellus De Morte Et Sepultura Henrici Regis Angliæ Junioris, Gesta Fulconis Filii Warini, Excerpta Ex Otiis Imperialibus Gervasii Tileburiensis. Ex Codicibus Manus*. Trans. Joseph Stevenson. Wiesbaden: Kraus, 1965. Print.

Ricardus, Canonicus Sanctae Trinitatis Londoniensis. *Chronicle of the Third Crusade: A Translation of the Itinerarium Peregrinorum et Gesta Regis Ricardi*. Trans. Helen J. Nicholson and William Stubbs. Brookfield: Ashgate, 1997. Print.

Ricardus, Canonicus Sanctae Trinitatis Londoniensis, William Stubbs, Osbern, and Neophytus. *Itinerarium Peregrinorum Et Gesta Regis Ricardi*. Ed. William Stubbs. London: Longman, Green, Longman, Roberts, and Green, 1864. Print.

Richard of Devizes. *The Chronicle of Richard of Devizes of the Time of King Richard the First (Cronicon Richardi Divisensis De Tempore Regis Richardi Primi)*. Ed. John T. Appleby. London: Nelson & Sons, 1963. Print.

———. *The Chronicle of Richard of Devizes of the Time of King Richard the First (Cronicon Richardi Divisensis De Tempore Regis Richardi Primi)*. Trans. John T. Appleby. London: Nelson & Sons, 1963. Print.

Robert le Moine. *The 'Historia Iherosolimitana' of Robert the Monk*. Eds. Damien Kempf and Marcus Graham Bull. Woodbridge, Suffolk: Boydell, 2013. Print.

Robert of Reims. *Robert the Monk's History of the First Crusade: Historia Iherosolimitana*. Trans. Carol Sweetenham. Burlington: Ashgate, 2005. Print.

Segré, Cesare, ed. *La Chanson De Roland*. Genéve: Droz, 1989. Print.

Seymour, M.C., ed. *The Bodley Version of Mandeville's Travels: From Bodleian MS. E Musaeo 116 with Parallel Extracts from the Latin Text of British Museum MS. Royal 13 E. IX*. Early English Text Society. Oxford: Oxford UP, 1963. Print.

———. *The Defective Version of Mandeville's Travels*. Oxford: Oxford UP, 2002. Print.

———. *Mandeville's Travels*. Oxford: Oxford UP, 1967. Print.

Shepherd, Stephen H.A., ed. *Turpines Story: A Middle English Translation of the Pseudo-Turpin Chronicle*. Oxford: Oxford UP, 2004. Print.

Short, Ian, ed. *The Anglo-Norman Pseudo-Turpin Chronicle of William de Briane*. Oxford: Anglo-Norman Text Society, 1973. Print.

Sir John Mandeville; Alfred W. Pollard; Giovanni da Pian del Carpine, Archbishop of Antivari; Willem van Ruysbroek; and Odorico da Pordenone. *The Travels of Sir John Mandeville: The Version of the Cotton Manuscript in Modern Spelling, with Three Narratives, in Illustration of It*. London: Macmillan, 1923. Print.
Sir John Mandeville; Alfred W. Pollard; Giovanni da Pian del Carpine, Archbishop of Antivari; Willem van Ruysbroek; and Odorico da Pordenone. *The Travels of Sir John Mandeville with Three Narratives in Illustration of It: The Voyage of Johannes de Plano Carpini, The Journal of Friar William de Rubruquis, The Journal of Friar Odoric*. New York: Dover, 1964. Print.
The Song of Roland. Trans. Glyn Burgess. London: Penguin, 1990. Print.
Vitalis, Orderic. *The Ecclesiastical History of Orderic Vitalis, Volume II: Books III and IV*. Ed. Marjorie Chibnall. Oxford: Clarendon, 1969. Print.
———. *The Ecclesiastical History of Orderic Vitalis, Volume II: Books III and IV*. Trans. Marjorie Chibnall. Oxford: Clarendon, 1969. Print.
William of Conches. *A Dialogue on Natural Philosophy (Dragmaticon Philosophiae)*. Trans. Italo Ronca and Matthew Curr. Notre Dame: U of Notre Dame P, 1997. Print.
———. *Guillelmus De Conchis, Dragmaticon Philosophiae*. Turnhout: Brepols, 2001. Print.
William of Malmesbury. *Gesta Regum Anglorum: The History of the English Kings, Volume I*. Trans. R.A.B. Mynors, R.M. Thomson and M. Winterbottom. Oxford: Clarendon, 1998. Print.
———. *Gesta Regum Anglorum, Volume I*. Eds. Roger Aubrey Baskerville Mynors, Rodney M. Thomson and Michael Winterbottom. Oxford: Clarendon, 1998. Print.
———. *Gesta regum anglorum, Volumen II*. Londini: Sumptibus Societatis, 1840. Print.
———. *William of Malmesbury's Chronicle of the Kings of England (From the Earliest Period to the Reign of King Stephen)*. Trans. J.A. Giles. London: Bohn. 1847. Print.
William of Tyre. *Crusader Syria in the Thirteenth Century: The Rothelin Continuation of the History of William of Tyre with Part of the Eracles or Acre Text*. Trans. Janet Shirley. Aldershot: Ashgate, 1999. Print.
———. *Guillaume De Tyr Chronique*. Ed. R.B.C. Huygens. Turnholti: Typographi Brepols, 1986. Print.
———. *A History of Deeds Done beyond the Sea, Vol. I*. Trans. Emily Atwater Babcock and A.C. Krey. New York: Columbia UP, 1943. Print.
Zupitza, Julius, ed. *The Romance of Guy of Warwick, Part I, Version I*. London: Pub. for the Early English Text Society by Trübner, 1875. Print.
———. *The Romance of Guy of Warwick, Part II, Version II*. London: Pub. for the Early English Text Society by Trübner, 1875. Print.

Secondary sources

Ahmad, Nafis. *Muslims and the Science of Geography*. Dacca: University Press Limited, 1980. Print.
———. *Muslim Contributions to Geography*. Lahore: Ashraf, 1972. Print.
Ahmad, S. Maqbul. "Al-Mas'ūdī's Contributions to Medieval Arab Geography." *Islamic Culture*. 27 (1953): 61–77. Print.
———. "Al-Mas'ūdī's Contributions to Medieval Arab Geography: Some Sources of His Knowledge." *Islamic Culture*. 28 (1954): 275–86. Print.

———. "Cartography of al-Sharīf al-Idrīsī." *The History of Cartography, Volume Two, Book One: Cartography in the Traditional Islamic and South Asian Societies.* Eds. J.B. Harley and David Woodward. Chicago: U of Chicago P, 1992. 156–74. Print.

———. *India and the Neighboring Territories in the Kitāb Nuzhat Al-Mushtāq Fi' Khtirāq Al-'Āfāq of Al-Sharīf Al-Idrīsī.* Leiden: Brill, 1960. Print.

Ahmad, Zaid. *The Epistemology of Ibn Khaldūn.* London: Routledge Curzon, 2003. Print.

Ailes, Marianne. "Otinel: An Epic in Dialogue with the Tradition." *Olifant.* 27 (2012): 9–39. Web. 28 Sept. 2015.

Allen, Roger. *The Arabic Literary Heritage: The Development of Its Genres and Criticism.* Cambridge: Cambridge UP, 1998. Print.

Allen, Rosamund, ed. *Eastward Bound: Travel and Travellers, 1050–1550.* Manchester: Manchester UP, 2004. Print.

Anidjar, Gil. *The Jew, the Arab: A History of the Enemy.* Stanford: Stanford UP, 2003. Print.

Ansari, Zafar Ishaq and John Esposito, eds. *Muslims and the West: Encounter and Dialogue.* Islamabad: Islamic Research Institute, 2001. Print.

Asbridge, Thomas. *The First Crusade: A New History.* Oxford: Oxford UP, 2004. Print.

Asin, Miguel. *Islam and the Divine Comedy.* Trans. Harold Sunderland. London: Murray, 1926. Print.

Atiya, Aziz S. *Crusade, Commerce and Culture.* Bloomington: Indiana UP, 1962. Print.

Bartlett, Robert. *The Making of Europe: Conquest, Colonization and Cultural Change 950–1350.* Princeton: Princeton UP, 1993. Print.

Bartlett, W.B. *The Last Crusade: The Seventh Crusade & the Final Battle for the Holy Land.* Stroud: Tempus, 2007. Print.

Beckingham, C.F. *Between Islam and Christendom: Travellers, Facts and Legends in the Middle Ages and the Renaissance.* London: Variorum, 1983. Print.

Bennett, Philip E. "The Storming of the Otherworld, the Enamoured Muslim Princess and the Evolution of the Legend of Guillaume d'Orange." *Guillaume d'Orange and the Chanson de Geste: Essays Presented to Duncan McMillan in Celebration of His Seventieth Birthday.* Eds. Philip E. Bennett and Wolfgang G. van Emden. Reading: Société Rencesvals British Branch, 1984. 1–14. Print.

Benson, C. David. *Public Piers Plowman: Modern Scholarship and Late Medieval English Culture.* University Park: Pennsylvania State UP, 2004. Print.

Billings, Anna Hunt. *A Guide to the Middle English Metrical Romances: Dealing with English and Germanic Legends, and with the Cycles of Charlemagne and Arthur.* New York: Holt, 1901. Print.

Bloom, Harold. *The Anxiety of Influence.* New York: Oxford UP, 1973. Print.

Boyarin, Jonathan. *The Unconverted Self: Jews, Indians, and the Identity of Christian Europe.* Chicago: U of Chicago P, 2009. Print.

Brault, Gerard J. *The Song of Roland: An Analytical Edition, I. Introduction and Commentary.* University Park: Pennsylvania State UP, 1978. Print.

Brehaut, Ernest. *An Encyclopedist of the Dark Ages: Isidore of Seville.* New York: Longman, Green & Co., 1912. Print.

Bridges, John Henry. *The Life & Work of Roger Bacon: An Introduction to the Opus Majus.* London: Williams and Norgate, 1914. Print.

Butterworth, Charles and Blake Andre Kessel, eds. *The Introduction of Arabic into Europe.* Leiden: Brill, 1994. Print.

Cahoone, Lawrence E., ed. *From Modernism to Postmodernism: An Anthology.* Cambridge: Blackwell, 1996. Print.

Calkin, Siobhain Bly. *Saracens and the Making of English Identity: The Auchinleck Manuscript.* New York: Routledge, 2005. Print.

Campbell, Mary B. *The Witness and the Other World: Exotic European Travel Writing, 400–1600.* Ithaca: Cornell UP, 1988. Print.

Chareyron, Nicole. *Pilgrims to Jerusalem in the Middle Ages.* Trans. W. Donald Wilson. New York: Columbia UP, 2005. Print.

Chaunu, Pierre. *European Expansion in the Later Middle Ages.* Trans. Katherine Bertram. Amsterdam: North-Holland, 1979. Print.

Chejne, Anwar G. *Muslim Spain: Its History and Culture.* Minneapolis: U of Minnesota P, 1974. Print.

Clegg, Brian. *The First Scientist: A Life of Roger Bacon.* New York: Carroll & Graf, 2003. Print.

Cohen, Jeffrey Jerome. *Of Giants: Sex, Monsters, and the Middle Ages.* Medieval Cultures 17. Minneapolis: U of Minnesota P, 1999. Print.

Connelly, Bridget. *Arab Folk Epic and Identity.* Berkely: U of California P, 1986. Print.

Cowan, Janet M. "The English Charlemagne Romances." *Roland and Charlemagne in Europe: Essays on the Reception and Transformation of a Legend.* Ed. Karen Pratt. London: King's College, 1996. 149–68. Print.

Cowdrey, H.E.J. *The Crusades and Latin Monasticism, 11–12th Centuries.* Aldershot: Ashgate, 1999. Print.

Crosland, Jessie. *The Old French Epic.* Oxford: Blackwell, 1951. Print.

Daniel, Norman. *The Arabs and Medieval Europe.* London: Longman, 1979. Print.

———. *Heroes and Saracens: An Interpretation of the chansons de geste.* Edinburgh: Edinburgh UP, 1984. Print.

———. *Islam and the West: The Making of an Image.* Edinburgh: Edinburgh UP, 1960. Print.

del Pulgar, A. Hernando. "Cronicas de los reyes de Castilla 1492." Trans. Teofilo Ruiz. *Medieval Iberia: Readings from Christian, Muslim, and Jewish Sources.* Ed. Olivia Remie Constable. Philadelphia: U of Pennsylvania P, 1997. 343. Print.

Devisse, Jean. *The Image of the Black in Western Art.* New York: W. Morrow, 1979. Print.

de Weever, Jacqueline. *Sheba's Daughters: Whitening and Demonizing the Saracen Woman in Medieval French Epic.* London: Garland, 1998. Print.

Duggan, Alfred. *The Story of the Crusades: 1097–1291.* New York: Pantheon, 1963. Print.

Duri, A.A. *The Rise of Historical Writing among the Arabs.* Trans. Lawrence I. Conrad. Princeton: Princeton UP, 1983. Print.

Easton, Stewart C. *Roger Bacon and His Search for a Universal Science: A Reconsideration of the Life and Work of Roger Bacon in the Light of His Own Stated Purposes.* New York: Columbia UP, 1952. Print.

Edbury, Peter W. *The Conquest of Jerusalem and the Third Crusade: Sources in Translation.* Brookfield: Ashgate, 1996. Print.

Edson, Evelyn. *The World Map, 1300–1492: The Persistence of Tradition and Transformation.* Baltimore: Johns Hopkins UP, 2007. Print.

El-Cheikh, Nadia Maria. "Byzantium through the Islamic Prism from the Twelfth to the Thirteenth Century." *The Crusades from the Perspective of Byzantium and the Muslim World.* Eds. Angeliki E. Laiou and Roy Parviz Mottahedeh. Washington, DC: Dumbarton Oaks, 2001. 53–70. Print.

Erdmann, Carl. *The Origin of the Idea of Crusade*. Trans. Marshall W. Baldwin and Walter Goffart. Princeton: Princeton UP, 1977. Print.

Faruqi, Nisar Ahmed. *Early Muslim Historiography: A Study of Early Transmitters of Arab History from the Rise of Islam Up to the End of the Umayyad Period (612–750 A.D.)*. New Delhi: Idarah-I Adabiyat-i Delhi, 1979. Print.

Finucane, Ronald C. *Soldiers of the Faith: Crusaders and Muslims at War*. London: Dent & Sons, 1983. Print.

Fischel, Walter J. "Ibn Khaldūn and al-Masʿūdī." *Al-Masʿūdī Millenary Commemoration Volume*. Eds. S. Maqbul Ahmad and A. Rahman. Calcutta: Little Flower, 1960. 51–60. Print.

Flori, Jean. *Richard the Lionheart: King and Knight*. Trans. Jean Birrell. Edinburgh: Edinburgh UP, 2006. Print.

French, Walter H. *Essays on King Horn*. Ithaca: Cornell UP, 1940. Print.

Friedman, John Block. *The Monstrous Races in Medieval Art and Thought*. Cambridge: Harvard UP, 1981. Print.

Giffen, Lois Anita. *Theory of Profane Love among the Arabs: The Development of the Genre*. New York: New York UP, 1971. Print.

Gilbert, Jane. "Putting the Pulp into Fiction: The Lump-Child and Its Parents in *The King of Tars*." *Pulp Fictions of Medieval England: Essays in Popular Romance*. Ed. Nicola McDonald. Manchester: Manchester UP, 2004. 102–23. Print.

Glick, Thomas F. *Islamic and Christian Spain in the Early Middle Ages*. Princeton: Princeton UP, 1979. Print.

Grousset, René. *Histoire des croisades, Vol. 1*. Paris: Plon, 1934–6. Print.

Hardman, Phillipa and Marianne Ailes. "Crusading, Chivalry and the Saracen World in Insular Romance." *Christianity and Romance in Medieval England*. Eds. Rosalind Field, Phillipa Hardman and Michelle Sweeney. Cambridge: Brewer, 2010. 45–65. Print.

Harvey, P.D.A., ed. *The Hereford World Map: Medieval World Maps and Their Context*. London: British Library, 2006. Print.

Heath, Peter. *The Thirsty Sword: Sirat ʿAntar and the Arabic Popular Epic*. Salt Lake City: U of Utah P, 1996. Print.

Hermes, Nizar F. *The [European] Other in Medieval Arabic Literature and Culture: Ninth-Twelfth Century AD*. New York: Palgrave Macmillan, 2012. Print.

Higgins, Iain Macleod. *Writing East: The "Travels" of Sir John Mandeville*. Philadelphia: U of Pennsylvania P, 1997. Print.

Hillenbrand, Carole. *The Crusades: Islamic Perspectives*. New York: Routledge, 1999. Print.

Holt, P.M. *The Age of the Crusades: The Near East from the Eleventh Century to 1517*. London: Longman, 1986. Print.

Housely, Norman. *The Crusaders*. Stroud: Tempus, 2002. Print.

Jotischky, Andrew. *Crusading and the Crusader States*. Harlow: Pearson, 2004. Print.

Jubb, Margaret. *The Legend of Saladin in Western Literature and Historiography*. Lewiston: Mellen, 2000. Print.

Kazmi, S. Hasan Askari. *The Makers of Medieval Muslim Geography: Alberuni*. New Delhi: Renaissance, 1995. Print.

Kennedy, Valerie. *Edward Said: A Critical Introduction*. Cambridge: Polity, 2000. Print.

Khalidi, Tarif. *Islamic Historiography: The Histories of Masʿūdī*. Albany: State U of New York P, 1975. Print.

Kimble, George H.T. *Geography in the Middle Ages*. London: Methuen & Co., 1938. Print.

Kline, Naomi Reed. *Maps of Medieval Thought: The Hereford Paradigm.* Woodbridge: Boydell, 2001. Print.
Kuhn, Sherman M. and John Reidy, eds. "Mahǒun." *Middle English Dictionary: Volume 6 (Lef-Minten).* Ann Arbor: U of Michigan P, 1975. 15. Print.
———. "Maumerīe." *Middle English Dictionary: Volume 6 (Lef-Minten).* Ann Arbor: U of Michigan P, 1975. 232. Print.
———. "Maumetrīe." *Middle English Dictionary: Volume 6 (Lef-Minten).* Ann Arbor: U of Michigan P, 1975. 233–4. Print.
Labarge, Margaret Wade. *Medieval Travellers: The Rich and Restless.* London: Hamilton, 1982. Print.
Lasater, Alice E. *Spain to England: A Comparative Study of Arabic, European, and English Literature of the Middle Ages.* Jackson: U of Mississippi P, 1974. Print.
Lewis, Bernard. *The Muslim Discovery of Europe.* New York: Norton, 1982. Print.
Lewis, Bernard, V.L. Ménage, Ch. Pellat and J. Schacht, eds. "Adjā'ib." *The Encyclopaedia of Islam, Volume III: A-B.* Leiden: Brill, 1960. 203–4. Print.
———. "Al-Idrīsī." *The Encyclopaedia of Islam, Volume III: H-IRAM.* E. J. Brill, 1971. 1032–5. Print.
———. "Bash*djirt*." [from "Bashkir"] *The Encyclopaedia of Islam, Volume III: A-B.* E. J. Brill, 1960. 1075–7. Print.
———. "Djughrāfiyā." *The Encyclopaedia of Islam, Volume III: C-G.* E. J. Brill, 1965. 575–90. Print.
———. "Ibn Fadlān." *The Encyclopaedia of Islam, Volume III: H-IRAM.* E. J. Brill, 1971. 759. Print.
———. "Ibn Khaldūn." *The Encyclopaedia of Islam, Volume III: H-IRAM.* E. J. Brill, 1971. 825–31. Print.
———. "IFran*dj*." *The Encyclopaedia of Islam, Volume III: H-IRAM.* E. J. Brill, 1971. 1044–6. Print.
———. "Rūs." *The Encyclopaedia of Islam, Volume III: NED-SAM.* E. J. Brill, 1995. 618–29. Print.
———. "Sakāliba." *The Encyclopaedia of Islam, Volume III: NED-SAM.* E. J. Brill, 1995. 872–81. Print.
Lewis, Reina. *Gendering Orientalism: Race, Femininity and Representation.* New York: Routledge, 1996. Print.
Lewis, Robert E., ed. "Sarasin(e)." *Middle English Dictionary: Volume 10 (S-Sl).* Ann Arbor: U of Michigan P, 1986. 86–7. Print.
———. "Turk." *Middle English Dictionary: Volume 11 (T).* Ann Arbor: U of Michigan P, 1993. 1159–60. Print.
Lock, Peter. *The Routledge Companion to the Crusades.* London: Routledge, 2006. Print.
Loomis, Laura Hibbard. *Mediæval Romance in England: A Study of the Sources and Analogues of the Non-Cyclic Metrical Romances.* New York: Franklin, 1969. Print.
Lozovsky, Natalia. *"The Earth Is Our Book": Geographical Knowledge in the Latin West ca. 400–1000.* Ann Arbor: U of Michigan P, 2000. Print.
Maalouf, Amin. *The Crusades through Arab Eyes.* Trans. Jon Rothschild. New York: Schocken, 1984. Print.
Macfie, A.L., ed. *Orientalism: A Reader.* New York: New York UP, 2000. Print.
MacKenzie, John M. *Orientalism: History, Theory and the Arts.* Manchester: Manchester UP, 1995. Print.

Madden, Thomas F. *The New Concise History of the Crusades: Updated Edition.* Lanham: Rowman & Littlefield, 2005. Print.
Mason, Peter. *Deconstructing America: Representations of the Other.* London: Routledge, 1990. Print.
Matthew, H.C.G. and Brian Harrison, eds. "Bacon, Roger." *Oxford Dictionary of National Biography, from the Earliest Times to the Year 2000: Volume 3 (Avranches-Barnewall).* Oxford: Oxford UP, 2004. 176–81. Print.
———. "Conches, William de." *Oxford Dictionary of National Biography, from the Earliest Times to the Year 2000: Volume 12 (Clegg-Const).* Oxford: Oxford UP, 2004. 916–17. Print.
Mayer, Hans Eberhard. *The Crusades.* 2nd ed. Trans. John Gillingham. Oxford: Oxford UP, 1988. Print.
McCann, Carole R. and Seung-Kyung Kim, eds. *Feminist Theory Reader: Local and Global Perspectives.* New York: Routledge, 2003. Print.
Menocal, Maria Rosa, Raymond P. Scheindlin and Michael Sells, eds. *The Literature of Al-Andalus.* Cambridge: Cambridge UP, 2000. Print.
Merrills, A.H. *History and Geography in Late Antiquity.* Cambridge: Cambridge UP, 2005. Print.
Metlitzki, Dorothee. *The Matter of Araby in Medieval England.* New Haven: Yale UP, 1977. Print.
Mittman, Asa Simon. *Maps and Monsters in Medieval England.* New York: Routledge, 2006. Print.
Monroe, James T. *Hispano-Arabic Poetry: A Student Anthology.* Berkeley: U of California P, 1974. Print.
Morrison, Karl F. *Understanding Conversion.* Charlottesville: UP of Virginia, 1992. Print.
Nicholson, Helen. *Chronicle of the Third Crusade: A Translation of the Itinerarium Peregrinorum et Gesta Regis Ricardi.* Brookfield: Ashgate, 1997. Print.
Nicholson, Helen. *The Crusades.* Westport: Greenwood, 2004. Print.
Nicholson, Reynold A. *A Literary History of the Arabs.* London: Kegan Paul International, 1998. Print.
Niyogi, Chandreyee, ed. *Reorienting Orientalism.* New Delhi: Sage Publications, 2006. Print.
"Nubdhat al-'asr". *Medieval Iberia: Readings from Christian, Muslim, and Jewish Sources.* Trans. L.P. Harvey and Ed. Olivia Remie Constable. Philadelphia: U of Pennsylvania P, 1997. 350–1. Print.
Parker, John. *Merchants & Scholars: Essays in the History of Exploration and Trade.* Minneapolis: U of Minnesota P, 1965. Print.
Phillips, Jonathan. *The First Crusade: Origins and Impact.* Manchester: Manchester UP, 1997. Print.
———. *Holy Warriors: A Modern History of the Crusades.* London: Bodley Head, 2009. Print.
Porter, Neil A. *Physicists in Conflict.* Bristol: Institute of Physics, 1998. Print.
Powell, James M. *Muslims under Latin Rule, 1100–1300.* Princeton: Princeton UP, 1990. Print.
Rabī', Muhammad Mahmoud. *The Political Theory of Ibn Khaldūn.* Leiden: Brill, 1967. Print.
Resnick, Irven M. and Kenneth F. Mitchell. *Albert the Great: A Selectively Annotated Bibliography (1900–2000).* Tempe: Arizona Center for Medieval and Renaissance Studies, 2004. Print.

Reynolds, Dwight Fletcher. *Heroic Poets, Poetic Heroes: The Ethnography of Performance in an Arabic Oral Epic Tradition.* Ithaca: Cornell UP, 1995. Print.
Richard, Jean. *The Crusades, c.1071-c.1291.* Trans. Jean Birrell. Cambridge: Cambridge UP, 1999. Print.
Ridyard, Susan J. and Robert G. Benson, eds. *Man and Nature in the Middle Ages.* Sewanee: U of the South P, 1995. Print.
Riley-Smith, Jonathan. *The Crusades: A History.* 2nd ed. New Haven: Yale UP, 2005. Print.
Riley-Smith, Louise and Jonathan Riley-Smith. *The Crusades: Idea and Reality, 1095–1274.* Eds. G.W.S. Barrow and Edward Miller. London: Arnold, 1981. Print.
Robinson, Arthur H. *Early Thematic Mapping in the History of Cartography.* Chicago: U of Chicago P, 1982. Print.
Rodinson, Maxime. *Europe and the Mystique of Islam.* Trans. Roger Veinus. Seattle: U of Washington P, 1987. Print.
Runciman, Steven. *A History of the Crusades, Volume I: The First Crusade and the Foundation of the Kingdom of Jerusalem.* Cambridge: Cambridge UP, 1951. Print.
———. *A History of the Crusades, Volume II: The Kingdom of Jerusalem and the Frankish East.* Cambridge: Cambridge UP, 1952. Print.
———. *A History of the Crusades, Volume III: The Kingdom of Acre and the Later Crusades.* Cambridge: Cambridge UP, 1954. Print.
Said, Edward W. *Orientalism.* New York: Vintage, 1978. Print.
Shafi, Mohammad. "Al-Mas'ūdī as a Geographer." *Al-Mas'ūdī Millenary Commemoration Volume.* Eds. S. Maqbul Ahmad and A. Rahman. Calcutta: Little Flower, 1960. 72–7. Print.
Sharafuddin, Mohammed. *Islam and Romantic Orientalism: Literary Encounters with the Orient.* London: Taurus, 1994. Print.
Shboul, Ahmad M.H. *Al-Mas'ūdī and His World: A Muslim Humanist and His Interest in Non-Muslims.* London: Ithaca, 1979. Print.
Shepherd, William R. *Atlas of Medieval and Modern History.* New York: Henry Holt and Company, 1932. Print.
Siddiqi, Akhtar Husain. "Muslim Geographic Thought and the Influence of Greek Philosophy." *GeoJournal.* 37.1. Ed. Wolf Tietze. Boston: Kluwer Academic, 1995. 9–15. Print.
Simon, Heinrich. *Ibn Khaldun's Science of Human Culture.* Trans. Fuad Baali. Lahore: Sh. Muhammad Ashraf, 1978. Print.
Simon, Róbert. *Ibn Khaldūn: History as Science and the Patrimonial Empire.* Budapest: Akadémiai Kiadó, 2002. Print.
Singh, Amritjit and Bruce G. Johnson, eds. *Interviews with Edward W. Said.* Jackson: UP of Mississippi, 2004. Print.
Smart, Lez. *Maps That Made History: The Influential, the Eccentric and the Sublime.* Kew: The National Archives, 2004. Print.
Snowden Jr., Frank M. "Greeks and Ethiopians." *Greeks and Barbarians: Essays on the Interactions between Greeks and Non-Greeks in Antiquity and the Consequences for Eurocentrism.* Eds. John E. Coleman and Clark A. Walz. Bethesda: CDL, 1997. 103–26. Print.
Southern, R.W. *The Making of the Middle Ages.* London: Pimlico, 1967. Print.
Sowayan, Saad Abdullah. *Nabati Poetry: The Oral Poetry of Arabia.* Berkeley: U of California P, 1985. Print.
Speed, Diane. "The Saracens of *King Horn.*" *Speculum.* 65 (1990): 564–95. Print.
Stetkevych, Jaroslav. *Muhammad and the Golden Bough: Reconstructing Arabian Myth.* Bloomington: Indiana UP, 1996. Print.

———. *The Zephyrs of Najd: The Poetics of Nostalgia in the Classical Arabic Nasib*. Chicago: U of Chicago P, 1993. Print.
Stetkevych, Susan Pinckney. *The Mute Immortals Speak: Pre-Islamic Poetry and the Poetics of Ritual*. Ithaca: Cornell UP, 1993. Print.
———. *The Poetics of Islamic Legitimacy: Myth, Gender, and Ceremony in the Classical Arabic Ode*. Bloomington: Indiana UP, 2002. Print.
Stock, Brian. *Myth and Science in the Twelfth Century: A Study of Bernard Silvester*. Princeton: Princeton UP, 1972. Print.
Strickland, Debra Higgs. *Saracens, Demons & Jews: Making Monsters in Medieval Art*. Princeton: Princeton UP, 2003. Print.
Taylor, Victor E. and Charles E. Winquist, eds. *Encyclopedia of Postmodernism*. New York: Routledge, 2001. Print.
Tolmacheva, Marina A. "Geography." *Medieval Islamic Civilization: An Encyclopedia, Volume I: A-K*. Ed. Josef W. Meri. New York: Routledge, 2006. 284–8. Print.
Tomasch, Sylvia and Sealy Gilles, eds. *Texts and Territory: Geographical Imagination in the European Middle Ages*. Philadelphia: U of Pennsylvania P, 1998. Print.
Tyerman, Christopher. *The Debate on the Crusades*. New York: Palgrave Macmillan, 2011. Print.
———. *Fighting for Christendom: Holy War and the Crusades*. Oxford: Oxford UP, 2004. Print.
———. *The Invention of the Crusades*. Toronto: U of Toronto P, 1998. Print.
Tzanaki, Rosemary. *Mandeville's Medieval Audiences: A Study on the Reception of the Book of Sir John Mandeville (1371–1550)*. Burlington: Ashgate, 2003. Print.
Uebel, Michael. "Unthinking the Monster: Twelfth-Century Responses to Saracen Alterity." *Monster Theory: Reading Culture*. Ed. Jeffrey Jerome Cohen. Minneapolis: U of Minnesota P, 1996. 264–91. Print.
Verdon, Jean. *Travel in the Middle Ages*. Trans. Beorge Holoch. Notre Dame: U of Notre Dame P, 2003. Print.
Watt, W. Montgomery. *The Influence of Islam on Medieval Europe*. Edinburgh: Edinburgh UP, 1972. Print.
Wehr, Hans. *A Dictionary of Modern Written Arabic (Arabic-English)*. 4th ed. Ed. J. Milton Cowan. Ithaca: Spoken Language Services, 1994. Print.
Weisheipl, James A., O.P. "The Life and Works of St. Albert the Great." *Albertus Magnus and the Sciences: Commemorative Essays, 1980*. Ed. James A. Weisheipl. Toronto: Pontifical Institute of Medieval Studies, 1980. 13–51. Print.
Whitfield, Peter. *The Image of the World: 20 Centuries of World Maps*. San Francisco: Pomegranate Artbooks, 1994. Print.
Williamson, Arthur H. "Scots, Indians and Empire: The Scottish Politics of Civilization 1519–1609." *Past and Present*. 150 (1996): 46–83. Print.
Woodward, David and Herbert M. Howe. "Roger Bacon on Geography and Cartography." *Roger Bacon and the Sciences: Commemorative Essays*. Ed. Jeremiah Hackett. New York: Brill, 1997. 199–222. Print.
Wright, John Kirtland. *The Geographical Lore of the Crusades: A Study in the History of Medieval Science and Tradition in Western Europe*. Concord: Rumford, 1925. Print.
Zambelli, Paola. *The Speculum Astronomiae and Its Enigma: Astrology, Theology and Science in Albertus Magnus and His Contemporaries*. Dordrecht: Kluwer Academic, 1992. Print.
Zwettler, Michael. *The Oral Tradition of Classical Arabic Poetry: Its Character and Implications*. Columbus: Ohio State UP, 1978. Print.

Index

'Abbāsid Caliphate 38, 41, 56, 58n18, 139, 165n3
'Abd al-Rahmān III (Caliph) 47
Abū 'Abdullah Muhammad ibn Muhammad ibn 'Abdullah ibn Idrīsī al-Sharīf *see* al-Idrīsī
Abū 'l-Hasan 'Alī ibn al-Husayn ibn 'Abd-Allāh al-Mas'ūdī *see* al-Mas'ūdī
Abū 'l-Qāsim 'Ubayd Allāh ibn 'Abd Allāh ibn Khurradādhbih *see* ibn Khurradādhbih
Abū 'Ubayd 'Abd Allāh b. 'Abd al-'Azīz b. Muhammad b. Ayyū al-Bakrī *see* al-Bakrī
Abu Shama 156
Abū Zayd 'Abd al-Rahman ibn Muhammad ibn Khaldūn Walī al-Dīn al-Tunisi al-Hadrami al-Ishbili al-Maliki *see* Ibn Khaldūn
Achebe, Chinua 9
Acre 66, 127, 148, 154, 156, 160–2, 175–6, 178–83
Æthicus Ister 23
Against the Pagans (Alain de Lille) 29
Ahmad ibn al-Tayyib al-Sarakhsi 42
Ahmad ibn Fadlān ibn al-Abbās ibn Rāshid ibn Hammād *see* Ibn Fadlān
Aigalonde (Saracen king) 69
'Ajā'ib al-Hind (Burzug ibn Shahriyār) 40
'ajā'ib literature 40, 63
Alain de Lille 29
Albertus Magnus 20–3, 127
Alexius Comnenus 139, 186n5
Almagest (Ptolemy) 39, 41
Ambroise 128–9

Anthropophagians 16, 22
Antioch 126, 137, 139, 155, 158
Apocrypha 23
Apparitions of Fixed Stars (Ptolemy) *see Appearance of the Stationary Stars*
Appearance of the Stationary Stars (Ptolemy) 39, 42
Arabs: Isidore's genealogy of 14–15; lack of attention to 14; mentioned by Albertus Magnus 22; Roger Bacon's account of 24–5
Aristotle 12, 20, 23, 39, 41, 42, 54
Armenian Christians 152, 153, 163, 191
al-Ashraf Khalil 180
astronomy 23, 34n62, 42; *see also* planets
Averroes (Ibn Rushd) 20
Avicenna (Ibn Sīna) 20, 23

Bahā' al-Dīn 156, 160–2, 175–80
Baibars 174, 180
al-Bakrī (Abū 'Ubayd 'Abd Allāh b. 'Abd al-'Azīz b. Muhammad b. Ayyūb al-Bakrī) 46–7
Baldwin III 147–8
al-Balkhī 42
Balkhī school of cartography 49, 61n77
Bartholomew, Peter 155, 158, 171n73
al-Battani 42
Battle of Hattīn 153
Baybars 127
Bible 23, 24
Bohemond of Apulia 174
Book of Roger (al-Idrīsī) 48, 52

The Book of the Two Gardens (Kitāb ar-Raudatain; Abu Shama) 156
Burzug ibn Shahriyār 40
Byzantine Christians 152, 153, 163, 169n47, 191, 193

Carl (grandson of Charlemagne) 45
chansons de geste 3, 77n2, 89, 129
Charlemagne 45, 69
Christians: Armenian 152, 153, 163, 191; Byzantine 152, 153, 163, 169n47, 191, 193; as Other 193, 194–6; in Syria and Lebanon 152
Christopher (saint) 108, 120n3
Chronicle of Richard of Devizes of the Time of King Richard the First 182
chronicles of the Crusades: Crusader-Muslim interaction 142–3, 162–3; focus on lack of Muslim leadership 141, 164–5, 165n1; foreign Saracens in 126–33; Muslim accounts of Crusader culture 141–2; Muslim accounts of military struggle 160–5; Muslim depictions of Franks 144–52; on religious motivations for the conflict 152–60
Church of the Holy Sepulcher 136n29, 140, 154–5, 169n53, 177
"climes," Greek concept of 20–1, 39, 43, 45, 58n6
Clotild 45
Clovis 44
colonization 9
Compendium Studii Philosophiae (Roger Bacon) 23
Constantinople 127, 133n3, 138, 152
Cosmographia (Æthicus Ister) 23
cross, as emblem of conquest 153
Crusaders: as *al-Ifranj* 140–1; Muslim accounts of culture and law 141–2
Crusader States 126–7, 137, 139, 164, 165n1
Crusades 6, 7, 51, 192; First 6, 126–7, 128–33, 133n9, 138, 159, 163, 172, 173; Second 126; Third 7, 126–7, 128, 133nn6–7, 153, 173, 174, 179–82; Fourth 127, 152; Fifth 127; and the defining of the Other 194; lack of interest in by Muslim historians 173; in literary discourse 194; religious dimensions of 153–60; Saracens in accounts of 126–33; Western European role in 137–41; *see also* chronicles of the Crusades
Cyprus 127

Damascus, siege of 126, 159
De Caelo (Aristotle) 23, 42
De multiplicatione specierum (Roger Bacon) 23
De situ et nominibus locorum Hebraicorum (Jerome) 23
De speculis comburentibus (Roger Bacon) 23
De vitae sua mutatione (Ovid) 26–7
Dome of the Rock 153, 158
Dragmaticon Philosophiae (Dialogue on Natural Philosophy; William of Conches) 18–19

Edessa 126, 137, 139
Egypt, Fatimid 38, 136n29, 138, 140, 142, 152, 165–6nn2–3, 166n9
Eleanor of Aquitane 180, 188n27
epics 63
Estoire d'Antioche 127
Estoire de la Guerre Sainte (Ambroise) 128–9, 181, 182, 183, 188n34
Ethiopians 16–17
ethnocentricity 1, 2, 22, 194, 196
ethnography 1, 2, 13, 18, 23, 70, 80
Etymologiae sive originum libri XX (Isidore of Seville) 13, 14–16
Europeans: Muslim awareness of 139–40; Muslim characterization of 40–1, 44–5, 47, 50, 54–7, 62n96, 64–7

al-Farghāni 23, 42
Fatimid Egypt 38, 136n29, 138, 140, 142, 152, 165–6nn2–3, 166n9
Fierabras 3, 4, 9n3, 89–91
Fifth Crusade 127
First Crusade 6, 126–7, 128–33, 133n9, 138, 159, 163, 172, 173
Flores Historiarum 5
Fourth Crusade 127, 152
Franks (*al-iFranj*): barbaric nature of 47, 146–7, 150–1, 158;

Crusaders as 140–1; duplicitous nature of 147–8; in early Muslim literature 40–1; Hospitallers 161–2; importance of the knight to 144–5; Al-Idrīsī's opinion of 50; moral laxity of 143, 148–50; kings of 44–5; al-Mas'ūdī's explication of 44, 46; Muslim stereotypes of 6, 193–5; naiveté of 158–9; religious fervor of 154–7, 159–60; Templars 161–2; as unclean 157; as warriors 145, 160–3; who have learned Muslim customs 151
Fulcher of Chartres 29

Galicians 46–7
Geminos 42
geographical literature 39–40
Geographikê Hyphêgêsis (Ptolemy) 39, 40, 41
geography 1, 2, 13, 18, 42, 63, 80–1, 86; according to Albertus Magnus 20–3; according to al-Bakrī 46–7; according to Ibn Khaldūn 52, 54, 57; according to al-Idrīsī 49–50; according to al-Mas'ūdī 45; in the Middle Ages 12, 39–42, 46; according to Muhammad ibn Mūsā al-Khwārizmī 39; according to Roger Bacon 23–4; according to William of Conches 19
Gesta Francorum et aliorum Hierosolimitanorum 130, 173
Guillaume cycle 104n23

al-Hākim (Fatimid caliph) 140
Hārun ibn Yahyā 41
Hermes 42
Historia Iherosolimitana 130
Historiarum adversus paganos libri septem (Paulus Orosius) 13, 14
History of Deeds Done Beyond the Sea (William of Tyre) 29

Ibn al-'Athīr 140, 153, 158
Ibn Fadlān (Ahmad ibn Fadlān ibn al-Abbās ibn Rāshid ibn Hammād) 40, 63, 77
Ibn Hawqal 49

Ibn Jubayr (Muhammad ibn Ahmad ibn Jubayr) 51, 65, 99
Ibn Khaldūn (Abū Zayd 'Abd al-Rahman ibn Muhammad ibn Khaldūn Walī al-Dīn al-Tunisi al-Hadrami al-Ishbili al-Maliki) 48, 51–7
ibn Khurradādhbih (Abū 'l-Qāsim 'Ubayd Allāh ibn 'Abd Allāh ibn Khurradādhbih) 39, 40, 42, 48
Ibn Rushd (Averroes) 20
Ibn Rusta 41
Ibn Sīna (Avicenna) 20, 23
Ibn Wasil 162
Ibn Ya'qūb 40
Ibrāhīm b. Ya'qūb al-Isrā'īlī al-Turtūsī (al-Turtūsī) 47
identity: Arab 193; Christian 191; European 100–2, 102n2, 103n10, 191; formation of 191; group 8, 191; *iFranj* 191; Jewish 191–2; Muslim 5, 80–1, 84, 191; religious 105n30; Saracen 88, 101, 191 (*see also* Saracen character types)
al-Idrīsī (Abū 'Abdullah Muhammad ibn Muhammad ibn 'Abdullah ibn Idrīsī al-Sharīf) 44, 47–51, 52, 54
al-iFranj see Franks
'Imād al-Dīn Zangi 142, 173, 179, 180
'Imād al-Dīn al-Isfahani 149–50, 153–5
Indians 16–17
Isidore of Seville 12–16, 23
Islam, Christian theologians' criticism of 27, 29; *see also* Muslims
Islam and the West (Norman) 8
Isma'īliyya "Assassins" 152
Itinerarium Peregrinorum et Gesta Regis Ricardi 180–1, 182, 183

al-Jāhiz 42
Jerome (saint) 23
Jerusalem 126, 129, 133n7, 133n9, 137–8, 139, 142, 153, 165n1, 169n55, 174, 180, 182
Jews: as religious Other 83; segregation and persecution of 192; in Western Europe 82–3
jihad 156, 170n58
Julius Solinus 12–13

al Kāmil fī'l-ta'rīkh (Ibn al-'Athīr) 140
Karbughā (Curbaram/Kerbogha)
    130–2, 134n13, 135n26
Al-Khwārizmī 40, 42, 51
al-Kindī 42
King Horn 12
The King of Tars 4, 5, 96, 99–100
kishwar system 39, 43
Kitāb al I'tibār (Book of Instructions with Illustrations; ibn Munqidh) 142
Kitāb al-'ibar (Ibn Khaldūn) 52
Kitāb al-Amsār wa 'Ajā'ib al-Buldān (al-Jāhiz) 42
Kitāb al-Masālik wa 'l-mamālik (*The Book of Itineraries and Kingdoms*; ibn Khurradādhbih) 39, 42
Kitāb al-Masālik wa-l-Mamālik (al-Bakrī) 46, 47
Kitāb Al-Tanbīh wa 'l-Ishrāf (Book of Indication and General View; al-Mas'ūdī) 41–2, 43, 45–6, 57
Kitāb Nuzhat al-Mushtāq fī' Khtirāq al-'Āfāq (The Book of Pleasant Journeys and Far Off Lands; al-Idrīsī) 47–50, 52, 57

La Chanson de Roland 4, 111–14
'Lance of the Messiah' 155, 158–9, 171n73
learned tradition 63, 77n1, 194, 195
Liber de natura locorum (Book of the Nature of Places; Albertus Magnus) 20–3
Louis IV (king of France) 44
Louis IX (Saint Louis) 174
Louis VI (king of France) 180, 188n27
Lucan 22
Ludrick (son of Carl) 45
Ludrick (son of Charlemagne) 45

Macrobius 12
Mamlūk Sultanate 127
al-Ma'mūn (Caliph) 42
Mandeville, John (Sir) 78n24
Mandeville's Travels 68, 70–5, 157; criticism of Christians in 75–6; on Muslim beliefs 73–7; on the Saracens 70–5
Marinos of Tyre 39, 42

Martianus Capella 12
al-Masālik wa 'l-mamālik (Ahmad ibn al-Tayyib al-Sarakhsi) 42
Masālik wa 'l-mamālik literature 40
al-Mas'ūdī (Abū 'l-Hasan 'Alī ibn al-Husayn ibn 'Abd-Allāh al-Mas'ūdī) 41–6, 47, 51–4
Metaphysics (Aristotle) 42
Meteorologica (Meteorology; Aristotle) 23, 42
Middle East, Western construction of 7–8
monstrous races 16, 29–30, 31n16, 32n24, 78n6
Mu'īn al-Dīn Anar 158
Muhammad ibn Ahmad ibn Jubayr *see* Ibn Jubayr
Muhammad ibn Mūsā al-Khwārizmī 39
Muqaddimah (Ibn Khaldūn) 51–3, 56–7
Murūj al-Dhahab wa 'l Ma'ādin al-Jawhar (Meadows of Gold and Mines of Gems; al-Mas'ūdī) 41, 43–6, 53, 57
Muslim Levant 8, 138, 165, 165n1
Muslim Near East 8, 58, 173, 193, 196
Muslim scholars 2, 39, 43, 54, 57
Muslims: beliefs compatible with Christianity 73–5; cultural and religious prejudice of 164–5; as Europeans 80, 82; as external Other 83, 87; liminal space of 11; as Other 192, 194–6; as Saracens 127; Shi'ite 152; in Spain 38, 60n64, 69–70, 80, 82–3, 102n2, 103nn8–9, 123n29, 140, 173; stereotypes of 4, 6–7, 17, 57, 194–5; Sunni 152, 165n3
muwashshah poetry 103n11
Mystery Plays 110–11, 121n16

Norman, Daniel 8
Nūr al-Dīn 126, 142, 165n1, 174, 180

Opus Majus (Roger Bacon) 23–6
Orientalism 7–8, 190n49
Orientalism (Said) 7
Orosius *see* Paulus Orosius
Other: and asymmetries of power 8–9; caricatures of 172; Christians as 1, 2, 3, 6, 7, 9, 159, 193, 194–6; Familiar

Saracen as 84, 87–8, 101; Foreign Saracen as 4, 107–9, 159; Jews as 83; Muslims as 1, 3, 5, 7–9, 11, 30, 83, 101, 127, 172, 191, 192, 194–6; political 90, 192; racial 30, 90, 101; religious 30, 83, 192; Saracen Converts as 90; and systemic oppression 9
Otinel (*chanson de geste*) 3, 5, 93
Outremer 129
Ovid 27

pagans 11, 12, 25, 29–30, 44–5, 76, 111, 129–30, 191–2
Party Kings (*al-Mulūk al-Tawā'if*) 38
Passion Play II 110
Passion Plays 110–11, 121n12, 121nn15–16
Paulus Orosius 11–14, 23
Peter of Cluny 28
Peter the Venerable *see* Peter of Cluny
Philip Augustus (king of France) 175
planets, Roger Bacon's account of 26–7; *see also* astronomy
Pliny 12–13, 23, 39
Pomponius Mela 12
Pseudo-Turpin Chronicle 68–9
Ptolemy, Claudius 12–13, 23, 39, 41–2, 48, 54

Qilīj Arslān I (sultan) 138
Qiwām al-Dawla Karbughā (Curbaram/Kerbogha) 130–2, 134n13, 135n26
Quadripartitum (Ptolemy) 42

Ramiro (King of Gallicians) 47
Rasm al-Ma'mūr min al-'Ard (al-Kindī) 42
religion, in the Middle East 28–9; *see also* Christians; Islam; Muslims
religious conflict 65; intra-religious 152–3; *see also* Crusades
religious tolerance 50–1
Richard I (king of England) 127, 169n47, 174; cruelty and duplicity of 178–9; inspiring fear in the Muslim armies 176; Muslim respect for 185–6, 186n8, 187n18; as shrewd politician 176–7; as warrior 175–6, 178

Risāla fī 'l-Bihār wa 'l-Miyāh wa 'l-Jibāl (Ahmad ibn al-Tayyib al-Sarakhsi) 42
Risāla fī 'l-Bihār wa'l-Madd wa 'l-Jazr (al-Kindī) 42
Roger (Norman king; son of Tancred) 50
Roger Bacon 23–6
Roger II (Norman king) 50–1, 60n64
The Romance of Duke Rowland and of Sir Ottuell of Spayne 4, 5, 84, 93, 131
Romance of the Sowdone of Babylone and of Ferumbras His Sone Who Conquered Rome 4
romances, vernacular 3–4, 63
Rūs, Ibn Fadlān's characterization of 64–5

Said, Edward 7
Salāh al-Dīn (Saladin) 7, 65, 68, 126–7, 142, 153–7, 161, 163, 165n1, 169n55, 174, 178, 180; blamed for massacre 178, 181, 183; European respect for 185–6, 186n8; as Familiar Saracen 183–4; as Foreign Saracen 184; Richard I's respect for 181–2, 183; as villain 183–5; as warrior-king 185; Western accounts of 180–6
Sallust 23
Saracen character types: Familiar Saracen 3–4, 6, 84–8, 183–5, 195; Foreign Saracen 3–4, 6, 107–19, 128, 159–60, 184; Saracen Converts 3–4, 6, 86, 88–9, 104n23, 195
Saracen literary characters: Astragoth 108–9; King Clarell (*Romance of Duke Rowland and of Sir Ottuell of Spayne*) 84–7, 95, 101–2; Orable (*Guillaume* cycle) 104n23; Ottuell 86–7, 93–6, 104n21, 105n33; Princess Floripas 89–92, 104n22; Saracen monarchs 110–11; Saracen monarchs (in *Chanson de Roland*) 111–14; Saracen monarchs (Laban in *Sowdone of Babylone*) 114–19; Saracen monsters 107–9, 119n1, 172, 195; Soudan of Dammas 96–100, 107–8
Saracens: in accounts of the Crusades 126–33; arrogant nature of 131–2;

defined 11; European stereotypes of 193–5; Isidore's explanation of 15; in *Mandeville's Travels* 70–5; mentioned by Albertus Magnus 22; as monstrous 30; Muslims as 127; racial and cultural features of 80–1; Roger Bacon's account of 24, 25, 27–8; use of term 11–12; as vanquished people 130, 132
Saracen Trinity 97, 105n36, 125n39
Sayf al-Dīn 181
Second Crusade 126
Seljuq Turks 138–9, 153, 165n3
Seneca 23
Sibt Ibn al-Jauzi 159
Sicily, Norman conquest of 50, 69
Sindbād the Sailor 40
sociology 51
Soudan of Dammas see *The King of Tars*
The Sowdone of Babylone and Ferumbras His Sone Who Conquered Rome 4, 89, 108–9, 114
Spain, Muslims in 82, 83
Spivak, Gayatri 8–9
stereotypes: of the Franks 66, 143, 147, 150, 158–9, 161; of Muslims 4, 6–7, 17, 57, 194–5; of the Rūs 65; of Western Europeans 47, 57, 143, 149, 158, 164–5, 186n1, 194–5
Summa totius haeresis Saracenorum (Peter of Cluny) 28

Al-Tanbīh wa 'l-Ishrāf (Book of Indication and General View; al-Mas'ūdī) 41–2
Tetrabiblon (Ptolemy) 39
Things Fall Apart (Achebe) 9
Third Crusade 7, 126–7, 128, 133nn6–7, 153, 173, 174, 179–82
topography 49, 70
travel narratives, medieval 2–3, 63, 77, 194
Tripoli 126, 137, 139
Troglodytes 16
True Cross 153–4, 181
Turks: lack of attention to 14; Seljuq 138–9, 153, 165n3
al-Turtūsī (Ibrāhīm b. Ya'qūb al-Isrā'īlī al-Turtūsī) 47
Tyerman, Christopher 8

Umayya b. Ishāq b. Muhammad b. 'Abd al-Rahmān 47
Umayyad Caliph al-Hakam 44, 45
Umayyad dynasty 38
Urban II (pope) 17, 29, 126, 142, 157
Usāmah ibn Munqidh 6, 142–52

vernacular romances 3–4, 63

Walter, Hubert 183
al-Wāqidī 52
Western Europeans: caricatures of in Muslim literature 143; Muslim portrayals of (by ibn Munqidh) 144–52; Muslim prejudices against 164–5; Muslim stereotypes of 47, 57, 143, 149, 158, 164–5, 186n1, 194–5; politics of 44; *see also iFranj*; Franks
William of Conches 18, 127
William of Malmesbury 17
William of Tyre (archbishop) 29
women: in Crusader battles 168n40; as wives of Franks 143, 148, 149; as wives of rulers 44, 111

Ya'qūb ibn Ishāq al-Kindī 39

zajal poetry 103n11